CORPORATE POWER AND SOCIAL CHANGE

CORPORATE POWER AND SOCIAL CHANGE

The Politics of the Life Insurance Industry

Karen Orren

THE JOHNS HOPKINS UNIVERSITY PRESS
Baltimore and London

The Johns Hopkins University Press, Baltimore, Maryland 21218
The Johns Hopkins University Press Ltd., London

Library of Congress Catalog Card Number 73-8118
ISBN 0-8018-1507-X

Library of Congress Cataloging in Publication data will be found on the last printed page of this
book.

For my parents,
Howard and Leila Orren

CONTENTS

TABLES

ACKNOWLEDGMENTS

If there is anything of merit in the following study the credit must be widely shared.

Dozens of busy people involved in the life insurance industry—company executives, mortgage officers and correspondents—spent long hours explaining their activities and objectives. Officials and staff of the American Life Convention provided essential information on legislation and the Urban Investments Program. Industry lobbyists candidly discussed their tactics. Most of these people are not mentioned by name in the text because they might disagree with the interpretations I have given their affairs. But without exception they have contributed to this project with enthusiasm, openness, and much patience.

Several members of the Illinois legislature and staff of the Illinois Insurance Department helped me to understand life insurance politics through their personal views and experiences. John McKnight, regional director of the U.S. Commission on Civil Rights, and Anthony Downs, of the Real Estate Research Corporation, gave me information helpful in analyzing the racial components of insurance investment. Officials in Mayor Daley's planning offices and the Chicago Housing Authority alerted me to problems of commerce and housing in the inner city.

Mr. Charles Giroux, an employee of the Chicago Title and Trust Company, lent cheerful and constant assistance during the many months I spent pouring over the tract books. Two friends, Kris Kleinbauer and Elizabeth Shalen, helped to prepare the mortgage and census data for processing. Ricardo Klorman, of the University of California at Los Angeles, was an unfaltering guide through my first computer program. Stephen Werner, also of UCLA, read the manuscript more than once and supplied moral support throughout.

While I was a graduate student at the University of Chicago and since then, I have benefited immeasurably from the teaching, encouragement, and scholarly example of Grant McConnell. He, J. David Greenstone, and Paul E. Peterson read the manuscript at an earlier stage and made many useful suggestions. The basic research was conducted in 1968 with the support of a NIMH training fellowship, administered by Theodore Lowi.

Finally, I am grateful to my research assistant Lindsay Desrochers for helping me bring the manuscript to publication.

CORPORATE POWER AND SOCIAL CHANGE

CHAPTER I

INTRODUCTION

In September 1967 the Life Insurance Association of America announced that its member companies had pledged to invest one billion dollars to bring housing and employment to the nation's slums. The announcement was made at the White House, President Johnson was present, and afterward the Chairman of the LIAA and the Secretary of Housing and Urban Development held a joint press conference. Considering the amount—life insurance companies invest nearly $200,000,000, or one-fifth of the pledge, on every working day—the general aura of self-congratulation may have been disproportionate. But the very fanfare attested to a gnawing political possibility: that corporate business may be the only institution today able to formulate policies and enforce decisions which have frustrated American government at all levels.

This is a study of the life insurance industry, but it is also an inquiry into the role of corporate business in American political life. Its goal is to begin to understand how business decisions impinge on public policy and conversely, within the broader context of social change. By understand is not meant just a good description or even "an analysis," but rather some inkling of fundamental relationships between business, government, and society which have shaped the present and which indicate, if only vaguely, prospects and pitfalls in the future. Since the study itself is necessarily limited to a rather narrow range of facts, this introduction is intended to suggest briefly the ideas which underlay how they were selected and arranged.

I

An adequate conception of business politics must accommodate changing conditions in business, in government, and in the relationship

1

between the two. With very few exceptions, students of politics interested in corporate business have emphasized one or another of these
facets at the cost of unified theory and, frequently, distortion of the
fragments analyzed.

The most common approach has been to consider corporate business
as a pressure group. Thus, a wide range of studies have been done on
how, through campaign contributions, media control, lobbying activities, the lending of personnel to public agencies, and so on, corporate
business has succeeded or failed in influencing a governmental decision.
While these studies tell us a great deal about government, they reveal
little about corporate business.

The pressure group approach has two important difficulties—two,
that is, apart from the fact that it can tell us nothing whatever about
corporate business power which has no desire or need for access to
government.[1] First, these studies fail to qualitatively distinguish corporate business from the congeries of other interests that attend government policymaking. While in the aggregate they indicate that the business community is less "latent" than certain other groups and has
greater access and resources than some others, such advantages are relative, varying with particular public issues and in different political
epochs, and have little to do with the characteristics of corporate business enterprise per se. Nor does the pressure group approach indicate
important social and economic changes within business institutions. A
perusal of this literature provides a fairly good history of the changing
patterns of American government seen from the perspective of American business—the direct election of senators, the independent regulatory commission, the technology and expense of a modern political
campaign, the growing importance of military affairs. But there is virtually nothing to suggest the "managerial revolution," the decline of
market competition, the absolute size and wealth and the organizational complexity of the modern business corporation; and nothing on
how these changes have affected even this limited pressure group role.

A second group of studies, which we may categorize as the structural
or office-politics approach, has the opposite difficulties. These have
analyzed in considerable detail the giantism of modern business, the
growth of oligopoly and its influence on management decision, the
demise of the stockholder, and the nuances of administrative structures.
But the concern with government has generally been limited to questions bearing directly on matters internal to the industry or company,
such as antitrust or legal protection of shareholders. A common variant

[1] This aloofness is discussed in respect to economic planning in Andrew Shonfield, *Modern
Capitalism: The Changing Balance of Public and Private Power* (Fair Lawn, N.J.: Oxford University Press, 1965), pp. 333–36.

of the office-politics approach skirts the question of business-government relations metaphorically by describing the corporation itself as a "private government." The notion of "private government" is a rich one; but to the extent that it ignores the wider political context of the corporation, it is an overly general idea, applicable to virtually any group, from the mafia to the political party, and tells us nothing specific about corporate business.[2]

Finally, a third approach, which may be expected to become increasingly influential in the analysis of business politics, is the so-called study of political economy. Political economy claims to confront the relations between business and government by describing both in terms of a blend of organization theory and welfare economics. Here, alongside private government, is a kind of public business system, wherein governments dispense public "goods," voters consume in a competitive market, and groups bargain according to the laws of marginal utility. Applied to corporate business, political economy has so far turned out to be a version of the pressure-group approach, refined with the overgeneralizations of "private government." The political economy approach does have the virtue of directing attention to the historical change in emphasis of government activities from primary concern with indivisible conditions of common welfare—administration of justice, protection of persons and property, etc.—to the divisible and tangible distributions of the welfare state to various social groups. But, again, there has been little attention paid to the importance (let alone the source) of these changes for government's relation to business.[3]

II

Much has been written about the public character of the modern corporation, and of the blurring of any distinction between government and business based on "public" and "private" affairs.[4] A development

---

[2]The literature in both approaches to corporate business is voluminous. A helpful if somewhat discursive summary of the studies with a pressure-group orientation is in Edwin M. Epstein, *The Corporation in American Politics* (Englewood Cliffs, N.J.: Prentice-Hall, 1969). A broad selection of primarily structural articles is in K. W. Rothschild, *Power in Economics* (Baltimore: Penguin Books, 1971). Although often reiterated by others, the most incisive statements remain those of A. A. Berle, including one of the more recent, *The American Economic Republic* (New York: Harcourt, Brace & World, 1965). On private government see Earl Latham, "The Body Politic of the Corporation," in Edward S. Mason, ed., *The Corporation in Modern Society* (New York: Atheneum, 1966); and Robert Engler, *The Politics of Oil* (Chicago: Phoenix Books, The University of Chicago Press, 1967). Engler does relate the internal politics of the oil industry to its role as a pressure group, and his book stands as one of the best available on corporate business.

[3]See for example Mancur Olson, *Logic of Collective Action* (New York: Schocken Books, 1968), and Gordon Tullock, *Private Wants, Public Means* (New York: Basic Books, 1970).

[4]See Michael D. Reagan, *The Managed Economy* (Fair Lawn, N.J.: Oxford University Press, 1963).

that is less commented upon, however, but of greater significance for a political conception of the life insurance industry and corporate business generally, is the fact that government and business alike operate in a milieu in which both public and private dimensions of experience and institutions have been eclipsed by their social dimension. By social dimension is meant a reference to the well-being, prestige, influence, behavior, survival, and so on, of individuals considered in their collective rather than singular condition.[5] Preoccupation with this social dimension is the essence of contemporary political discourse. It is evident in the business community's quest for a conscious and conscientious role in society. These are not faddish perspectives, but rather reflect deep changes in the processes of modern life. The institution of life insurance is itself based on the socialization of a private situation: with the disappearance of the extended family as an interdependent economic unit, financial security is regained by reintegration with a larger group through actuarial science. Moreover, the corporation, as has been frequently pointed out, is distinguished from the proprietary firm not by its functions or economic behavior, but by its social organization and mobilization of social wealth.[6] And perhaps the most dramatic transformation of all has occurred in the organization and policies of the modern democratic state.

In the United States the representative political form of the socialization of private behavior is the interest group. Although the group process and the "role" are concepts now commonplace to political science, it is worth recalling that their importance rests on the historical emergence of groups whose members earlier had been perceived neither by others nor by themselves as having any particular interests in common.[7] The effects of successive interest-group activity on government institutions have recently been analyzed elsewhere.[8] But certain additional considerations are basic to our inquiry.

Apart from occasional lobbying, American interest groups have not, for the most part, been political in the sense that they have sought control or reordering of government structures. Nor, at least since the Civil War and with the possible exception of the farmers' revolt in

[5] An extremely suggestive discussion of the contemporary domination of the social dimension is in Hannah Arendt, *The Human Condition* (Garden City, N.Y.: Doubleday Anchor Books, 1959), chapter II.

[6] On the corporation as a social institution, see Peter F. Drucker, *The Future of Industrial Man* (New York: The John Day Company, 1942), chapters III and IV.

[7] An instructive study of emergence of group consciousness is E. P. Thompson, *The Making of the English Working Class* (New York: Pantheon Books, 1963). Also see P. E. Kraemer, *The Societal State* (Meppel, The Netherlands: J. A. Boom En Zoon, 1966), chapters I and II; and on social movements, E. J. Hobsbaum, *Primitive Rebels* (New York: W. W. Norton, 1965).

[8] Grant McConnell, *Private Power and American Democracy* (New York: Alfred A. Knopf, 1966).

the 1890s, have they been economic in that they have advocated fundamental changes in the manner of production or consumption. Rather, their primary aim, in respect to government and generally, has been to secure or maintain a measure of status relative to other social groups, or control and rationalization of certain socioeconomic processes.

Prior to the Civil War important interest groups coincided roughly with territorial divisions, and status and control outside of government was protected by the balances of the representational system, the maintenance of which occupied the best efforts of statemen for three generations. Following the Civil War and ever since, however, interest groups have sought government's protection and promotion of privileges and powers entirely outside those regional interests which the federal system had been designed to accommodate. Interest-group aims have variously assaulted and endorsed the status quo, but have almost always required positive measures in the form of new agencies and laws. Organizationally, this has meant the imposition of an informal system of functional representation on the formal, geographic one. The net policy result has been, as McConnell and others have documented, a fragmented and frustrated tangle, with scant regard for inclusive public interests. The cumulative predicament is a commitment to a variety of social prerogatives which government is incapable of providing. And it is these circumstances that shape government's present relationship to corporate business.

The development of the predicament may be understood in terms of the three major social changes in this century—the consolidation of industrial capitalism, the organization of labor, and the so-called Black Revolution—and their corresponding interest-group activities. The first saw the spread of trade associations, particularly of the "open-price" variety in the decade before 1920, which, while requiring no state powers for their operations per se, did need official protection from the antitrust laws. Conditions made for an easy cooperation. The collection of information on business finance and prices coincided with the aims of the new Department of Commerce and Labor and the associations' purpose—"to effect greater stability in business conditions in order that profits may be made, if not greater, at least more steady, dependable and calculable from year to year"—found eager government endorsement in the exigencies of World War I.[9] Nor were there any immediate political difficulties. The associations were already, or readily could be, organized within specific industries. No new government powers were necessary; in fact, this approach made new mechanisms of positive intervention in the business sphere superfluous. Finally, these develop-

[9] Quoted in Harold U. Faulkner, *The Decline of Laissez Faire*, 1897-1917 (New York: Harper and Row, 1969), p. 173.

ments nicely paralleled the Progressives' scheme for business regulation by independent commissions. Establishing the pattern for future entrenchment, the smooth passage of the associations into permanent officialdom was aided, not hindered, by "antibusiness" groups.

The second important interest group foray was by the labor organizations of the 1930s. Although labor did seek limited tangible guarantees of security, such as the minimum wage, and even flirted with the idea of challenging the preeminent status of business in production decisions (as in the Reuther plan for war mobilization), the primary goals were achieved through Section 7 of the National Labor Relations Act: the rights to organize and bargain collectively. As in the case of business, this grant of privileges presented no extraordinary obstacle to government, particularly to an administration resigned to the opposition of the business community. Labor organization was an accomplished fact in certain industries and well under way in others. The privileges accorded had to do with a specific and established sphere of operations, the factory, and they required only minimum, back-up intervention by government.

The third category of interest group, representing the thrust toward social equality by American blacks, has presented government with a far more troublesome problem. The problem is not, however, as is often claimed, mainly due to official "racism" or to the extremity of the group's demand: a sustained and expanding commitment to the blacks' general aspirations has been a fixture of official policy since the Brown decision, and certainly labor organization represented a greater revolution in social principles than the civil rights movement. Nor can the greater difficulties be explained simply in terms of public resistance: the labor movement met bitter, violent, powerful, and better organized resistance. The nub of the problem lies, rather, in its social shape. It is this shape, as much as the substance, which makes customary methods of response, even by the most well-meaning government, inadequate for coping with such an interest group.

In the first place (and this analysis may be applied to other recent mass interest groups, such as other minorities, consumers, and women), the group itself has no definite organization. Since any actual organization is bound to represent only a fraction of the group's membership, government tactics of preemption and cooptation have the principle effect of calling forth new and bolder leadership, as has been amply demonstrated by the results of the appointment of Negro cabinet members and other such appointments. Second, there is no limited sphere, like the industry or the factory, in which status rights are sought and may be granted. In fact, government has attempted to single out and promote changes in those spheres under its immediate control, such as the civil service, for instance, and the community action boards of the War on Poverty created specifically for this purpose. More important, educational institutions have been designated as the center rings of social change, largely because they are among the few basic and widespread institutions subject to direct governmental manipulation; thus, this proverbially most public of policies has become a ground for intense interest-group skirmishes. Finally, government has confronted the issue of shapelessness juridically, in piecemeal redefinition by law and adjudication of privileges guaranteed by the Constitution, with the government in the role of advocate of group rights.

The reliance on education and the courts, virtually by default, illustrates vividly the present predicament of government and its position in respect to corporate business. Changes through education are slow and limited; the judicial system is already overburdened. And, as the disappointing succession of job corps, public housing projects, poverty programs, and small business incentives have demonstrated, important levers of pertinent social change are found outside the scope of government. More specifically, many of these levers are located in the institutions of corporate business.

Decisions concerning the variety and pricing of consumer products, the level and personnel of employment, the location of plant facilities, the availability of adequate housing—these and other categories of business decision have a direct and immediate impact on social change far beyond the reach of the antidiscrimination statutes. Whereas, like accommodation to industrial capitalism and the labor movement, preliminary responses to the civil rights movement were accomplished with minimum appropriations of power from nongovernmental institutions, and relied instead on a rearrangement of powers within the federal system, present circumstances face government, should it wish to accede to this latest interest-group demand, with the prospect of making significant incursions into the domain of business (and likely also, organized labor), either by incentive methods or more radical means of coercion.

It is here that the cumulative character of the deadlock is apparent. The repeated strategies of cooptation and functional representation, the building of interest-group satrapies extending through the Congress, the administrative agencies, the state governments, have been carried out at considerable cost to government in political maneuverability. Business, in particular, has consolidated its status in the bureaucracies, the legislatures, and political parties. Its resources of capital, organization, technical expertise, and political experience are well adapted to the prevention of government inroads into its domain. And in a government which has become the creature of interest groups this largely means prevention of a coalition between, say, labor, blacks, and liberal politicians—a collection with sufficient internal strains to be vulnerable to a less than massive assault from the outside.

III

All of this assumes that corporate business will not respond to social change voluntarily, either directly, or as Galbraith has predicted, by attaching itself to the goals of the federal bureaucracy in return for the state's continued support of expensive technology.[10] Indeed, for two decades there has been a heightened concern among businessmen for the "conscience of the corporation." In large part, this concern is a manifestation of the socialization that has affected all modern activities and the standards of evaluation applied to them, and which has accelerated with the pace of the social revolution occurring outside executive offices. It is also the result of increased options available to corporations, including the option to obey its conscience or ignore it, which have accompanied changes in business structure.

Essentially, these well-known and widely documented changes boil down to the discretion of corporate executives in the matter of profits.[11] First, and perhaps most important in the long run, is the decline of the competitive market as a constraint on prices. The oligopolistic structure of major industries, characterized by the price leadership of a single large firm, in effect allows certain companies to levy a tax on public consumption for corporate projects. This taxation, as it were, may be for such conventional projects as higher profits, company growth, or executive amenities; on the other hand, it might be put, at the discretion of management, to low-yield investment in slums, minority training projects, or air and water depollution. Second, the techniques of advertising have further separated the consumer from company decision and provide the basis for administered prices through more regularized, predictable income.

Third, corporations have increasingly relied on internal financing for necessary funds, through the retention of income rather than its distribution as profits. In the last decade well over half of industrial corporation finance has been from internal sources. This development has removed an important constraint on management, since profit levels previously had to remain high in order to insure a market for future securities.

Finally, there is the freedom of corporate managers from stockholder control. The notorious ease with which managers perpetuate themselves in office, because of the number of stockholders, their anomalous legal

[10] John Kenneth Galbraith, *The New Industrial State* (Boston: Houghton Mifflin, 1967), pp. 337 ff. and passim.

[11] See ibid., and structural writings cited in footnote 2 above.

position, and their general disinterest and ignorance of management affairs, permits as great a management disregard for the profits of existing "owners" as for profits of potential, future ones. The contemporary manager is often erroneously contrasted with the proprietary tycoon of an earlier era. But, in fact, from the standpoint of autonomy and power within the company, these two are quite alike. The appropriate contrast to the autonomous manager is the manager at the behest of a less dispersed and more active group of stockholders than characterize the prototype modern firm.

It must be emphasized that these structural changes indicate the discretion available to corporate business and, as such, may determine the eventual course of government action. In so far as they facilitate concerted industry strategy and provide funds for political spending, they may raise the efficiency of political prevention against government interference. But, except as these changes themselves contribute to or effect the conditions of social dislocation and interest-group demands, they do not fundamentally alter government's predicament as it has been described here. A business sector of many competing firms under close stockholder control might present a more formidable task of coordination to government, but would be no less an obstacle to government's accommodation of group demands.

This point is important in light of arguments made by students of the corporation that it is the illegitimacy of management power, resulting from the disintegration of private property, and thus the devolution of responsibilities traditionally imposed by law, that makes the position of modern business in a democratic society highly precarious. Quite aside from the fact that entire civilizations have flourished under conditions of illegitimacy (one need, for example, only read Burckhardt's account of the Italian Renaissance), these arguments ignore the history of industrial capitalism. It is a continuous story of violations against established property rights, beginning with the expropriation of the peasants and the Church, and is laced through with illegalities of all types; yet there has been no serious erosion of business power as a result. A much better argument might be made that wealth, as distinct from landed property, has always been an object of the claims of the whole society, with the market system in economic theory an implicit expression of these broader interests in the common wealth. To the extent that the socialization or dispersion of ownership of wealth has been accompanied by the desocialization or concentration of power over its use, government controls might be considered a reassertion of traditional claims.[12]

---

[12] See Gunnar Myrdal, *The Political Element in the Development of Economic Theory* (Cambridge, Mass.: Harvard University Press, 1954), chapter 6. Of course, the question of legitimacy may be an essential part of the business executive's "identity crisis" and, as such,

IV

Having delineated the social context of the contemporary conflict between government and corporate business, and having described certain conditions within these institutions, we are moving toward a general characterization. Although this introduction has emphasized the pressures of a social-group demand, there are, of course, other circumstances which may produce similar tensions, such as war mobilization or severe inflation.[13] What is lacking in our conception is a statement of what controls or activities of corporate business are of intrinsic political concern. Even given certain parameters—for example, Talcott Parsons's definition of *political* as those actions or decisions which influence a goal of the wider community—the interdependency of an industrial nation and the rapid accumulation of goals guarantees a virtually infinite taxonomy. Thus, in the situation of war, for example, a company which utilizes a scarce raw material (let us say a radio company with a back supply of mica—these were frequent cases just before World War II), suddenly acquires political importance of the first order. On the other hand, a mere acknowledgment of this interdependency begs the question, for it gives no sense of specific conflicts, or of the direction they might take. Nor, finally, is there theoretical satisfaction in an ad hoc accounting based on community goals, since goals and "values" are established by corporate business as well as by conventional political agencies.

The problem may be given some shape by directing attention away from specific goals and their required resources, and focusing instead on social processes which provide or restrict facilities for the achievement of a variety of goals and determine the conditions of their achievement. After Parsons, we may refer to these as situational controls.[14] A list of situational controls in a modern society would include control over the means of violence; the mass communications; legislation, in Weber's sense of prescribing norms which determine that certain factual situations are to have certain legal consequences; in more primitive societies one would add the control of witchcraft; and so on. These situational controls are distinguished by their detachment from any specific or

---

may influence his decisions, but this becomes important only within the larger context of business and government as it has been outlined here. For a sensitive insider's view see David Finn, *The Corporate Oligarch* (New York: Simon & Shuster, 1969), chapters 8-11.

[13]Indeed, the inadequacy of government's traditional powers to fulfill its mandate within the status quo has been demonstrated by the extraordinary economic stabilization measures of the Nixon administration. See also Grant McConnell, *Steel and the Presidency* (New York: Norton and Company, 1963) and Bernard Nossiter, *The Mythmakers* (Boston: Beacon Press, 1964), chapter 4.

[14]Talcott Parsons and Neil J. Smelzer, *Economy and Society* (New York: The Free Press, 1965), p. 56. Their usage is somewhat different from the one employed here.

tangible goal; rather they are in the nature of media, highly generalized with respect to purpose. They are also characterized by their *direct* relation to the situation in question. In stable regimes these controls tend to be located within particular social institutions—the military, the independent press, the priesthood, etc. Disputes over the location of these controls is an important theme in political history and their distribution and redistribution the substance of political change.

It is the argument of this study that the relationship between government and corporate business may be understood in terms of the situational control of credit. To adopt Schumpeter's description, credit is the means of detaching existing resources from the circular flow of production, savings, and consumption, and moving them to new combinations for economic development.[15] In its simplest form, credit enables a homeowner, say, to obtain a mortgage on his house, or a businessman to obtain a loan on the security of his machinery or something he has produced. In its more important and complicated form, credit creates purchasing power to which no existing commodities correspond: it, credit, is what *enables* the entrepreneur to purchase the materials and labor he needs for his projected enterprise. To extend credit to a homeowner or a businessman, or for that matter, to the government, is to provide general purchasing power for a variety of goals; to deny credit is to restrict facilities by direct control of the situation. As Veblen aptly remarks, credit gives one who controls it the "legal right of sabotage."[16]

Because of their socially strategic role and the powers they imply, the mechanisms of credit have been throughout history pivots of controversy. During premodern eras, credit and credit standing with the moneylenders were a foremost preoccupation of rulers ever anxious to supplement their chronically deficient tax revenues, usually to pay for the expenses of warfare. In 1917 the first act of the Supreme Council of National Economy of the new Soviet Union was the nationalization of the state bank. In the early years of this country, Alexander Hamilton, perhaps alone among the founders in his acute understanding of the dynamics of industrial society, wrote that credit was "not a mere matter of private property, but a political machine, of the greatest importance to the state." And although the battle over the Bank of the

---

[15] Joseph A. Schumpeter, *Theory of Economic Development* (Fair Lawn, N.J.: Oxford University Press), chapter 3. Parsons and Smelzer in their system of boundary-exchanges describe credit creation as a subtype of the "control of the situation . . . one of *two* primary outputs of the polity. The other . . . is the capacity to command support, i.e., the necessary motivational commitment of the individual and collective units of society." *Economy and Society*, p. 58.

[16] Thorstein Veblen, *Absentee Ownership and Business Enterprise in Recent Times* (Boston: Beacon Press, 1967), p. 66.

United States was finally settled in favor of a financial system largely independent of federal control, that credit was primarily a matter of private business, rather than an institution of public service to be governed by representative institutions, was an idea accepted only gradually.[17]

Consider the history of American banking. In the 1830s Tennessee, Kentucky, Arkansas, Georgia, Illinois, Vermont, South Carolina, and Alabama operated state-owned banks; Indiana and Ohio joined them in the 1840s. Florida, Arkansas, Louisiana, and Mississippi established their own real estate banks. Portions of the profits of these institutions were earmarked by the legislatures for public schools, turnpikes, canals, and the like. Although the state-owned banks were found where capital for establishing private banking was in short supply, many other states, including those with the most developed economies, turned for similar financing to the private banks they chartered. New York, for example, required the Manhattan Company to build a water supply system, and the Dry Dock Bank to build wharfs as conditions of their charters. In Louisiana, the New Orleans Light and Banking Company was obliged to install gas lights. Several states chartered so-called banking and railroad companies. Also, private banks were often expected to invest a part of their funds on a continuous basis in specified state projects, most often railroads, turnpikes, and state bonds, and to extend long-term loans to the states at special rates set by statute. Frequently, when a new project was devised, such as Maryland's plan to build a turnpike westward to Cumberland, and no appropriate new bank obligingly sought a charter, financial support was made a condition for renewing the charter of one already established. Another common requirement was that banks give favored treatment to citizens of their own states. Pennsylvania, for instance, required that 20 percent of bank funds be loaned at 6 percent interest "for one year to farmers, mechanics, and manufacturers of their districts." Moreover, the notion that banks should be controlled by social institutions devoted to the public welfare was not confined to control by government. Connecticut prescribed in 1807, for example, that banks "at all times" accept subscriptions to their capital by churches, schools, and charitable institutions, which stock was non-

[17]For a provocative discussion of credit in premodern economies see John Hicks, *A Theory of Economic History* (London: Oxford University Press, 1969), chapter V. A discussion of the place of credit institutions in the Bolshevik financial program appears in Edward Hallett Carr, *History of Soviet Russia*, vol. 2, *The Bolshevik Revolution* (Harmondsworth, England: Penguin Books, 1966), p. 136 ff. Carr points out that the nationalization of the banks, along with the annulment of existing debts, was the only concrete item in the entire program. Also see Robert A. Brady, *Business As a System of Power* (New York: Columbia University Press, 1947), chapter III, on the importance of control over credit in the rise of the Zaibatsu in Japan. For a comparative treatment, see Rondo Cameron, *Banking in the Early Stages of Industrialization* (New York: Oxford University Press, 1967). Hamilton is quoted in Carter Goodrich, ed., *The Government and the Economy, 1783–1861* (Indianapolis: Bobbs-Merrill, 1967), p. 279.

transferable and redeemable for subscribers on six months notice. This law continued until the Civil War.[18]

It must be emphasized that these measures most often proceeded from an inclusive conception of the public interest in education, public works, and a growing economy. Although it may in fact have been the case that certain sections of the population benefited more than others, the laws aimed at advantages to "farmers, mechanics, and manufacturers" alike, and thus could not be more unlike the intensely interest-group distributions of the modern welfare state's porkbarrel and "contracting out." The significant "group" reference was to the economy and citizens of a particular state, in preference to other states. The main lines of political opposition to these financial policies were not drawn between businessmen and "debtor classes"—in that period, like today, almost everyone, and particularly the merchants, speculators, enterprisers, were debtors—but rather between the financial community and the more broadly representational governments.[19]

The cultural, economic, and political triumphs of industrial capitalism, consolidated at the beginning of this century, have generally obscured the conflict. The Populist movement was the last serious assault on "free banking." The impact of Keynesian economics, for all of its emphasis on investment and the varieties of potential state manipulation, has been limited largely to fiscal schemes for modulating the level of investment, leaving the direction of credit allocation to business rather than government decision.[20] The welfare state finances its turnpikes, schools, and hospitals by supplementing tax revenues with securities that compete on the market with other credit instruments. Recently, however, the social requirements of the Black Revolution, and the obvious failure of government's traditional methods of interest-group accommodation, has again brought to the surface the question of credit as a situational control.

The relationship of business and government and their respective relationships to society via the mediation of credit may be seen sharply in the case of the "core" or "inner" city. While not all of the social

[18]Bray Hammond, *Banks and Politics in America* (Princeton, N.J.: Princeton University Press, 1967), chapter 7; and Louis M. Hacker, *The Course of American Economic Growth and Development* (New York: John Wiley & Sons, 1970), pp. 123 ff.

[19]Hammond, *Banks and Politics*, pp. 326 ff., convincingly argues against the thesis that Jacksonian democracy was a blow to capitalism or the "money power." Rather, it represented the diffusion of enterprise, Wall Street's jealousy of Chestnut Street, state politicians' resentment at the Bank of the United States' interference with states' rights, and the local businessman's dislike of federal controls. The gradual emergence of corporate enterprise from under the wing of the state, and the early disassociations of sectional and corporate interests which prefigured the post-Civil War alliance of finance and businessmen against agricultural groups, is analyzed by Louis Hartz *Economic Policy and Democratic Thought: Pennsylvania, 1776–1860* (Cambridge, Mass.: Harvard University Press, 1948).

[20]See Robert Lekachman, *The Age of Keynes* (New York: Vintage Books, 1966), chapter 11.

problems bound together in these euphemisms can be understood in terms of credit and investment, several of the major ones can. Consider housing, for example. The scarcity of sound housing in the inner city is the direct product of a credit system that has consistently funnelled loans for new housing and home improvements into other sections of the city and the suburbs, leaving behind the slums (and the unscrupulous speculator to prey on the black resident still determined to own his home.) This is not to analyze the *causes* of bad housing: they are arguable and diversified. But the nonavailability of credit created a major condition for the deterioration, and a reversal would require judicious manipulation of finance. The same is true for the location of new industrial and service facilities. One could, indeed, extend the argument and discuss the problems of air pollution as decisions of corporate business to invest its profits in new plants and expanded production instead of cleaner methods—although here, because of the only recent consciousness of ecology, one might speak more accurately of "non"-credit "decisions."[21]

Clearly, by credit decisions is not meant only those decisions made by financial institutions. A half-century ago a study of the life insurance or banking industries could confidently assert that it was working at the nerve center of the capitalist system. In the new industrial state, however, the nerves have spread throughout the productive body. Thus, when Galbraith, for example, cites at length the declining role of capital, he is not actually describing the disappearance of credit mechanisms, but rather the extent to which corporations have become their own banks, from which they may borrow on favorable terms and with scarcely a demurrer from their stockholders for the purposes of expanding production *or any other goals of their own choosing.*

V

A few remarks now to introduce the following study. Life insurance is a thoroughgoing example of the socialization of enterprise. As already suggested, the very principle of insurance rests on a collectivizing of private needs for financial security. Structurally, a life insurance company is a prototype of the corporation with amorphous, dispersed "ownership"—especially if it is a mutual company, as are most of the largest. Economically, the industry's function is to aggregate individual savings and channel them into various commercial and industrial ventures, thereby enhancing the liquidity and efficiency of the nation's

---

[21]Nondecisions refers to policy options filtered out, as it were, by various biases in cultural and political institutions. For an interesting treatment of nondecisions on the subject of air pollution and generally, see Matthew A. Crenson, *The Unpolitics of Air Pollution* (Baltimore: The Johns Hopkins University Press, 1971).

credit system. The some two hundred billion dollars in life insurance assets comprise approximately one-quarter of all outstanding nonfarm mortgages, one-third of farm mortgages, and 70 percent of the outside capital finance for American industry.

Our concern is entirely with life insurance companies as institutions of credit. That credit is a primary activity of the industry, and not merely incidental to the sales and servicing of insurance policies, is evident in the industry's origins. Although official company histories often tell of some founder's extraordinary sympathy for widows and orphans, a considerable incentive to promoters and entrepreneurs has always rested in the fact that a life insurance company demands little or no capital investment besides that put up by the policyholders. To choose one of the oldest companies as an example, the New York Life and Trust was founded by William Bard in 1830 as a vehicle for investing Dutch-controlled money in New York real estate mortgages.[22] Moreover, as will be demonstrated below, the industry's position in the world of finance has determined the expansion and choice of sales products beyond the straight life insurance policy, and protection of its investment autonomy has been its fundamental political aim.

As in the case of banking—and for identical reasons—the states from the beginning took an active interest in the charters and operations of life insurance companies. No state followed the English example of granting tax remittances to policyholders as a reward for contributing to development capital; but they did exclude insurance companies from the general incorporation laws for many years, since their establishment consistently presented new possibilities for public finance and state sponsored investment. Again, to select one example among many, Massachusetts in 1818 granted a state monopoly to Massachusetts Hospital Life (today Massachusetts Mutual, the tenth largest American company) in return for investing one-third of company profits in the Massachusetts General Hospital.

Also, as with banking, the Populist movement, which called for the nationalization of insurance, mounted the last broad-scale attack against the private direction of insurance funds. During this century the principles of "free" life insurance, regulated only to protect the safety of policyholders' funds, have maintained the political offensive. Life

[22] During the medieval period, monasteries, towns and states, as well as guilds and individuals, circumvented church prohibitions against usury by selling life annuities to raise capital. In sixteenth-century Germany, the burgomaster of Nuremburg sought to enhance the town treasury by requiring compulsory insurance of children through a deposit made upon birth—which deposit remained in the treasury if, as was frequent, the child died before a designated age of maturity. See R. Carlyle Buley, *The American Life Convention 1906–1952* (New York: Appleton-Century-Crofts, 1953, vol. I, pp. 13 ff.). For general industry history also see J. Owen Stalson, *Marketing Life Insurance: Its History in America* (Cambridge, Mass.: Harvard University Press, 1942).

insurance politics, the active intercourse between the industry and the government, has been dominated by lobbying, campaign contributions, and insurance men in public office—for which the industry has a great penchant, both here and abroad.[23]

Most of this activity is at the state level, because, except for the important area of federal taxation, most of the provisions concerning company operations are established by the states. This somewhat complicates our analysis of the business-government relationship on the nexus of credit. Life insurance companies are vitally important to state finance and state economies through the taxes they pay, the jobs they provide, the investments and bank deposits they make. But it is at the national level that the social problems which bring government into conflict with corporate business are most often posed for solution. This complication is no political accident; it is, as we shall see, a result of prolonged industry strategy.

The study which follows will concentrate on the state of Illinois. Although Illinois is not one of the four or five leading states in dollar volume of assets domiciled there, Franklin Life, Continental Assurance, and State Farm Life are domestic (in-state) companies among the largest forty life insurers nationally, and all of the major foreign (out-of-state) companies do business and pay taxes there. In terms of the simple number of domestic companies, Illinois ranks only behind Arizona and Louisiana. As an important industrial and agricultural state, Illinois is a leading depository of life insurance investment. In the area of farm and nonfarm mortgages, the state is fourth after California, New York, and Texas, in amount of credit extended. Finally, Illinois was among the first states to consider legislation proposed by the national industry in the currently central policy areas of equity investments and holding companies.

On the other hand, it must be emphasized that this is not intended as a state study, sealed off from the broader picture of which each of the other states and the national government are parts. Insurance politics in Illinois are representative rather, in that the same network of foreign and domestic companies, their lobbyists and associations, as well as the circumstances arising from the ambiguities of power in a federal system, are common to the others. Furthermore, the role of government in life insurance credit, the range of options available to the states in a state-regulated industry, and the social problems engendering the need for choice, are also generally characteristic.

The following chapters apply, in the case of one major industry, the general approach sketched above. First, they are concerned with the

[23]See for example, H. G. Nicholas, *The British General Election of 1950* (London: Macmillan, 1951), pp. 51 ff., and subsequent election volumes in the same series.

tension that has historically prevailed between the state and the life insurance companies over the matter of investment, and the importance this tension has had and continues to have in the industry's political strategy. Second, they study the manner in which the life company manager makes his credit allocations, the degree to which he is constrained in his choice of investment goals, and the likelihood that he will attach himself to the goals of the federal bureaucracy or by some other method lessen the conflicts between business profits and the social demands on government. Third, they examine questions of the so-what variety with respect to one major investment area, residential mortgages. Life insurance mortgages in the metropolitan area of Chicago over a period of three decades are analyzed for their role in a variety of social changes, including neighborhood development and decline, which, with its racial components, creates an important strain on the status quo between government and corporate business. Fourth, they evaluate the implementation of the recent Life Insurance Urban Investments Program in Chicago as an example of socially conscious investment by corporate business.

The capabilities of the corporation for engineering social change again raises the problem of government's relation to business in the context of group demands. The degree to which business discretion and autonomy is synonymous with power to achieve desired social results is an important consideration in the question of alternative government-business arrangements and policies for coping with the present impasse, and is the subject of the final chapter.

CHAPTER II

VARIETIES
OF STATE
POLICY

Coming to the study of present-day life insurance politics from the direction of the previous Introduction, one experiences a sudden withering of confidence in the framework set forth. To be sure, there are statutes regulating investment, along with those regulating virtually every other facet of the business, filling two thick volumes of the Illinois Annotated Code. But neither their perusal nor an acquaintance with the details of their passage suggests the slightest tension between the state and the industry over the question of credit allocation. On the contrary, the state of Illinois appears to have no policy except that of providing for the smooth and profitable operations of the companies.

It is only after some study of the evolution of this pattern that the benign present begins to take shape as the status quo: that is, as a situation different from certain alternatives and with vested interests against them. Historically, the investment of life insurance assets has been the object of a variety of policies, manifest in laws long superseded and in proposals narrowly defeated in the legislature. Each posits a different relationship of the state to the industry, each a greater or less infringement on company discretion.

This chapter analyzes the history of Illinois investment policy and argues that life insurance politics is preoccupied with maintaining company autonomy. As will be shown, the federal system, the configuration of separate states and a national government, provides the industry with both its main strategy and its most effective tactics. Autonomous control of the assets is at once the industry's principal objective and its strongest weapon. These facts demonstrate the importance of credit in industry politics and are concrete support for our abstract scheme.

The factual details, useful and theoretically satisfying as they may be, must not, however, obscure the more general point. The relationship between government and business is always governed by *a set of possible state policies* concerning credit, ranging from absolute state control to absolute company autonomy. This proposition holds whether or not such possibilities have ever been realized in the form of laws and proposals. It is on this ground that the action among state institutions and techniques and industry strategies and tactics is played out, and on which the otherwise deceptively commonplace "pressure-group" politics described in chapter III may be understood.[1]

Life insurance investment laws in Illinois may be analyzed in three categories, or more precisely, three policy modes. First, *mandatory* laws oblige the company to invest a portion of its assets in specified securities or in designated localities.[2] Second, *inducing* laws encourage or endorse a particular type of investment, sometimes providing rewards or compensation for compliance, more often merely the recognition of company good will by state officials. Third, *enabling* laws authorize the investment of funds in a designated manner but with no legislative intent of channelling money in a preferred direction.

These categories are constructed according to the degree of coercion applied by the state on the life company. From one perspective, of course, all laws may be said to be coercive, in that they exact certain penalties for their abuse. But a mandatory statute requires as a condition of doing business one particular type of investment, or it so radically eliminates alternatives that it imposes requirements by default. An enabling statute, on the other hand, merely permits certain investments among a relatively wide range of alternatives, while an inducing statute is in the middle realm of persuasion.

The categories, moreover, have been associated historically with different legislative purposes. Mandatory and inducing statutes have usu-

[1] This chapter suggests a certain superficiality in recent arguments that "policy determines politics" as much as the more traditionally held "politics determines policy." See the writings of Theodore J. Lowi, particularly his seminal "American Business, Public Policy, Case Studies and Political Theory." *World Politics* 16, no. 4 (July 1964): 677-715. In our view an industry regulated by a "distributive" policy (Lowi's terms) must be understood as primarily devoted to warding off a "redistributive" one.

[2] A subcategory of mandatory laws might comprise those laws which expressly prohibit any investment in a given type of security. An important law in this subcategory could be the prohibition against insurance company ownership of real estate except under certain limiting conditions. This provision was probably an inheritance from the English law of mortmain, which expressed popular fears of unlimited ownership in land by organizations that do not die. See Lester W. Zartman, *The Investments of Life Insurance Companies* (New York: Henry Holt & Co., 1906), p. 157. Also in this subcategory could be placed prohibitions against ownership in mining and manufacturing concerns.

These prohibitions share with mandatory laws the same properties of coercion and external constituency reference. And they attempt to channel funds and credit, although away from, rather than to, specific economic sectors. See below, p. 23.

ally been intended to change or redistribute the availability of credit in order to assist the economic development of particular economic groups, or sectors of the state economy, or the state economy as a whole. Enabling statutes, on the other hand, have aimed to maximize business profit and, allegedly, to safeguard the integrity of the policy-holders' funds.

Finally, these categories refer to different constituencies, and the constituencies vary with respect to their relationship to the insurance industry. Mandatory and inducing statutes are concerned with constituencies external to the companies, such as citizens of Illinois, poorly housed city dwellers, local industrial corporations, and so on. Enabling statutes, on the other hand, are concerned with internal life insurance constituencies—stockholders and policyholders—as well as the general public in its special capacity as potential and future policyholders.

Not all investment laws fall neatly as mandatory, inducing, and enabling. Early laws in Illinois, for example, were enabling in the sense that they did provide for a wide range of possible investments and then added the mandatory provision that these various investments must be within the boundaries of the state. Since attention here is directed to the positive efforts of the state to channel insurance assets, the mandatory provisions of a complex law take precedence in determining its classification. Nor are the clusters of characteristics associated with each type of law always true to form. For example, there have been bills proposed from time to time which would require a life insurance company to grant its policyholders mortgages on their homes: in other words, to force extension of credit to benefit an internal, rather than external, constituency. Again, because of the focus of this study, the coercive aspects of a law are determining, and this law would be classified as a mandatory one.

Chapter III will suggest different legislative and popular coalitions which might be expected to form in support of, or opposition to, different policy modes, or specific laws within them. Here, however, it should be reemphasized that each of the categories posits a different relationship between the state and the insurance industry. In the case of mandatory statutes, the state infringes on the investment discretion of the life insurance company for the benefit of some constituency external to it. In a real sense, the state appropriates a measure of company decisionmaking. With the enabling statute, the state acts on behalf of policyholders and stockholders in declaring a given type of investment or distribution among investments to be consistent with the profitability and the safety of the funds. Though enabling statutes may be said to impair insurance company autonomy, there is no question of appropriation.

II

In the history of Illinois insurance law, mandatory investment statutes are most common during the nineteenth century and the early stages of state economic development.[3] The very first investment laws, in the form of charters incorporating individual companies, were most often of the enabling type, specifying real estate, corporations in Illinois or any state, and loans "upon such security as [the companies] think proper," as permissible investments. From the beginning there were also instances of mandatory provisions which would later become general laws: for example, one company was allowed by its 1834 charter to loan money on state bonds and real estate mortgages in any state, but to individual persons only if they were citizens of Illinois. But generally the state's policy toward investment was haphazard and laissez faire. This laxness probably was due first, to a desire to encourage the organization of insurance companies in Illinois by allowing maximum leaway for growth and profit. Second, the state legislators could have had little understanding of the enormous funds life insurance reserves would generate. In fact, early laws refer only to the investment of capital stock, and many years would pass before mention is made of "surplus funds," and "accumulations."

By the 1850s the eagerness of the state to foster Illinois' capital-hungry industries and farms—not to speak of the state treasury—is reflected in the new emphasis on mandatory legislation. The charter incorporating the Northwestern Mutual Life Insurance Company in 1857 is typical of the period:

The directors shall have power to invest a certain portion of the premiums received, not to exceed one half thereof, in public stocks of the United States or of this State. The whole of the premiums received which are not so invested, excepting such portion thereof as the directors shall reserve for immediate losses and expenses, shall be invested in 1st class mortgages and securities upon unincumbered real estate within the state of Illinois.

When, in 1869, the legislature passed the first general life insurance law, the mandatory pattern was followed. The law provided that any company doing business in Illinois must invest a guarantee capital of at least $100,000 in securities issued by the United States or the state of Illinois, in bonds and securities of any Illinois city or town, or in first mortgages on Illinois real estate; and that in-state companies invest their "funds and accumulations" in these same categories, with the addition of national bank securities. But an exception provided for in this early law is equally noteworthy, for it indicates a pitfall which has continued to vex modern advocates of mandatory state legislation. It provided

[3]No individual statute citations are provided here. All statutes referred to or quoted may be found in appropriate volumes of Illinois Laws, beginning with 1834.

that if an Illinois company sold insurance in another state, it could invest in that state's "like securities." The measure was undoubtedly inspired by the recognition that the largest reservoirs of life insurance capital were based in the East—Massachusetts, New Jersey, New York, Pennsylvania—and legislation of these states to inhibit their own home companies from investing in Illinois was a grim financial prospect.

This early period raises the question of the original aims of life insurance regulation. It is a truism of life insurance textbooks that the safety of the policyholders' funds has always been the cardinal principle guiding the government's involvement in insurance affairs. While this may be the case for certain other states, in Illinois it is clear that the temptations of mercantilism were a good deal stronger than the counsels of consumer protection. It must have been obvious to legislators that, say, the bonds of several prosperous Eastern states were safer than first mortgages on Illinois real estate. But the exception in the 1869 law which made such sound investments possible was a concession to fears of retaliation rather than a positive objective. Moreover, provisions for public scrutiny of business operations, that sine qua non of protective regulation, do not appear until some twenty years after the first general investment laws were passed; and even then these provisions are crude, perfunctory, and naive.[4]

Safety through publicity and public examination did not become the preoccupation of Illinois insurance regulation until the national wave of insurance reform during the first decade of this century. Public concern about the financial reliability of insurance policies was excited by the rash of company failures in the depression of 1902–3 and the disclosure of mismanagement and fraud in the 1905 Armstrong investigations in New York. And the demand for effective state surveillance of insurance affairs, the main thrust of reform, was now coupled with the companies' own constant insistence on liberalized investment laws. Having sorely chafed under mandatory statutes and having achieved gradual relief from restrictions during the economic expansion of the 1880s and 1890s, the industry had a new, effective rationale for still greater autonomy over their assets: the best guard against a bankrupt company was a profitable company, and profits required that the untrammeled and invisible hands of the national money market replace the parochial grasp of the state legislature.[5]

---

[4] On this point see Edwin Wilhite Patterson, *The Insurance Commissioner in the United States: A Study in Administrative Law and Practice* (Cambridge, Mass.: Harvard University Press, 1927), pp. 525–29.

[5] For a description of politics and investment in the 1880s and 1890s see Harold F. Williamson and Orange A. Smalley, *Northwestern Mutual Life, A Century of Trusteeship* (Evanston, Ill.: Northwestern University Press, 1957), chapter VIII. A balanced account of the Armstrong

The turn toward the enabling mode is evident in the 1907 law permitting Illinois companies to invest capital, surplus, and other available funds in United States stocks and bonds, the stocks or bonds of any state, or of a county, town, or municipality in any state or Washington, D.C.; in the first mortgages and trust deeds on real estate in any state; in the mortgage bonds of railroad companies; and in the stocks, bonds, or notes of any American corporation except for mining companies and the stocks of companies known as industrials. The last provision modified in actual practice, reflected the desire of a legislature dominated by rural interests to keep funds from heavy industry, thereby preserving a credit advantage for farmers. This aim, accompanied by the general rural hostility toward the cities, was common to many other state insurance codes of the time.

Through the next several decades, enabling statutes gradually broadened the investment field. Some of the most important authorizations were guaranteed or preferred stocks of industrials (1931); a limited investment in common stock (1935); provisions for participation with other life insurance companies in large mortgages (1947); mortgages on oil- and gas-producing properties (1953); a provision that 5 percent of assets may be invested with the total discretion of the company—the "leaway" or "basket" clause (1963); and participation in downstream holding companies (1967).

Beginning in the depression years of the 1930s, this steady liberalization has been accompanied by a number of inducing laws designed to facilitate the flow of life insurance funds to impoverished or needy sectors, without, however, actually forcing investment and without any reward but political good will. The basic idea behind such laws is indicated in the text of a 1932 statute authorizing investment in municipal tax anticipation warrants:

Whereas, on account of the nationwide business depression and the resultant and unusual condition of banking facilities, the marketability of municipal tax anticipation warrants has been and now is seriously impaired, and

Whereas, certain municipalities of this state now find it difficult and impossible to market their tax anticipation warrants, and

Whereas, such municipalities must find an immediate market for such anticipation warrants, for that reason an emergency is hereby declared to exist and this Act shall take effect from and after its passage.

Inducing statutes have been used most frequently to channel money into housing, beginning with a 1935 authorization of the bonds of the National Mortgage Association and the Homeowners Loan Corporation,

---

investigations and its aftermath may be found in Morton Keller, *The Life Insurance Enterprise, 1885–1910: A Study in the Limits of Corporate Power* (Cambridge, Mass.: Belknap Press, Harvard University Press, 1963), chapter XV.

and mortgages insured by the Federal Housing Authority. In 1939 were added the shares of state-chartered building and loan associations and federal savings and loan associations insured by the Federal Savings and Loan Insurance Corporation, and in 1945 mortgages guaranteed by the Veteran's Administration. When Chicago began its program of slum clearance in 1948, the legislature passed a law inducing investment in bonds and other obligations of the Illinois Housing Authority and mortgages financed under the Neighborhood Redevelopment Act, and in 1955 approved the bonds of the Illinois Building Authority. Inducing laws have also been used to finance education with life insurance funds, by sanctioning as investments the University of Illinois Foundation (1939); the Board of Trustees of the University of Illinois (1949); the Teachers College Boards of the State of Illinois, the Board of Trustees of Southern Illinois University, and the Southern Illinois University Foundation (1957). Other projects designated have included the Illinois Armory Board (1939) and the International Bank for Reconstruction and Development (1951).

In practice, then, mandatory laws have been supplanted by enabling and inducing laws as the dominant modes of investment regulation. But this progression must not be taken as an indication that the attractions and possibilities of the vast sums collected in life insurance premiums have become invisible to Illinois legislators. During this century mandatory laws have been proposed many times and often only narrowly missed passage. The most common form has been the so-called compulsory investment law. While mandatory laws in the nineteenth century had usually attempted to tap the investment assets of domestic companies, compulsory investment laws were based on the realization that the lion's share of the money that Illinois citizens paid out for life insurance premiums was transferred into the treasuries of large Eastern companies which were entirely immune from the old laws. This newer type of mandatory statute would keep capital at home by requiring that a sizable portion, usually 75 percent, of the premiums collected in Illinois be invested in Illinois corporations, either public or private. Such a law has been proposed fourteen times since 1900, most recently in 1945. It was never passed, but sentiments supporting its aim, if not necessarily its specific remedy, were widespread. For instance, in 1947 the state senate adopted a resolution voicing the mood of those legislators who would take stronger action. The resolution called "attention to the fact that nationally-known life insurance companies which maintain headquarters in New York City, have invested approximately $100,000,000 in housing projects in such city to the exclusion of similar investments in other large cities in the nation" and requested the director of insurance to report to the senate "his recommendations for such legislation as he may deem necessary to correct this situation."

III

The use of mandatory investment statutes, the attempt by the state to appropriate life insurance investment decision, has largely determined the industry's changing preference for state or federal regulation. The passage of these laws, or, equally effective, the threat that they might be passed, has provoked major segments of the industry to call for a shift in regulatory jurisdiction away from the usurping government in question. This has occurred with a consistency that betrays present-day rhetoric about keeping regulation close to the people and that attests to the central position of investment activities in life insurance politics.

The evolution of Illinois investment laws partakes of a broader national pattern, against which the industry as a whole has shaped its attitudes toward the locus of supervision.[6] The period of the late 1850s and 1860s saw New Jersey, New York, California, Iowa, Kansas, Kentucky, Ohio, and Wisconsin join Illinois in passing general insurance laws that forced large portions of investment capital to remain in a company's home state.[7] Thus, when the Chamber of Life Insurance convened in New York in 1866 to "form one grand union of all the companies of America for objects promotive of the common welfare," the very first object promoted was the federal regulation of insurance. In order to escape the "spirit of persistence and injurious hostility" and a "temper of extortion" which the states had expressed through their laws demanding "forced loans," the Chamber arranged for a bill to be introduced in Congress providing for the federal incorporation of life insurance companies and the establishment of a National Bureau of Insurance within the Treasury Department.[8] The bill failed to pass then, however, and failed again on its reintroduction in 1868. Also, during this period life insurance companies were among those groups who campaigned longest and most vigorously in support of the Fourteenth Amendment as an alternate means of protection against adverse state legislation.[9]

The Supreme Court decision in Paul v. Virginia (1869)—that an insurance policy was a contract of indemnity, not a transaction in commerce, and thus not subject to federal jurisdiction—temporarily stalled

[6]Henry A. Warshall, assistant general counsel of the American Life Convention, has calculated that between 1910 and 1968, when he was interviewed by the author, mandatory investment laws have been introduced 254 times in 41 states. (This excludes laws in the subcategory discussed in footnote 1, p. 19.) See also p. 34 below.

[7]Zartman, *Investments of Life Insurance Companies*, pp. 162–63. Much of the following information on nineteenth-century laws of states other than Illinois comes from Zartman, passim.

[8]R. Carlyle Buley, *The American Life Convention, 1906–1952: A Study in the History of Life Insurance* (New York: Appleton-Century-Crofts, 1953), vol. I, pp. 82–83.

[9]See Howard Jay Graham, "The Conspiracy Theory of the Fourteenth Amendment: Part 2," *Yale Law Journal* (December 1938): 171 ff.

the drive for federal regulation. The Supreme Court's blow was somewhat softened, however, by the expectation that with economic expansion after the Civil War the days of odious state legislation would soon be over. In 1871 the National Convention of Insurance Commissioners held their first meeting and announced that from now on "the true object and aim of governmental supervision should be to afford the fullest possible protection to the public, with the least possible annoyance or expense to, or interference with, the companies," and the gradual liberalization of investment laws during the late seventies and 1880s fired the Commissioners' hopes.[10]

The 1890s brought new attacks on life insurance assets and a renewed campaign by the industry for federal regulation. Populist legislators, concentrated mainly in the western and southern states, put insurance companies alongside railroads and eastern bankers as prime targets in the assault on high-handed finance, and they introduced a multitude of proposals ranging from increased taxation to compulsory investment to outright nationalization of insurance. Although a massive infusion of life insurance monies into state and national elections succeeded in preventing passage of the most offensive statutes, the industry unsuccessfully tried again in Congress in 1892 to create a national commissioner of insurance and, in 1897, to officially define as interstate commerce all company activities pursued outside its home state.

It is curious to note that the life insurance industry frequently argued its case for federal regulation in terms of the financial benefits which would accrue to the federal government upon assuming supervision—the precise advantage it was trying to deny the states. "A bureau of national insurance," urged the president of a large New York company, which "would receive deposits of stocks of the United States government pledged for the security of policyholders would both bring confidence to the insured and create a home market for a large amount of government stock."[11] These words may have returned to haunt the industry forty years later, but for the time being they must have seemed justified by the intensely hostile climate in the states. "It is possible," an important trade journal mused,

that legislatures come by their milking proclivities from the fact that a majority of the members are farm bred. Quite likely from early association "touchin" on and "appertainin" to the swelling udders of the kine, swine, geese and ducks; use doth breed such a habit that the desire is keen to lead this phase of pastoral life even in the temples of state. The sow of Aeneas has thirty tits, but how many does the granger think should adorn a life company?[12]

[10] Buley, *The American Life Convention*, p. 84.
[11] Ibid., p. 144.
[12] *Insurance Field* 12 (July–December 1905), July 13.

In 1903 Illinois "grangers" proposed that 90 percent of the capital collected in Illinois business be invested inside the state, and legislators in several other states thought the same.

As the fight for federal supervision continued into the new century the industry had the support of President Theodore Roosevelt and, as a champion in the Congress, John F. Dryden, president of the Prudential Life Insurance Company and recently elected senator from New Jersey. But bills introduced in 1904, 1905, and 1906 to put insurance under federal regulation failed to pass. Dryden's bills unfortunately kept landing in the Committee on the Judiciary, which was headed by Senator John C. Spooner of Wisconsin. Senator Spooner's own state had been one of the first to pass mandatory investment legislation and in 1907, under the leadership of Progressive Governor LaFollette, would pass a package of bills perhaps more repellent to life insurance companies than any before in history.[13]

That the notorieties of the 1905 Armstrong investigations had the effect of slowing the drive for federal regulation is somewhat ironic. The evidence of self-serving investments and general mishandling of funds by the officers of the giants of life insurance—the Equitable, Mutual of New York, and New York Life—certainly justified the worst epithets hurled eastward by the Populists. Nineteen hundred and seven was a bumper year in several states for mandatory investment bills, climaxed by the passage of a compulsory investment statute in Texas. But three developments stemming from the investigations were of much greater long-range importance to the future regulation of the industry. One was the new emphasis on safety and profitability discussed earlier. The second was a crack in the united front of companies on the issue of federal regulation. The smaller, western life insurers bitterly blamed their worsening public relations with their state capitals less on home-grown radicals than on the miscreants in the New York companies, and they were becoming increasingly suspicious of the idea of a single federal agency which might be dominated by these powerful competitors whose aims and methods they now distrusted. Finally, and ultimately most important, the Armstrong Committee's report had recommended remedial legislation for New York, and a Committee of Fifteen, chosen by the National Conference of Insurance Commissioners, had drawn up a group of model bills in order to implement similar legislation in other states. The extensive consultation between the commissioners and the life insurance companies which ensued during the shaping of these

[13] See Williamson and Smalley, *Northwestern Mutual Life*, pp. 142 ff. See also Spencer L. Kimball, *Insurance and Public Policy: A Study in the Legal Implementation of Social and Economic Public Policy, Based on Wisconsin Records, 1835-1959* (Madison, Wis.: University of Wisconsin Press, 1960), passim. Also Buley, *The American Life Convention*, pp. 306-9.

model bills marked a new high level of accommodation and cooperation between the state regulators and the industry. The future success of this working alliance, moreover, was promised by the passage of several of these model measures in eight of the dozen states in which they were introduced, including the state of Illinois.[14]

The next few years abounded in insurance legislation, likened by *Insurance Field* to "the confusion of Babel." The resurgence of mandatory investment bills, however, did not occur until 1915, when they were considered in Illinois and eleven other states. Again there was an industry drive for federal regulation, led by Darwin P. Kingsley, president of New York Life. Kingsley had a resolution introduced in Congress to submit to the states a constitutional amendment stating that insurance was interstate commerce.[15] But this time the eastern companies acted without the support of their western colleagues, who were no longer inclined to trade increasingly smooth relations with supervisory officials at home for a far-away federal regulation which might turn out to benefit only those who were so vociferously demanding it. This suspicion was symbolized by the existence of two trade organizations—the American Life Convention (ALC), based in Chicago and founded in 1906 expressly to oppose federal regulation, and the Association of Life Insurance Presidents (ALIP), dominated by the New York group.

So high was the hostility between the two industry factions that some rather extreme weapons were brandished. In 1913, for example, when the Secretary of the ALC learned that lobbyists for the eastern companies were pressing for certain laws detrimental to companies in the west, he warned the ALIP "either to keep hands off or a 'Robertson Law' would be passed." The Robertson Law was the name given to the Texas compulsory investment statute.[16]

An important additional factor in the declining enthusiasm of many companies for federal regulation was doubtless the changing political character of the federal government itself. Life insurance lagged behind most of the financial community in feeling that their business affairs were threatened by Washington. For bankers, security dealers, and corporation lawyers, disaffection had begun during the administration of Theodore Roosevelt and his dissolution of the Northern Securities Company.[17] But the large life companies, accustomed to having friends

[14] The 1907 Illinois investment statute discussed in the previous section above was an adaptation of the Committee of Fifteen's model bill.

[15] In New York Life v. Deer Lodge County (1913), the Supreme Court had reaffirmed the decision of Paul v. Virginia that insurance was not commerce, but was rather a personal contract subject to state laws.

[16] Buley, *The American Life Convention*, p. 409.

[17] See G. W. Edwards, *The Evolution of Finance Capitalism* (London: Longmans, Green and Co., 1938), pp. 190 ff.

in the national court—William Howard Taft would become chairman of the board of the Life Extension Institute, a research organization of the large firms, and Grover Cleveland, chairman of the ALIP—found that Roosevelt's plan to curb corruption in life insurance through uniform federal regulation coincided with their own plans for escaping radical state controls. Roosevelt's recommendations, in fact, consisted largely of proposals drawn up jointly by the industry and the state insurance commissioners in the wake of the Armstrong investigations.

Woodrow Wilson, however, presented a more serious problem. He was on record as opposed to the "monopoly of big credits," and had appointed to his cabinet one of the Populist arch-foes of the insurance industry, William Jennings Bryan. More ominous yet, Wilson was known to be greatly influenced in economic affairs by Louis D. Brandeis, an unrelenting critic of the financial manipulations of life insurance companies and of the laxness of state supervision, who had gone so far as to advocate state-operated life insurance companies as an alternative to an inefficient and wasteful private system.[18] In Congress the main assault against the edifice of security capitalism came with the 1912 hearings before the House Committee on Banking and Currency, chaired by Arsene Pujo of Louisiana. In 1913 the life insurance industry only narrowly defeated a section of the income tax bill which would have taxed dividends on life insurance policy premiums. Ex-President Taft, now with the Life Extension Institute, characterized the political atmosphere and the industry's fear for its assets in a speech before the National Association of Life Underwriters:

In the agitation regarding social changes and radical innovations in economic and governmental policy, much of which tends toward socialism, we hear much of the great results that are to be anticipated from the impartial and beneficial use of the capital of the whole country by governmental agencies, and the more equitable distribution of the profit from its use among all the people.[19]

The emergence of World War I abruptly pushed the idea of "the impartial and beneficial use of capital" into the background. But now the industry saw the general economic mobilization and in particular government-run war risk insurance, as a shove down "the greased slide of which the ultimate end is strangely like autocracy, absolutism, Prussianism." Nor was the industry reassured when, shortly following the armistice, Senator James Hamilton of Illinois introduced a resolution calling for nationalization of railroads, telegraph and telephone lines, fuel production, and interstate shipping, and it was rumored that the

---

[18]Wilson is quoted in ibid., p. 193. Bryan, in his more radical days of the late 1880s, had advocated the nationalization of insurance companies along with railroads. On Brandeis's views see Louis D. Brandeis, *Business—A Profession* (Boston, Mass.: Small, Maynard and Co., 1914), pp. 109-97. On the question of state life insurance as it was argued during this period, see W. F. Gephart, *Insurance and the State* (New York: Macmillan Company, 1913).

[19]Buley, *The American Life Convention*, p. 430.

insurance business was next on the list.[20] Many years later industry historians would agree that these fears had been exaggerated, that the real result of the war was increased cooperation among the companies and a firm implanting of the idea of life insurance in the minds of millions of young servicemen and their families. But for the time being the prospect of a federal government deeply involved in the national economy worked to reverse whatever momentum remained in the movement for federal regulation.

In the prosperous atmosphere of the 1920s, the issue of mandatory investment remained dormant, and, alongside it, the demand for federal regulation. The life insurance industry enjoyed unprecedented growth. As important contributors to the economic vitality of their home states, companies found relations with supervisory officials and legislators increasingly cordial and cooperative. Even after the stock market crash of 1929 life companies continued to expand their business, and industry forecasts remained optimistic. Only at the end of 1931, with the national economy collapsing all around, did the euphoria begin to sag. The misfortunes of others once again raised the specter of mandatory investment or other schemes to grab insurance assets: the manager of the American Life Convention wrote his fellow members that constant repetition of figures boasting about the volume of life insurance in force and the aggregate assets of the industry might not be "entirely advantageous," since it was bound to attract the attention of "all legislators and future legislators."[21]

Industry tensions were generally heightened by Franklin Roosevelt's election, but, while mandatory laws became a renewed threat in the states, it remained uncertain how the federal intrusion might occur. Then the Fletcher bill, approved June 10, 1933, authorized the Reconstruction Finance Corporation to purchase preferred stock of insurance companies, raising the unnerving possibility that the federal government might control life insurance assets by becoming a major stockholder. In 1934 it was anticipated that a congressional committee investigating abuses in various kinds of receiverships would recommend federal regulation of life insurance through the power to control the mails. Finally, the New Dealers appeared to show their hand in the hearings of the Temporary National Economic Committee (TNEC). In the industry's

[20] See Walter H. Bennett, *The History of the National Association of Insurance Agents: Fifty-Eight Years of a Stabilizing Force in Insurance* (Cincinnati: National Underwriter Co., 1954), p. 68.

[21] Buley, *The American Life Convention*, p. 711. The industry continued to prosper throughout the Depression, increasing its assets 32.8 percent without an appreciable rise in insurance in force. See Marquis James, *The Metropolitan Life, A Study in Business Growth* (New York: Viking Press, 1947), chapter XVII. On state mandatory activity, see Williamson and Smalley, *Northwestern Mutual Life*, p. 254. On the industry's view see James, *The Metropolitan Life*, chapter XXI.

view, the TNEC hearings were arranged to pillory the life insurance industry and prepare the ground for federal regulation, and it was expected that a bill for federal control would be introduced in the first session of Congress following the TNEC's report.[22]

The American Life Convention, at its annual meeting in October, 1939, reaffirmed its support for state regulation. But the statement—which was widely circulated with an accompanying letter urging all company executives to discuss its contents with their senators and representatives—did not simply oppose federal regulation per se. Notably, it tied its position to the issue of mandatory investment. Control by a single federal agency would of course arouse

apprehension of political tampering with the investment of trust funds of the most sacred character. We frankly fear that the power of coercion inherent in supervision by a single federal bureau might be used to force the financing of Federal projects, economic experiments and pet political schemes. Any proposal for Federal supervision and control would not emanate from policyholders—its aim would be political—and should cure indirect but effective domination over the thirty billion dollars held in trust by the companies, its accomplishment would be a calamity. Few things are more important to more people in America than keeping politics out of life insurance.[23]

The chances that the industry's old program for federal regulation might soon be realized against its will seemed even better with the 1944 Supreme Court decision in US v. South-Eastern Underwriters Association. The South-Eastern Underwriters' case concerned a prosecution by the Justice Department of a conspiracy of fire insurance companies to fix rates in several southern states. The Supreme Court majority said that the business of insurance was interstate commerce and fell, therefore, under the powers of Congress. This decision overturned Paul v. Virginia which had thwarted the industry's earlier plans for shifting regulation away from the radical state legislators.[24]

The fire and casualty companies responded to the South-Eastern Underwriters decision by angrily calling for, first, an amendment to the Constitution exempting insurance from regulation under the commerce clause and, second, congressional action exempting insurance from federal antitrust legislation. The life companies, however, after quietly making certain that the decision applied to *all* types of insurance, typically took a more circumspect view, one in the tradition of protecting as paramount the inviolability of their assets. Antitrust was not the

[22] See U.S. Temporary National Economic Committee, *Investigation of Concentration of Economic Power*, Monograph 28, Gerhard A. Gesell and Ernest J. Howe, "Study of Legal Reserve Life Insurance Companies," 76th Cong., 3rd sess., 1941.

[23] Buley, *The American Life Convention*, p. 848.

[24] See "Decisions," *Columbia Law Review* 44, no. 4 (July 1944): 772–73. Also James B. Donovan, "Regulation of Insurance Under the McCarran Act," *Law and Contemporary Problems* 14, no. 4 (Autumn 1940): 472–92. Also see Elmer Warren Sawyer, *Insurance as Interstate Commerce* (New York: McGraw-Hill, 1945), p. 140.

issue, argued industry executives. Federal regulation could end only as a means for funneling additional billions into the Treasury to be spent for New Deal programs. The life companies were joined in this position by the National Association of Insurance Commissioners, understandably reluctant to part with their jobs as state officials. If the government was successful in "swallowing" the insurance companies, said Illinois director Paul F. Jones, "Millions of the people's savings would be made available for foreign aid and domestic bribery." Additional support came from the Insurance Committee of the American Bar Association, composed primarily of lawyers for insurance companies, who warned against a federal grip on the vast funds of life insurance "to support this or that social or economic theory, or even to balance the budget, or make loans to various pressure groups."[25]

Attorney General Biddle, who had prosecuted the South-Eastern Underwriters case, repeatedly announced that the Department of Justice had no such grandiose ambitions: the sole desire and purpose, he explained, was to proceed against a limited number of practices which were in violation of the Sherman Antitrust Act.[26] But the nerves of the life companies had been worn thin by the several highly publicized, even if not especially effective, forays against finance capital, particularly the investigations of the TNEC. The anxiety was heightened still further by other prominent opponents of the New Deal, such as Governor John Bricker of New York and Congressman John Vorys of Ohio, who similarly interpreted the administration's purposes. The editorial of the *Washington Evening Star* is representative of conservative press reaction:

> For several years now it has been evident that the New Dealers wanted to get their hands on the insurance business because of the vast control of funds involved therein.
> Attorney General Biddle has said there is not present intention to enter into regulation of the insurance business. But he cannot speak for the bureaucrats who have been planning a long while to set up a Federal agency to control insurance.
> News of the case was blanketed by the invasion but it remains the most sensational happening on the home front.[27]

But by the time the McCarran-Fergusson bill was on its way through Congress, life companies, along with the rest of the insurance industry, had regained both their composure and the political initiative. The bill itself had been drafted by the American Life Convention, the National Association of Insurance Commissioners, the Association of Insurance

[25] Buley, *The American Life Convention*, p. 848.

[26] See, for example, his statement in U.S. Congress, Senate and House Committees on the Judiciary, *Joint Hearings, Insurance*, 78th Cong., 2nd sess., pp. 634–36.

[27] Bricker is quoted in "Decisions," *Columbia Law Review*. Vorys and the *Washington Evening Star* are quoted in *Congressional Digest* 23 (October 1944): 255.

Agents, the National Board of Fire Underwriters, and other insurance organizations. It provided for a three-year moratorium on enforcement of the Sherman, Clayton, and Federal Trade Commission Acts, and made these statutes applicable thereafter only "to the extent that such business is not regulated by state law." In other words, Congress would delegate its new power to regulate the insurance business back to the states, pending only good behavior on the matter of antitrust.

The hearings on the bill were punctuated with disavowals by public officials to the effect that neither certain Congressmen nor the administration, nor, in particular, Attorney General Biddle—by now the Nemesis of the insurance industry—had any intentions whatever of disturbing the system of state regulation. The most exuberant disclaimers of all were reserved for the subject of possible mandatory investment activities by the federal government. Senator Joseph O'Mahoney, chairman of the Joint Committee conducting the hearing and former chairman of the TNEC, directed his closing remarks to the nefarious opinion that "the Government of Washington intended to lay its heavy hand upon the treasuries of the insurance companies." Senator O'Mahoney reassured those gathered that the Joint Committee—or for that matter the TNEC or the SEC—had not "ever suggested any such thing. . . . It was never considered . . . that there should be federal supervision or any attempt to take over the funds of life insurance companies."[28]

The easy passage of McCarran-Fergusson (Public Law 15) signaled a tempering of the controversy over federal regulation. Since that time, proposals for mandatory investment in the states have been less frequent, and in 1967 the Texas Robertson Law was rescinded.[29] At the federal level the matter has been raised by the government indirectly in relation to the economic concentration of the industry and the effectiveness of state antitrust procedures.[30] In 1948 the O'Mahoney Subcommittee on Investments (of the Committee on the Economic Report) initiated an extended investigation of industry financial practices but made no recommendations to upset the status quo. Since 1970, in response to the shortage of home mortgage funds, several suggestions have been offered by public officials, notably Congressman Wright Pat-

[28]U.S. Congress, Senate and House Committees on the Judiciary, Insurance, p. 640 and passim. For a general account of the bill in Congress, see Congressional Quarterly Almanac (Washington, D.C.: Congressional Quarterly, 1945), pp. 104 ff.

[29]On the post-World War II period see Winston Clingen Beard, "The Financial and Economic Effects of Geographical Restrictions upon the Investment Policies of Life Insurance Companies," Ph.D. dissertation, University of Illinois, 1961.

[30]See Charles C. Center and Richard M. Heins, Insurance and Government (New York: McGraw-Hill Book Company, 1962), especially the papers by John C. Stedman and Robert L. Bicks. Also see the speech by Paul Rand Dixon, chairman of the Federal Trade Commission, "Federal Anti-trust Laws and the Insurance Industry," Proceedings of the Sixtieth Annual Meeting of the Legal Section of the American Life Convention (1967): 243-51.

man and Senator William Proxmire, to insulate housing credit from the
strains of the business cycle through mandatory measures. The Nixon
administration has proposed inducements to the same end in the form
of tax advantages. But, in g .eral, the tone of recent years has changed
from the staged inquisitions of the New Deal to the sober studies and
concerned assessment of trends by the now rather domesticated federal
watchdog, and life insurance has not been singled out from among the
wider financial community for special treatment.

There is evidence, nonetheless, that the prospect of mandatory investment laws continues to shade the industry's political outlook. From
1965 to 1972 nineteen compulsory laws were introduced in thirteen
states, all easily defeated.[31] The possible advantages of a national system of regulation have been suggested, somewhat diffidently, by a few
of the larger New York companies. But the majority of life insurance
executives and companies have opposed the change, and industry
lobbyists have resisted such federal inroads as might come through SEC
jurisdiction over their variable annuity activities. Among the reasons
stated in the Illinois interviews the potential for federal manipulation or
seizure of the assets figured prominently. The argument of the president of one of Illinois' fastest growing life companies was characteristic: "The integrity of our assets is a major consideration. Once you
mix money and the federal government you're in bad trouble." As will
be discussed in chapter VI, the policy decision to invest one billion
dollars in American slums was influenced by the expectation that Congress might require such allocations by large financial institutions by
law. The midwest lobbyist for one of the nation's largest life companies
explained in an interview: "The Federal government won't be able to
show cause of such legislation in light of the Urban Investments Program. I'm quite certain this was one of the main objectives." A merger
of the ALC and LIAA to become the American Life Insurance Association, and the movement of headquarters from Chicago and New York
to Washington, D.C., may signify a greater attention to federal rather
than state encroachments.

IV

The federal system of American government, specifically the division
among the national government and the several states, imposes on life
insurance politics an important structural dimension, one no less important for its rather mechanistic character. Thus, while a particular mode

---

[31] The states included Arkansas, Delaware, Hawaii, Kansas, Maryland, Mississippi, Montana,
New York, North Dakota, South Dakota, Tennessee, Virginia, and West Virginia. Most of these
bills were aimed at channeling funds into home mortgages and required the investment of from
20 to 75 percent of the premiums collected inside the state.

of legislation—the mandatory investment law—has largely determined the companies' preference for state or federal regulation, the fact that the seat of regulation has continuously been in the states has afforded vital strategic opportunities for preventing the enactment of laws obnoxious to the insurance industry. The simple existence of a federal alternative creates an immediate vulnerability of state officials to the strictures and demands of the industry—in this case a vulnerability enhanced by the long history of constitutional uncertainty and the present probationary status of state regulation. The foregoing section has documented the salience of the federal alternative as a recurring issue in insurance politics. But other, more workaday considerations serve to remind state legislators and regulators of this particular sword of Damocles.

The first and most important reminder is taxation. In the fiscal year 1967–68 the Illinois Department of Insurance collected for various insurance licenses, examinations, and assorted privileges, over forty-six million dollars for the state treasury, most of which sum would be forfeited under a system of national regulation.[32] This potential financial loss to the states has been skillfully exploited by the companies as a means of avoiding a wide range of state legislation.[33] Another sacrifice to a system of federal regulation would be the Department of Insurance personnel, and especially the office of director or superintendent. Although since the days of the Armstrong Investigations the office has been wrapped in the garb of professionalism, in Illinois, as elsewhere, the directorship is an important bit of political largesse for a new governor, and it carries with it the usual appurtenances of an operation surveiling billions of dollars in business. The National Association of Insurance Commissioners (NAIC) has been an important and effective pressure group against federal encroachment and has been instrumental in achieving uniform standards for computing reserves, taxation, investments, and so on. Through the labors of the professional staffs of the numerous state departments rather than the peripatetic commissioners, the NAIC has acquired a reputation for disinterested expertise in the service of a viable system of state regulation. The successful resistance against federal control, however, depends on maintaining the industry's support for the status quo in regulation. This has resulted in an entente

[32]John F. Bolton, Jr., *Annual Report by the Director of the Department of Insurance*, 1968, p. 27.

[33]For example, see *Congressional Record, Proceedings, and Debates of the 79th Congress, 1st Session*, vol. 91, Part 1, (January 3, 1945–February 23, 1945), Washington, 1945, pp. 478, 1085 ff., 1093 ff., 1477 ff. Members of Congress from North Carolina, New York, Iowa, Texas, and others complained that their state insurance departments were having or anticipating trouble collecting taxes in the wake of the South-Eastern Underwriters Association decision, and they argued for the swift passage of the McCarran-Fergusson bill as the remedy.

between the NAIC and the industry, marked by amiability, cooperation, and the implicit understanding that any NAIC policies or recommendations which are too distasteful might provoke the companies into
taking the federal option.[34]

Quite apart from the constraints imposed on state policy by the
alternative of federal regulation are those resulting from the multiplicity of state jurisdictions. This multiplicity has created a field played
by the life insurance industry with great skill and to consistent advantage. Any state law promulgating regulations or taxes at variance with
the laws of another state and less advantageous to the industry is faced
with two contingencies. The first is the withdrawal of domestic companies to some other state. For instance, in 1947 the Prudential threatened to leave New Jersey unless a tax proposal considered onerous to
the company was defeated.[35] The second contingency is the tactical
withdrawal of foreign insurance companies from business in the state.
This was the industry's response to the Texas Robertson Law: twenty-
nine companies, including virtually every major foreign company operating in Texas, withdrew immediately. Similarly, progressive insurance
reforms in Wisconsin precipitated a flight of twenty-three companies,
holding almost one-half of Wisconsin life insurance.[36] In the latter case
the losses in jobs to agents and company employees, rental payments,
and the rest are somewhat less severe than with the departure of home
companies, but they are sufficiently prohibitive to stay the hand of a
capricious legislature.

The constraints arising from this multiplicity of jurisdiction are reinforced by the competition among the states to provide a favorable
climate for business growth and profit. Should one state pass a law
offering advantages to companies domiciled within its borders there is
the immediate inducement for laggard states to follow suit. A recent
example is the pressure felt by the State of New York Insurance Department to imitate Illinois and other states in liberalizing restrictions
on insurance holding companies.[37]

[34]On the NAIC see Wade O. Martin, Jr., "The NAIC and State Insurance Department
Functions," *Insurance Law Journal* 356 (September 1952): 538-87.

[35]Earl Chapin May and Will Ousler, *The Prudential: A Story of Human Security* (Garden
City, N.J.: Doubleday and Co., 1950), p. 196. On the same tactic in the 1890s see Williamson
and Smalley, *Northwestern Mutual Life*, p. 130. The authors describe lobbying methods, then
comment: "Where these efforts were not effective, it was always possible to stop doing business
in the state in question; this was done in a number of instances."

[36]See Winston C. Beard, *The Effects of State Investment Requirements for Life Insurance
Companies.* Prepared for the Arkansas Insurance Commissioner by the University of Arkansas
College of Business Administration, Industrial Relations and Extension Center in cooperation
with the Arkansas Industrial Development Commission, 1958, mimeo.

[37]See State of New York Insurance Department, *Report of the Special Committee on Insurance Holding Companies*, February 15, 1968.

Another aspect of this state competition is the protection of locally based companies from the pernicious regulation of other states. This is the domain of the retaliatory or "reciprocal" laws. Since their first passage in 1851, the retaliatory laws have provided commissioners with an effective weapon to force policy changes outside their own jurisdictions. The Illinois law states that:

> Whenever the existing or future laws shall require of companies incorporated or organized under the laws of this state as a condition precedent to their doing business in such other state or country, compliance with laws, rules, regulations, and prohibitions more onerous or burdensome than the rules and regulations imposed by this State on foreign or alien companies, Illinois will exact the same requirements of foreign insurance companies incorporated in the offending state.

An Iowa mandatory investment law, for example, requiring a percentage investment in Iowa farms and housing as a condition for selling insurance in Iowa would mean that Iowa companies must make identical percentage investments in Illinois (and all other states which have such retaliatory laws), even though Illinois itself has no such investment requirements. Retaliatory laws thus perform a double service: they protect domestic companies from competitive disadvantage, and they serve as an effective deterrent against all types of innovation opposed by the industry. This last has been particularly significant in the field of mandatory investment.[38]

States, on the other hand, are denied parallel tactics which would allow them to play one segment of the industry against another, or offer special inducements to business from other states. This is largely the accomplishment of the NAIC, which has worked closely with life insurance trade organizations for uniform state laws. While these so-called model bills have been somewhat less popular in the areas of investment and taxation than in policy provisions, examinations, and fair trade practices, they nonetheless represent a united front—industry and commissioners—that limits an individual state's maneuverability.[39] The fact that the value of uniformity is widely accepted as an essential condition of McCarran Fergusson gives such model bills added symbolic importance as a check on local initiative.

Finally, renegade states are faced with the industry's adroit use of its own investment funds. The withdrawal of capital is an extremely delicate tactic because of its widespread ramifications on the local economy, in which life companies may already have sizable investments. Also it may eliminate certain opportunities for profits on loans to

[38] Interview with Henry A. Warshall, footnote 6.

[39] See Henry A. Warshall, "Review of State Legislation," *Proceedings of the Sixtieth Annual Meeting of the Legal Section of the American Life Convention* (1967), pp. 394–97. Warshall tabulates the success of the various model bills in the states through 1967.

enterprises within the state. In the 1890s capital withdrawal was used against states deemed "politically unstable" because of Populist majorities.[40] A similar stoppage was affected against Texas after the passage of the Robertson Law, although companies soon returned to participate in the exploration of oil. This tactic has particular relevance to the federal structure, since the ability to isolate legal entities for punitive treatment would be eliminated under a system of national regulation.

The interplay between state policy, regulatory structure, and industry strategy may be conceptualized more concisely in terms of the *mobility* of capital and the *rigidity* of state jurisdictions. The mobility of capital is most clearly illustrated in the case of the withdrawal of investment funds. The same concept applies equally, however, to the departure of companies from their home states. The insurance industry is virtually pure capital. Allowing perhaps for an untimely sale of a home office building and the loss of some trained employees, a life company may move its base of operation to another state with no serious impairment to its business. In this respect life insurance is in a significantly different position from industries which are necessarily more stationary. One extreme example of the latter is an industry engaged in the development of a natural resource. If it is true that Montana is captive to Anaconda mining and Maine to the timber companies, there are likewise important implications in the fact that the reverse captivities are also a political reality. The attribute of mobility may be underscored by the threat of the New York Stock Exchange in 1966 to leave New York City unless tax relief was forthcoming. While this option was open to an institution as culturally entrenched as the stock exchange, it is an impossibility for Anaconda.[41]

The mobility of capital functions as an important aspect of life insurance politics only against the stationary rigidity of the state laws. The state is powerless to retaliate against a company which chooses to withdraw rather than conform to some local regulation. It cannot reach across its borders to penalize a company that chokes off investment funds from the local economy. Paradoxically, retaliatory laws heighten this rigidity by reducing available legal stances the state might take toward foreign companies. These problems of stationary rigidity are a result of the sphere of industry operations being more extensive than any one unit of regulation, and would be meaningless in a national system with no "free" zones.

[40]Morton Keller, *The Life Insurance Enterprise*, p. 136.

[41]The idea of industry mobility has sometimes been noted in passing by students of federalism. Thus, Daniel Elazar: "Or, in yet another kind of problem, until the federal government made it advantageous for all states to adopt unemployment compensation programs, those which wished to do so were handicapped by threats of major employers to move elsewhere." "The States and the Nation," in Herbert Jacob and Kenneth N. Vines, *Politics in the American States: A Comparative Analysis* (Boston: Little, Brown, 1967), p. 454.

Ultimately, of course, the mobility of capital is itself dependent on a state policy dominated by the *enabling* mode. In other words, the protection of the assets from state control, the chief object of industry politics, is the precondition for the industry's most powerful defensive weapon. In a nation governed by mandatory laws, capital manipulations would be restricted or entirely stopped. At this point, international considerations become relevant.[42] Also, life insurance relations with state officials and the public, and political circumstances other than the mobility of capital, would assume chief importance. These relations and circumstances are the subject of the next chapter.

---

[42] We have confined our remarks to national boundaries, but an international perspective is by no means far-fetched. For an interesting discussion of one nation's dilemma between dependence on outside capital and the desire for repatriation of business control, see Kari Levitt, *Silent Surrender: The American Economic Empire in Canada* (New York: Liveright, 1971).

CHAPTER **III**

THE
POLITICS OF
SAFETY

Life insurance investment is not a prominent issue in contemporary Illinois politics. If a state legislator is asked about insurance politics, he will inevitably start to talk about the problems of passing a bill providing no-fault automobile insurance or fire coverage for dilapidated sections of the cities. If pressed about *life* insurance, he might refer to legislative battles over the accidental death limits, or the bill to put life insurance proceeds under the inheritance tax laws.

Nine bills directly related to investment were passed by the 75th General Assembly of the Illinois legislature, the session studied in this chapter as a case of the life insurance industry's relationship to the governmental process. Two of these bills, concerning holding companies and variable annuities, were of major importance for the future financial role of the large life companies. But very few legislators remembered them as highlights of the so-called "Session of Insurance Reform".

This lack of differentiation—between investment issues and other life company issues, and between life insurance and other branches of the insurance industry—may be partly explained in terms of the categories set forth in chapter II. None of the bills proposed in the 75th General Assembly were mandatory laws; all of them were enabling laws. Since mandatory laws aim to benefit a specified segment of the community which is external to the insurance industry, we might expect that within the larger field of insurance legislation, these laws would be political questions in their own right, as deliberate public policies toward particular goals, and with the support of noninsurance groups. Enabling laws, on the other hand, are associated with benefits to the insurance industry, the internal constituency of companies and customers. Invest-

ment has no special place among such areas as capitalization requirements or payment provisions. Thus, we might expect enabling investment laws to be part of the same processes, coalitions, strategies as
other life insurance legislation.

A similar explanation applies to the currently undifferentiated place
of life insurance among the politics of the various branches of the
insurance industry. Mandatory laws to provide credit have always been
directed at life companies, because life companies are the members of
the industry richest in assets. Enabling laws, on the other hand, which
ostensibly seek safety, have been part of a general policy that encompasses the entire insurance industry. To study the legislative and administrative politics of investment laws in Illinois, then, necessarily entails
study of the politics of insurance laws in general and, to some extent,
the politics of the insurance industry as a whole.

The previous chapter described the overall development of state regulation of life insurance investment. Having had a look at the forest, we
turn now to a few trees. This chapter analyzes the political thicket
through which investment laws in Illinois are passed: the origins of
insurance legislation, the role of the legislators, the Department of Insurance, the industry lobby. The fact that all of the investment bills
proposed in the session are enabling laws, however, again raises the
problem of nondecisionmaking. In Illinois politics, mandatory investment is a dead issue, or, more precisely, an issue which is sleeping
soundly. This chapter is also concerned with identifying political tactics, institutions, legislative attitudes which support the status quo and
obscure alternative policies of greater state control over life insurance
assets. Since, historically, a great deal of life insurance energy has been
devoted to this end, these findings are at least as important as the
details of lobbying techniques and legislative voting patterns.

I

The 75th General Assembly of the Illinois Legislature passed some
fifty insurance laws, most of them part of the Department of Insurance's program to "provide the most sweeping and extensive moderni-
zation of the Illinois Insurance Code in thirty years."[1] The program
had been inspired by a rash of company insolvencies that had aroused
the press and embarrassed the Governor and his Insurance Department.
At first glance, the case of insurance politics during 1967–68 would
seem to provide a good example of a state government exerting its
power over a recalcitrant industry.

[1]John F. Bolton, Jr., *The Illinois Program: A Two Year Plan to Modernize Regulation of the
Insurance Industry; A Regulatory White Paper Prepared for the Use of Members of the 75th
Illinois General Assembly*, 1967, p. 1.

That first glances are often misleading is indicated by an event which took place on the evening following the submission of the Insurance Department's "white paper" to the legislature. That evening nine hundred insurance executives paid twenty dollars a plate for a testimonial dinner at Chicago's Palmer House Hotel in honor of Director of Insurance John F. Bolton. Also attending were some hundred Illinois politicians; Mayor Daley of Chicago, Governor Kerner, and leaders of the General Assembly were seated alongside industry luminaries at the head table. After dinner, the group presented Bolton with a plaque citing his contributions to the "financial security and welfare of all the people of Illinois." Bolton, in turn, gave a short speech urging the companies to support the new legislative proposals, warning against the evils of federal control, and praising the assembled industry for its role in the state's economic growth.[2]

The testimonial dinner was certainly exceptional as a show of friendship, but the cordial relations between the insurance director and the industry he regulates is a regular pattern of Illinois government. This pattern, familiar to students of other clientele agencies, involves, first of all, the recruitment and rotation of personnel among the Insurance Department, the companies, and law firms that serve as counsel for the industry. Of the last nine insurance directors preceding Bolton, extending in office from 1933–65, seven had been lawyers for large insurance companies, and four of these seven had also been company directors or officers before assuming the directorship. An eighth had been a district agent for a large life company before coming to the department as assistant director. The ninth was in the real estate investment business and a life company director. Bolton, while serving as director, remained active in his old law firm of Bolton, Keane, and Bolton, which numbers several insurance companies among its clients, including the largest domestic life insurer in Illinois.[3] Upon retirement from the department, directors and lower officials frequently take positions with insurance companies they regulated while in office.[4]

In addition to personnel, the companies provide a wide range of service for the poorly staffed and financed Insurance Department.

[2] *Chicago Daily News*, January 20, 1967.

[3] Bolton's law partner, Thomas J. Keane, is a Chicago Alderman who is close to Mayor Daley and considered by many to be the second most powerful politician in the city.

[4] For example, in September 1967, the executive assistant to Bolton, James C. Cage, resigned to enter business as a consultant to the industry. Before joining the department in 1963, Cage had been board chairman of ICT Insurance Company of Dallas, Texas. That company failed in 1957, and a $15 million suit as a result of the failure was still pending against Cage during his service under Bolton. Cage had also been executive vice-president of Cosmopolitan Insurance Company of Chicago, against which a pending suit charged its officers with defrauding policy and stockholders, false financial statements, rigging the value of stocks owned by the company, and fraud.

These services include loaning house accountants for company examinations, providing company statistics for department studies, serving on advisory commissions, and lobbying for department-sponsored legislation. This creates a condition of department dependency on the industry which is self-perpetuating. For example, Bolton has singled out a task he found especially helpful: the big companies

helped in aiding the department in drawing for the first time what I consider a very realistic and sensible budget. They came and testified on my behalf before the Budgetary Commission. . . . And they did the job where they broke down the number of companies that might have to be examined in the next year, they divided it by the number of examiners, field examiners, I now have, and they came out with how many hours, and they suggested to the Legislature that we employ "this many" people. This is how far they went.[5]

After the budget in question was approved, the Insurance Department had 80 examiners for 1,300 companies. The department's budget showed, and has continued to show, the lowest ratio of operating funds to receipts of any state agency in Illinois.[6]

The insurance industry's attitude of cooperation is fostered by the governor's customary consultation with leading insurance executives on the selection of the director, and the extreme unlikelihood that any man objectionable to the industry would be appointed. This practice reflects in part the penetration of company representatives into all levels of the political machinery of both Illinois political parties and the industry's financial contributions to state campaigns.[7] Friendly dispositions are reinforced by the atmosphere of consultation. Life company officials describe their relations with Bolton as "entirely satisfactory," "friendly," "amicable." Typical are the remarks of a life company executive who heads a trade organization of Illinois companies and is active in Republican politics:

Bolton had the same trouble you see in most of these Chicago politicians. You couldn't get to him. He spent one day in Springfield, another up here in Chicago. But after 4:30 or whenever they close up down there, he'd sit around and talk to you the whole night. He'd take off his coat, sit around in his shirt sleeves he loves to talk. And I don't remember having any disagreement with Bolton. What he could support, we could support, and what he opposed, we could also oppose.

This shirt-sleeve congenialty infects even those few who are initially less inclined to cooperate. Another company executive describes the conversion of a young lawyer on the Insurance Department's legal staff:

[5] Certified Stenographic Report of Proceedings Held at the Public Hearing of the Joint House of Representatives and Senate of the State of Illinois Insurance Study Committee, April 14, A.D. 1967, Chicago, Illinois, p. 86.

[6] New York had at this time 322 examiners for 913 companies. 3.6 percent of taxes paid to the Department of Insurance are used to run the department. New York spends 10 percent. The national average is 4.8 percent.

[7] See pp. 48ff. below.

D. was hired to assist the man in charge of drafting legislation, then the other man quit. The job requires a familiarity with every angle of the insurance code and in his first presentation we made a monkey out of him. . . . When D. came in he was going to represent "the people" and defend them against the big bad insurance companies. But as he got to know some of us and become more familiar with the history of some of these things, his attitude changed. I found I could work very well with D.

The idea that the department ought to represent "the people" and defend them against the insurance companies has been explicitly denied by Bolton, who sees the problem of representation somewhat more circumspectly:

My feeling is that the Department of Insurance was set up to regulate the insurance industry in all of its phases and we shouldn't put ourselves up as either plaintiff's attorneys, nor should we put ourselves up as company attorneys in trying to regulate it. It is a job that must be done as fairly as possible, without prejudice against the rights of the companies that do, as a large measure, a real big and wonderful job in our State of Illinois.[8]

Bolton specified two general goals of the Insurance Department under his leadership. First, "solvency and honesty of the companies, agents, solicitors and brokers—in short, safety for the insuring public." Second, "to preserve insurance as a source of State revenue."[9] During fiscal year 1968 the Department of Insurance collected 46.2 million dollars for the state treasury, and Bolton estimates the contribution of the insurance industry to the economy of Illinois as "incalculable."[10]

The goal of safety was discussed in the last chapter as a distinctive characteristic of enabling legislation and will be considered here in the concluding section. The concentration on safety has had special effects on the Department of Insurance, however, which may be understood in terms of a process of administrative natural selection. This process has already been implied in the lack of differentiation of life insurance from the insurance industry generally. More specifically, the process of administrative natural selection works to deflect attention away from life companies to less financially stable sectors of the industry, like fire and casualty insurance. Within the life insurance industry itself, the process works to turn scarce department resources to the surveillance of financially weak life companies, leaving stronger (and usually larger) companies fairly unhampered in their operations. Administrative natural selection influenced the contents of the 1967–68 legislation, and has been important in the department's enforcement of existing insur-

---

[8] *Certified Stenographic Report* . . . , pp. 34–35. Also see Bolton's speech before the Union League Club, *Chicago Daily News,* January 30, 1966.

[9] John F. Bolton, Jr. *Annual Report by the Director of the Department of Insurance,* 1967, p. 5.

[10] Bolton, *The Illinois Program* . . . , p. 2.

ance laws. For example, the remarks of the Examiner in Charge of Office Auditing illustrate the principle of the survival of the fittest in respect to the conflict-of-interest laws:

> We aren't concerned with the big companies like Continental or New York Life. We're concerned about companies that would go under and hurt the policy-holder. . . . If we got a complaint, even then I don't think we could realistically go into it. But we're really not interested anyway. Even if there was a potential conflict, it would be alright if it wasn't hurting the company, even though the officer might benefit. Looking at it realistically, Continental or New York Life would probably never go out of business.

The role of revenue and taxation in creating a solicitous attitude of public officials was mentioned in chapter II and is worth reemphasizing. Bolton has repeatedly underscored the "economic fact" which makes "the business of insurance . . . particularly appropriate for regulation at the state level," and has been a chief spokesman for the National Association of Insurance Commissioners on the dangers of federal regulation.[11] He has boasted that successful Illinois regulation has meant that "dollars that once were drained to other states and other regions are remaining at home."[12] While Insurance Department officials are not ones to spend time thinking about abstractions like the mobility of capital, they are well aware of the financial realities. With respect to the life companies, the concern for revenue has considerably offset the inherent political advantages of home companies over foreign companies. In response to a question about the feasibility of a law requiring foreign life insurers to invest Illinois premiums inside the state, the Legislative Assistant to the Director replied that it was unlikely that the department would ever support such legislation because, among other reasons, foreign life insurance companies contribute more money to state revenue than do the domestic companies.

The framing of the insurance reform package in 1967 presents a condensed version of the abiding relationship between the Department of Insurance and the insurance industry. The reformist spirit in a department which for thirty years had alternated between benign and corrupt passivity came as a response to a protracted public demonstration that the celebrated program of safety for Illinois insurance funds was a complete failure. Twenty-six insurance companies, several of them life companies, had been liquidated since 1960. These liquidations presented a political threat, since the failure of an insurance company destroys the savings and security of thousands of persons—and voters. If

[11] Bolton headed the NAIC Committee for the Preservation of State Regulation. For his views see "State Supervision Has Earned the Right to be Proven Wrong," a speech delivered before the Conference for Young Life Insurance Companies, sponsored by the Continental Assurance Company, September 28, 1966. Also see *Chicago Sun-Times*, August 24, 1967.

[12] *Chicago Sun-Times*, January 20, 1967.

the company happens to be a mutual or reciprocal company, as many of those liquidated were, the erstwhile policyholder is further enraged to find that he owes the state of Illinois money on the liabilities of "his" defunct company. Newspapers around the state joined angry legislators in calling for an investigation of insurance regulation.[13]

Anxious to head off trouble, Governor Kerner instructed Director Bolton to take the initiative for cleaning out his own house—the lease to which Bolton had acquired after the preceding director displayed the hypocrisy of the safety regulations by becoming involved in a scandal over these same liquidations. Bolton promptly delegated the job of drawing up proposals to an Insurance Advisory Committee. The committee was a nice model of Bolton's theories on representation. It was designed to represent "elements of the insurance industry: our state educational institutions, the General Assembly, the Courts of Illinois, the accounting profession, and most importantly, the insurance-buying public."[14] There were twenty members: five were executives of insurance companies; three represented company trade organizations; four were members of law and accounting firms with an extensive insurance clientele; one man was a professor at the University of Illinois who was a regular paid consultant to life insurance companies. Three were public officials: first, apparently representing the judicial branch, the administrative assistant to the Circuit Court of Cook County, a politician in Mayor Daley's Democratic machine, of which Bolton had once been a member; second, the chairman of the Insurance Committee of the Illinois House; and third, the chairman of the Insurance Subcommittee of the Committee on Financial Institutions of the Illinois Senate, who was in private life a director of two life insurance companies. Finally, one

---

[13] Scholarly treatments of public policy generally downplay the element of corruption in official behavior. Our study is no exception, although malfeasance in office, conflict of interest, and so on is pervasive throughout insurance politics, and the Department of Insurance in particular. The details of Bolton's executive assistant's career are mentioned on page 42 (note). Even more interesting is the case of Joseph Gerber, Director of Insurance under both Republican Governor Stratton and Democratic Governor Kerner. While in office, Gerber's two assistants formed a law firm, Berman and Woodruff, which in 1961 and 1962 collected $78,809.46 in retainers and fees from six insurance companies, including Cosmopolitan Life Insurance Company. During this period, Cosmopolitan Life was under investigation for insolvency. Gerber delayed a determination for seven months, then allowed Guarantee Reserve Life Insurance Company of Hammond, Indiana, to reinsure $100 million worth of policies written by Cosmopolitan. Gerber resigned from the department in 1963, and became head of a new law firm, Gerber, Berman, and Woodruff. Gerber then took a job as legal advisor to Cosmopolitan Life and a director of Guarantee Reserve Life. Berman became secretary of Guarantee Reserve Life. In the closing months of 1963 and the beginning of 1964, the law firm collected over $82,000 in fees and expenses from these two companies and several other insurance company clients, which, like Cosmopolitan Life and Guarantee Reserve Life, had received their original charters under Gerber's directorship.

See C. W. Owsley Sheppard and Robert Class, "Shady Insurance Firms Can Thrive under State Laws," *Chicago American*, October 3, 1966.

[14] Bolton, *The Illinois Program* . . . ,p. 4.

member represented the consumers—the "insurance-buying public"—, an official responsible for purchasing insurance for the Inland Steel Corporation.

The actual work was done elsewhere. The bills on casualty insurance were drawn up jointly by the department staff, a group of casualty companies who had organized themselves into the Illinois Casualty Insurance Industry Legislative Committee, a move coinciding with efforts of casualty companies nationally to tighten up state controls in order to forestall federal regulation.[15] Most of the life insurance bills were drafted by the department staff, after advisement with individual companies and the American Life Convention.

Of the nine investment bills, four, including the bill on holding companies, were drafted by individual companies; one was drafted by the American Life Convention; three were drafted by the department's examination staff at the behest of life companies; and one was drafted by the department's legal staff on its own initiative and was proposed after subsequent consultation with the industry. The investment bills, then, were framed entirely outside of the Advisory Committee. In Bolton's speech to the legislature they were listed in the enumeration of reform proposals but were given no mention in his long explanation of the purposes of the reforms. Presumably, they were included under the general rubric of "many other specific measures designed to meet problems developing in the new insurance marketplace."[16] In fact, none of the investment bills were "reforms," unless changing provisions for higher profitability be considered a reform. The various proposals liberalized laws concerning investment in leases, mortgages, conditional bank obligations, real estate, and bank accounts and other investments in foreign countries.

The most important was S. 138, clearing the legal way for a life insurance company to pyramid its investments through the device of a holding company. S. 138 permits a life insurance company to participate with other investors in a finance company, which in turn may purchase stocks and make other investments. The advantage to the life company is that this device geometrically extends the purchasing or investment power of its own assets. By controlling the finance company it has more money at its disposal, while the law concerns itself only with fractional ownership in computing conformities to the insurance code with respect to diversity and permissible percentages in given investments. This "downstream holding company" device was a prime target of the Armstrong investigations of 1905. In his "white paper"

---

[15] *Wall Street Journal*, February 23, 1967.

[16] Bolton, *The Illinois Program* . . . , p. 4.

Bolton explains the legislation: "To prevent pyramiding of small, weak companies by requiring a surplus."[17] The thrust of the legislation, however, was not at small weak companies at all, but was intended to enable the pyramiding of large companies.

The place of life insurance in the reform program and the place of investment laws in particular bear out remarks above about administrative natural selection. Three representatives of life insurance companies were appointed to the Advisory Committee in order to lend their prestige. But most of the reforms were aimed at the casualty companies. An official of the department explained, "Sure, there's plenty wrong with life company operations. But the situation in casualty is the worst, and quite frankly, the most obvious."

The industry-dominated Advisory Committee functioned in three important ways. First, its existence provided the image to the public and the press that something was being done, that a highly expert body was busy reforming the code. In fact, they met infrequently and held few hearings, but these details of their "activity" escaped public notice because of Bolton's strict avoidance of all publicity on the promised reforms. Second, the committee acted as a veto group for legislation unpalatable to the industry: several proposals of department staff members were withdrawn on anticipation of Committee disapproval. Third, it provided an expert and respectable endorsement for the package of bills, including several which had nothing to do with reform. In his regulatory "white paper," Bolton presented the legislation to the General Assembly as the hard work of the Insurance Industry Advisory Committee.

II

For some issues in Illinois politics, like taxation or education or public assistance, the distance between executive endorsement and legislative approval can be something of a chasm. For life insurance proposals, the move is more like stepping off one bus and on to another. In 1967 the Democrats held the governorship and the Republicans controlled both houses of the General Assembly. But these ordinarily troublesome political circumstances had no apparent effect on the easy course of the Advisory Committee's reform program.

The General Assembly is an important branch of the insurance industry's "sub-government," to use Cater's phrase, and only in the most formal sense can be considered part of a separation of powers.[18] Insur-

---

[17]Ibid., p. 10. The variable annuity legislation, providing for "separate accounts" not subject to investment limitations, was not part of Bolton's reform package but was written by the ALC and introduced by a bi-partisan group of senators, several of them actively affiliated with the life insurance industry.

[18]Douglass Cater, *Power in Washington* (New York: Random House, 1966).

ance is unique among nonfarm interest groups in the extent to which industry personnel sit as key public officials in the executive, the legislature, and the courts.[19] Even to speak of a separation of functions is a distortion. The Insurance Department, for example, has important judicial and—as in the reform proposals under study here—legislative functions.

Next to lawyers, insurance is the largest occupational group inside the legislature. During the 75th Session of 1967–68, 21 percent of the Senate and 19 percent of the Assembly were in the insurance business, and these proportions have been fairly stable over recent years (see table 1). In the Senate, insurance members have most often been

Table 1. Number and Percent of Senators and Representatives
of the Illinois General Assembly Engaged in the
Insurance Industry in Private Life, 1961–68

	No. Democrats	No. Republicans	Total	%
	SENATE			
72nd G.A. (1961–62)	5	9	14	22.3
73rd G.A. (1963–64)	4	10	14	22.3
74th G.A. (1965–66)	5	11	15	24.1
75th G.A. (1967–68)	2	11	13	20.5
	HOUSE			
72nd G.A. (1961–62)	17	16	33	18.7
73rd G.A. (1963–64)	17	16	33	18.7
74th G.A. (1965–66)	22	8	30	16.4
75th G.A. (1967–68)	20	15	35	19.2

[19] Besides persons in the Department of Insurance and the legislature, which shall be discussed below, many other important Illinois officials have direct connections with the life insurance industry. During the 75th General Assembly they included State Superintendent of

Republicans, while the House has had a more even distribution between the parties. There is a good deal of diversity among these insurance legislators. They are roughly evenly divided between company executives and insurance agents, but except in respect to certain bills on agents' status, they may be considered a phalanx of support for the companies. Nor does the distinction between members from different branches of the insurance industry create any factionalism, although certain legislators become spokesmen on issues concerning their own branch.

To limit the insurance group to those members who list insurance as their official occupation is to greatly underestimate its natural strength. The occupation represented most heavily in the legislature after insurance is real estate, and many real estate brokers also sell insurance. Another source of support for the insurance industry is among the lawyers, many of whom count insurance companies as important clients.[20] Finally, many members who list "politics" as their profession are insurance brokers.[21]

But it is in the positions of legislative leadership that the industry's influence has been unparalleled. During the 75th Session, the Senate majority leader, Russell Arrington, and the majority whip, Joseph Peterson, were executives of Illinois life insurance companies. One of the three members of the Committee on the Assignment of Bills was a life insurance company executive. And 40 percent of the Committee on Committees were in the insurance business, including the chairman. In the House these various leadership powers are combined in the speaker, who, in 1967–68, was a lawyer. In previous sessions, however, the speakership has also been held by a member of the industry. For ex-

---

Public Instruction George T. Wilkins, chairman of the board of Nathan Hale Life; Samuel C. Bernstein, employment secretary, Illinois Department of Labor, who is also a director of Fidelity Life Insurance; William E. Smith, assistant director of the Department of Conservation, president and director of Georgetown Life; Chicago Superintendent of Schools Benjamin Willis, director of Northwestern Mutual Life; Judge Creel Douglas, chief justice of the Circuit Court in Springfield, vice-president and director of Nathan Hale Life; Alderman Thomas J. Keane of Chicago, counsel for Continental Life Assurance Company. This list is merely suggestive. Judge Douglas, for example, has defended his custom of going to the Insurance Department on company business by asserting that he knew of six other judges with similar insurance interests. See *Chicago American*, February 7, 1966.

[20] A useful, if incomplete, guide to the insurance clients of state legislators and other lawyer officials is the *Martindale Hubbell Law Directory*, Illinois section, vol. 2 (Summit, N.J.: Martindale Hubbell, 1968). The directory is a good indicator of the extent to which insurance companies disperse their vast litigation among many influential firms. On the role of lawyers in the Illinois legislature, see James H. Andrews, *Private Groups in Illinois Government: Final Report and Background Papers, Assembly on Private Groups in Illinois Government*, University of Illinois Bulletin, vol. 62, no. 63 (Urbana, Ill.: University of Illinois Press, 1965).

[21] An experienced reporter of Illinois politics, Jack Mabley, has estimated that at least a quarter of all senators and representatives in the Illinois General Assembly have an occupational link with the insurance industry. See *Chicago American*, June 24, 1966.

ample, from 1959–63, the speaker was Democrat Paul Powell, a life insurance director. (During the 75th Session, Powell was serving as secretary of state.)

Insurance members sit on the committees which deal with insurance legislation in even greater proportions than in the legislature as a whole. In 1967–68 they made up 33.3 percent of the House Insurance Committee, and 58.3 percent of the Insurance Subcommittee of the Senate Committee on Financial Institutions (hereafter referred to as the Senate Insurance Committee) (see table 2). This percentage was somewhat higher than in recent previous sessions, perhaps as a precaution against possible impending trouble amidst the public dismay over the state of insurance regulation. The chairman of the Senate Insurance Committee was an officer and director of two Illinois life insurance companies.

Table 2. Number and Percent of Members on the Insurance Committees in the Illinois General Assembly Engaged in the Insurance Industry in Private Life, 1961–68

	SENATE		
	Size of committee	No. insurance members	% insurance members
72nd G.A. (1961–62)	18	6	33.3
73rd G.A. (1963–64)	16	5	31.3
74th G.A. (1965–66)	17	7	41.2
75th G.A. (1967–68)	12	7	58.3
	HOUSE		
72nd G.A. (1961–62)	27	7	25.9
73rd G.A. (1963–64)	28	7	25.0
74th G.A. (1965–66)	24	5	20.8
75th G.A. (1967–68)	18	6	33.3

The customs of the Illinois legislature, combined with a healthy supply of assemblymen and senators in the insurance business, generally preclude the need for vulgar pressures by the industry to secure committee assignments for employees and friends. Committee assignments are made by the party leadership of each party according to the expressed preference of legislators. The norms of the legislature do not discourage a member from involving himself directly in the legislative business of his own livelihood, and even encourage such involvement on the grounds of divisions of labor and expertise.[22] On the other hand, the industry has exerted pressure to keep members it finds particularly obnoxious off the committees. In the 75th session, for example, one legislator openly critical of the insurance industry was kept from being appointed to the House Committee at the last moment through industry intervention with Democratic party leaders in Chicago. But this leverage is used with restraint. The Chairman of the House Committee in the 75th session was generally disliked by the insurance industry— one of the most powerful insurance executive-senators referred to him in an interview with the author as an "imbecile" and a "disgrace." But no attempt was made to dislodge him. The evidence suggests that the industry will step in when threatened with overt hostility in the ranks of the committees, but will tolerate a committeeman whom they disrespect on grounds of personality or competence, provided he is neutral or supportive of industry positions.

One member of the House Insurance Committee who claims he is in principle opposed to committees with members who have an occupational interest cited the working conditions of the legislature as partially responsible.

The legislature is hideous, a gigantic bucket of worms. You don't have an office, just your little desk with one drawer. You share a steno pool and every two years they give you fifty bucks for stamps and stationary. The committee system may be the only solution. . . . Besides, insurance is technical as hell. You need somebody on there who has some vague idea of what's going on.

The argument that the hellish technicality of insurance legislation requires, or at least justifies, that several members of the insurance committees be from the insurance industry is dubious in light of actual practice. Another member of the House committee, for example, had been counsel for several companies on liability and personal injury litigation. He had asked to be appointed because "I felt I knew something about it, so I felt I could be of some help. But I was completely wrong. . . . It would take years to figure it out. On almost everything I listen to the experts, and follow their lead." A lawyer for insurance

---

[22] See on this point Malcolm Jewell, *The State Legislature: Politics and Practice*, 2nd edition (New York: Random House, 1969), p. 97.

companies, a company agent, an independent broker—even a member of the board of directors of an insurance company—is unlikely to have a technical understanding which encompasses the diverse legislation that passes before the committees. A few members do have this expertise, at least for their own industry branch: the life company president-chairman of the Senate Committee is one, but he is the exception. At a minimum, it may be stated that what is gained in expertise is not equal to what is lost in disinterested legislative judgment.

This technical rationale for committee vested interests may be considered a variation on the theme of technicality which runs through the entire process of insurance politics. Its effect in the legislature is, among other things, to create a pattern of regressive decisionmaking, in which each legislative body relies largely on the decisions of somebody that considered the matter previously. This may be seen, first of all, in the committees, where most members rely on the experts.

The experts, who give prepared testimony at hearings, are the representatives of the Department of Insurance and the industry lobbyists. In the 75th session, the department spoke in favor of the bills in the reform program and industry lobbyists spoke for bills introduced independently. There is, of course, some double bookkeeping in this distinction, since much of the legislation in the reform program was devised and even worded by the companies. Every bill must be sponsored by a legislator, and usually a bill will have multiple sponsors from both parties. But this is a mere formality. One senator, a member of the Senate Insurance Committee, who had been the chief sponsor and co-sponsor of many insurance bills during the 74th and 75th sessions, told the author shortly after adjournment of the 75th session that he could not remember the substance of a single bill to which he had lent his name. He insisted he wasn't "putting anybody on. I could maybe look each one up and remember something. But offhand, no. Besides, most of the bills are administration bills drawn up by the Department of Insurance that are brought to my desk to be signed. These bills are so technical. . . . It's a complicated and gargantuan business." A life insurance lobbyist recalled with a smile how the chief Senate sponsor of several of the reform program bills would nervously shuffle his papers at the hearing and announce, "The next bill is number 'X.' And now I will let Mr. W. (the legislative assistant of the Insurance Department) explain to the committee the purposes of this legislation."[23]

The spokesman for the Insurance Department, usually the director's legislative assistant, is the most important figure at the hearings. Of the

[23]The Senate chief sponsor was Alan Dixon, former lieutenant governor, 1949–53. Dixon's law firm of Dixon, DeVine, Ray, and Morin listed among their clients in 1967 Prudential Life Insurance Company of America; The Travelers Insurance Company; Bankers Life of Des Moines; American Associated Insurance Company; Aetna Casualty and Surety Company.

nineteen life insurance bills introduced in the Senate, the department endorsed eleven as part of the reform program; of the eleven House bills, the department endorsed three. The others were introduced independently, most often by insurance industry legislators. But on these bills as well the department's position is important. A House committeeman describes the procedures: "The Department sends their man. The first question somebody will ask is, 'Is this bill alright with the Department?' If he shrugs his shoulders, and that's just about always, okay." No legislator interviewed could remember favorable committee action on a bill opposed by the Department of Insurance.

The atmosphere at committee hearings is generally harmonious. In the occasional case of conflict, the hearing serves to identify opposition and to amend legislation to the satisfaction of the objecting parties. For example, in the 75th session there was considerable acrimony between the large and small companies over the employment of unlicensed agents on a temporary basis, but all sides were able to support the bill after it was watered down by several amendments. Says the lobbyist for the Illinois Life Convention: "We'll spend more time getting a word knocked out, then we can support almost anything." Representatives of the public, whether "insuring public" or otherwise, never appear at hearings.

Although bills are frequently tabled (see table 3), this doesn't necessarily represent the committee's killing a bill in response to opposition. Rather, as in every case in the 75th session, a bill is tabled because the sponsor has withdrawn support, or because the bill is set aside in anticipation of a substitute bill with the same legislative intent but more

Table 3. Committee Action on Life Insurance Bills, 74th and 75th Illinois General Assemblies

	Recommend do pass	Recommend do pass as amended	Table	Recommend do not pass
	No. bills	No. bills	No. bills	No. bills
74th G.A. (1965-66)				
Senate	10	8	3	1
House	2	5	1	0
75th G.A. (1967-68)				
Senate	7	7	4	1
House	6	3	4	0

carefully worded or slightly different in detail. Similarly, amendments
are not always conciliatory but more often are either technical corrections in the printed text or amendments agreed upon in advance by,
say, the industry sponsor and the Department of Insurance. In the
words of another House committee member: "It's an absolutely boring
committee."

Students of the Illinois legislature generally give the standing committees a minor role in which the committee recommendation has very
little influence on the final disposition of a bill.[24] This is clearly not the
case with the insurance committees. As table 4 indicates, only once

Table 4. Floor Action on Life Insurance Bills Which Carried Do Pass
Recommendations from Insurance Committees, 74th and 75th
Illinois General Assemblies

	Pass	Fail to pass
	No. bills	No. bills
74th G.A. (1965–66)		
Senate	16	1
House	7	0
75th G.A. (1967–68)		
Senate	14	0
House	9	0

during the last two sessions did a bill with a "do pass" recommendation
fail to pass in the respective legislative chamber. Nor is there evidence
that these industry-dominated committees act in a spirit of "let the bill
live."[25] True, during the 75th session, no bills were tabled because of
committee disapproval of substance. But in recent past sessions the
committee disapproval did serve as a filter for the industry.[26] During

[24] Gilbert Y. Steiner and Samuel K. Gove, *Legislative Politics in Illinois* (Urbana, Ill.: University of Illinois Press, 1960), pp. 60–66, 82–83.

[25] Ibid., p. 63.

[26] On this point insiders are clearly at odds with students like Steiner and Gove and in
agreement with the argument presented here. Legislators interviewed all perceived the committees as screens for hostile legislation, and as deterrents against the introduction of opposition
bills. See also Senator Paul Simon's remarks in *The Alton Evening Telegraph*, September 6,
1966: "The insurance lobby in Illinois doesn't operate in the same way as other lobbyists.
Insurance operators work to stop legislation by getting their friends in the legislature on the
state insurance committees.... It would be the same as if the state created a race track
committee to clean up practices in racing and then appointed to the committee all the people
connected with the track." Also Adlai E. Stevenson III: "Legislative committees have great

the 74th session, committees of both houses killed legislation designed
to clarify terms of policy cancellation; to abolish wrongful death limits;
to provide for privilege taxes on foreign insurers operating in Illinois.

There was one bill in the 75th session which is the exception that
proves the rule—or, more accurately, disproves the rule of "let the bill
live" as an operating principle of insurance committees. A bill was
introduced in the House Insurance Committee to require companies to
state within a specified period of time the reason for turning down an
application for insurance coverage. Although similar legislation had
been killed in the committee in previous years, on the particular day
that this bill was considered in committee several members were absent
and industry lobbyists were attending another hearing. The bill emerged
with a "do pass" recommendation. When the slip was discovered, the
bill was immediately tabled on the floor by its own sponsor, who had
introduced it for personal political reasons but had fully expected it to
get no further than the committee. Such slips are rare, however, and in
any case are likely only in the House where, unlike the Senate, proxy
voting in committee is not permitted.

The importance of the committees may be underscored by two insurance bills which bypassed the committees and passed on the floor,
much to the dismay of the life insurance industry. The first bill, called
by the lobbyist for one of Illinois' largest life companies "the most
dastardly thing ever introduced," placed all life insurance proceeds over
$20,000 under the inheritance tax laws. This legislation, introduced in
the last few days of the session by the Speaker of the House, reflected
the general search for ways of augmenting state taxes rather than any
special hostility to the insurance industry. (The law was subsequently
repealed after intense lobbying.) Another bill, which had been for many
years bottled up in the Senate Insurance Committee, changed limits on
payment for death caused by a wrongful act or neglect. Although various explanations are given by legislators for the sudden approval of this
long-opposed law, the most common opinion is that Republicans were
angry at Majority Leader Russell Arrington for having forced through
several pieces of liberal legislation, including a bill on open housing, and
his colleagues passed the new wrongful death law as a means of revenge.
(The majority leader, it will be recalled, is a life insurance executive.)

These two bills also point up the role of the insurance committees in
isolating insurance issues from other questions of public policy, a characteristic of the enabling mode. The division of legislative business

---

power over certain regulated industries such as insurance, liquor, banks, savings and loans.
These committees are dominated by legislators with economic interests in the very industries
they are intended to regulate. . . . Legislators with economic interests or long experience in any
industry are too likely to be subservient to industry views and bereft of new ideas for construc-
tive regulations in the public interest" *Chicago American*, June 24, 1966.

along functional lines further institutionalizes the technical aura surrounding insurance affairs, with insurance bills a matter for insurance experts who sit on the insurance committees. On rare occasions when insurance bills bypass the committees they are found to readily articulate with broader policies, such as revenue needs or opposition to open housing. The insulation of insurance from other policies has the accompanying effect of preventing clear lines of conflict from forming on insurance in the manner that they form on other issues such as welfare, education, and housing. And, in particular, insulation works against the stabilization of conflict along party lines.

The degree to which life insurance is exempt from the ordinary conflicts of Illinois legislative politics is manifest in actions taken on the floor. As shown in table 5, during the two sessions analyzed the floors

Table 5. Floor Action on Life Insurance Bills, 74th and 75th Illinois General Assemblies

	Senate		House	
	No. bills	% bills	No. bills	% bills
74th G.A. (1965–66)				
Pass	23	92.0	20	80.0
Fail	2	8.0	3	12.0
Table	0	0.0	2	8.0
Total	25	100.0	25	100.0
75th G.A. (1967–68)				
Pass	20	95.3	21	100.0
Fail	1	4.7	0	0.0
Table	0	0.0	0	0.0
Total	21	100.0	21	100.0

of both houses systematically and rather routinely ratified the life insurance bills proposed. The lack of conflict is emphasized in the number of life insurance bills passed by unanimous vote (see table 6). Perhaps even more significant, the spoilers of this unanimity form no coherent opposition from bill to bill. A bill to permit certain kinds of foreign investment drew dissent from a few suspicious rural senators. The bill concerning variable annuities, which has the effect of placing large and increasing shares of life company assets beyond the scope of the investment regulations, received scattered "nay" votes from several

Table 6. Number and Percent of Life Insurance Bills Passed by Unanimous
and Nonunanimous Votes, 74th and 75th Illinois General Assemblies

	Senate		House	
	No.	%	No.	%
74th G.A. (1965–66)				
Unanimous	20	86.9	18	90.0
Nonunanimous	3	13.1	2	10.0
Total	23	100.0	20	100.0
75th G.A. (1967–68)				
Unanimous	19	95.0	16	76.2
Nonunanimous	1	5.0	5	23.8
Total	20	100.0	21	100.0

House members beholden to smaller insurance companies concerned
about competitive disadvantage. An amendment on a detail of investiga-
tive procedure divided the House along party lines. There is virtually no
debate on the floor. The most frequently asked question during the
75th session was, "Is this legislation approved by the Advisory Committee?"—in a sense, bringing the legislative process to full circle.

Paradoxically, the present immunity of the life insurance industry
from serious opposition may be illustrated by the composition and
activities of the so-called anti-insurance bloc. The bloc is a loose group
of members of the House, with a core of four or five members, joined
from time to time by an outer group of three or four others. These
members are divided roughly between the parties, are relatively young,
and generally politically liberal. There is no real leader. The most vocal
member is Anthony Scariano, a suburban Chicago Democrat who is
described by other legislators interviewed as a "radical," "a stock liberal," "a loudmouth," and who is even criticized by some other members of the bloc as "ineffective" because "when he gets up to talk
everybody turns off." The orientation of the bloc is toward an honest
system of insurance regulation, unlike the present one infiltrated by the
insurance industry, rather than opposition to specific policies as such.
The group has been critical of the Department of Insurance and the
composition of the House and Senate insurance committees, and
Scariano in particular has voiced these criticisms to the press, to civic

groups, and in professional journals.[27] Although they are critical of regulation of the industry as a whole, they are subject to the process of natural selection described above and have concentrated their fire on the casualty field.

The fate of the plan for a thorough legislative investigation of insurance regulation is instructive in the ways of insurance politics. There had been sporadic legislative criticism of insurance regulation for many years, but the failure of life and casualty companies in the 1960s gave a direction to the discontent. In 1965 the House dissidents called for the establishment of a commission to study the insurance laws. Because the bill was to establish a legislative investigation it was directed to the House Executive Committee, where it was approved and was subsequently passed on the floor. In the Senate the bill squeezed through the Insurance Committee by one vote, and the fight finally broke out on the floor of the Senate. Led by Insurance Committee Chairman Egbert Groen and Majority Leader Arrington, both directors and officers of life insurance companies, intense pressures were put on senators of both parties. According to one, "those two guys gave promises of everything but the kitchen sink." The tactics were successful. The final vote in the Senate was 26–13 for passage, many votes short of the required two-thirds. When the roll-call began, several senators of both parties, including the Majority Leader, staged a walk-out, thereby defeating the legislation without going on public record against an investigation.

By the time the 75th session opened, those House members pressing for an investigation had a new and influential ally. The speaker, Ralph T. Smith, was under sharp criticism by his hometown newspaper, the *Alton Evening Telegraph*, for the legislature's failure to investigate insurance regulation, and he was prepared to support a watered-down version of the original proposal. Through a joint resolution the Senate and House agreed to a preliminary six-week study, directed by the chairman of the House Insurance Committee, Peter J. Miller, to determine whether a full investigation of insurance laws was justified.

Despite the study committee's subsequent claim that testimony was taken from agents, brokers, industry spokesmen, and members of the general public, almost all of the time in the three rather desultory hearings was taken up by representatives of the industry and the Director of Insurance. Industry representatives argued against any broader

---

[27]See, for example, Anthony Scariano, "Changes for Automobile Claims?" *Law Forum* 1967 (Fall): 596–99. Scariano has suggested that the Chicago press have become less willing to print articles unfavorable to the insurance industry because the newspapers now sell insurance through their circulation departments. The *Chicago Tribune,* the *Chicago American,* and the *Chicago Sun-Times* received their charters from Bolton.

investigation: "This is a private matter. . . . The industry can clean itself up. . . . The industry can police itself."[28] Director Bolton agreed with the industry. His department was "neither for nor against the establishment of an Interim Legislative Commission," but, he said, such an investigation might "hinder the operation of the Department. . . . by giving it excessive publicity, where we are trying to work on one particular detail."[29]

Some weeks after the hearings, without any voting, Chairman Miller issued a report which outlined the organization of the Insurance Department, summarized department and industry bills pending in the legislature, and concluded:

It is the conclusion of the committee that the remedial legislation proposed by the Department of Insurance and other legislation in the 75th General Assembly will be adequate to deal with the problems presently confronting the insurance industry within the State of Illinois, and on the basis of the investigation conducted by this committee there is at the present time no need for the establishment of an interim commission.[30]

Two of the committee members, Scariano and Republican Edward Copeland, refused to sign the report. They charged that it had been written by industry lobbyists and not by the Chairman, who, according to Scariano, "hasn't written a complete sentence since he got out of the eighth grade."[31] Instead the two issued a minority report highly critical of the Department of Insurance: "Bolton is a captive of the industry. He should be living in a goldfish bowl. If he thinks insurance regulation belongs to him, he has got another think coming. That department belongs to the people." The minority report chastized the committee for not making recommendations forbidding department employees from taking jobs with companies under department investigation, and questioned the propriety of Bolton's law practice with Chicago Alderman Keane, and their firm's representation of several life insurance companies. As for the dinner at the Palmer House, the minority report commented: "That's like having the crime syndicate throw a testimonial dinner for the United States Attorney."[32]

Smarting from bad publicity in the press and threatened with a floor fight over the report, Speaker Smith and industry lobbyists persuaded Miller to withdraw the report and issue a call for a two-year investigation. Now two senators refused to sign, the Democrat announcing that he was "not going to be a party to any maligning of the Illinois insur-

[28] *Certified Stenographic Report* . . . , p. 89.

[29] Ibid., p. 90.

[30] "Report of the Insurance Problems Investigating Committee," mimeographed, p. 13.

[31] *Chicago Daily News*, May 12, 1967.

[32] Ibid., May 15, 1967.

ance director," then relenting.[33] The final decision was left up to the General Assembly.

After first providing that the proposed investigation be conducted entirely by the House and Senate insurance committees, Speaker Smith shepherded a bill providing funds for the investigation through passage in the House. In the Senate, however, the bill was stopped in the Executive Committee chaired by Senator Arthur Bidwell, the one hold-out who had refused to sign the report; whereupon life insurance executive and Senator Peterson successfully moved on the floor that all bills at that moment in committees be tabled. Still determined, and irritated by the defeat, Speaker Smith now attempted the strategy of amending a noncontroversial bill in the House and returning it to the Senate for a second try with an attached letter to Republican senators: "I have tried to take good care of your bills as they have come over to us. I would consider it a real personal favor if you could support me."[34] But on the final vote there were only 17 yes votes, 13 short of passage. Again senators, including Arrington and most of the Democrats, left the chamber as the roll-call began, and the most important battle of the "anti-insurance bloc" ended in defeat.

The efforts of the anti-insurance bloc foundered on the well-worn rocks of Illinois insurance politics: industry-dominated insurance committees; reliance on views of the department and the industry; the power of the industry on the floor; the inchoate lines of conflict. There are, in addition, other characteristics of the bloc that make it an unlikely challenger to the status quo. Scariano, Copeland, and the others view problems of insurance from an essentially "good government" perspective. They are disturbed that the department and so many legislators are influenced by the industry that Scariano calls "the most vicious lobby in Springfield. They're dirty, corrupt, and corruptors. It's just another case of the regulated becoming the regulators." Beyond this, however, the bloc has gone no further than the shibboleths of the industry and the department in enunciating goals for policy. Scariano and the others want insurance regulation to provide insurance that is safe and economical, and they have supported new legislation in the casualty field, the so-called Keaton-O'Connell Basic Protection Plan.[35]

The lack of any special orientation is evident in the anti-insurance bloc's voting records on insurance legislation, particularly life insurance legislation, when it comes to the floor of the House. Most often, these members voted along with the various unanimous decisions to liberalize

[33] Ibid., May 19, 1967.
[34] Ibid., June 26, 1967.
[35] See Scariano, "Changes for Automobile Claims?"

regulation. But even on the bills passed with less than unanimous approval they voted in virtually every case with the majority.

From the point of view of the industry, the anti-insurance House members are a nuisance. They play on the more sensational aspects of industry abuse, and by doing so open up the possibility of closer public scrutiny or even a thorough revision of the 1937 Insurance Code. But there is no likelihood that this group, or even a larger or more respectable one like it, will attempt or succeed in fundamentally altering investment policies dominated by the enabling mode. First of all, their concern is wholly directed toward the internal insurance constituency—dishonest companies, exploited policyholders, hapless victims of automobile accidents, and, in the words of Scariano, "schlock" life policies. Second, while these legislators are liberals on matters of public welfare, housing, education, minority programs, and benefits, they make no connection between these goals and the potential contributions of the insurance industry. There has been some recent precedent for such a policy linkage in Illinois. One example is Treasurer Adlai Stevenson's program for depositing state funds in a manner to encourage banks to finance minority businesses; or, less pertinent perhaps, the 75th Assembly's passage of an assigned-risk plan for fire coverage in urban ghettos, in an effort to induce rebuilding and redevelopment in depressed and riot-torn areas.

Inducing statutes in Illinois have traditionally been supported by the group hoping to benefit, such as the Chicago Housing Authority or the natural gas producers, and the insurance industry. Mandatory statutes have been supported by various groups needing funds and credit for survival or development, such as local businessmen or farmers. Today Illinois, like other states, has severely and self-consciously undernourished sectors of the economy, but they have not yet rallied to mandatory investment programs. So far there is little evidence that certain potential constituencies, say blacks, or their potential allies and spokesmen, are thinking along lines such as requiring financial institutions like life insurance companies to invest a portion of their assets in slum housing—although this particular group has demanded financial support of other agencies, including the churches. Obviously, there would be formidable obstacles to be overcome before such mandatory investment laws could be passed in Illinois. But at present there is no political force within the legislature which can be expected even to initiate this kind of fundamental change in insurance politics.

III

The life insurance lobby plays an important role in maintaining the status quo in insurance regulation. In our analysis this means the perpetuation of a system of enabling laws permitting maximum company control of investment. Lobbyists are busy and preeminently practical men not easily absorbed in the fascinations of insurance law history, but they realize the persistent tensions between government and the life insurance companies over the industry's assets. In response to the author's question: "Are there any groups which are sometimes in opposition to life insurance interests?," the lobbyist for one of the largest Illinois life companies explains:

Unfortunately, yes. The insurance industry finds itself in the position where people think that all the industry has is money to spend. What the public doesn't seem to understand is that we're merely custodians of this money. Everybody has their hand out today. There are people in Springfield who would grab it for tax purposes and Lord knows what else. This is an old story, one we've always had to contend with.

During the 75th session the inheritance tax was perceived as such a grab and was ultimately repealed. Most lobbyist energy, however, is spent promoting or resisting legislation which is of varying financial importance but which does not disturb existing regulatory arrangements or principles. This concluding section will consider these regular lobbying activities in terms of their own relationship to the status quo. This relationship must be emphasized in light of recent analyses of business politics, particularly the research of Bauer, Pool, and Dexter in *American Business and Public Policy*, a painstaking but somewhat oversubtle study which concludes that the "lobbyist becomes in effect a service bureau. . . . rather than an agent of direct persuasion."[36] The life insurance lobby in Illinois does conform in part to this "service bureau" description. But the "service bureau" role directly corresponds and contributes to the specific mode of current state policy toward life insurance.

There are a great number and variety of life insurance lobbyists. Several of the domestic companies—Continental Assurance, Allstate, Washington National, the Kemper Group, State Farm—have their own "legislative specialist" who devotes full time to lobbying and related political work. The Prudential Life Insurance Company has a lobbyist

---

[36]Raymond A. Bauer, Ithiel de Sola Pool, and Lewis Anthony Dexter, *American Business and Public Policy: The Politics of Foreign Trade* (New York: Atherton Press, 1963), p. 353. Several of the central elements of the foreign trade situation are absent in Illinois life insurance politics. The most important, perhaps, is the absence of pressure groups on the opposing side of issues, and thus the absence of an alleged restraint on lobbying. (On this point, see also Lester M. Milbraith, *The Washington Lobbyists*, [Chicago: Rand McNally, 1963], pp. 348 ff.) Another difference is that in the foreign trade case participant corporations, because of their size and diversity of operations, often had something to gain *and* lose however the tariff issue was decided. In the life insurance case the interests are clear. Rather, our case approximates the situation suggested by Bauer et al., when the stakes are clear, when one group has much to gain and no one has much to lose, and where the "magical" results so often attributed to lobbies may be observed. *American Business*, p. 399.

in its Chicago mid-America office who often also represents other large foreign insurers. Two organizations lobby in behalf of groups of Illinois companies, the Illinois Life Convention, representing some thirty medium-sized companies, and the Association of Life Companies, representing forty-eight smaller companies. The American Life Convention (ALC) and the American Association of Life Insurance (AALI) are the main national trade associations, and they coordinate their lobbying activities, with the ALC, based in Chicago, usually representing the national industry in the Illinois legislature. Finally, there are numerous organizations, such as the National Life Insurance Association, made up of black-owned companies, and the various individuals usually from small companies who occasionally lobby for selected bills of special interest to them.

The lobbyists themselves are men with wide political experience and connections. The lobbyist for Continental Assurance is William H. "Bud" Perkins. Perkins, who has been with the company since 1949, was sergeant-at-arms for the Democratic National Conventions of 1952 and 1956; special assistant to the Democratic national chairman in 1960; on the Presidential Inauguration Committee in 1961 and 1965; a member of the Illinois Atomic Energy Commission, 1963–67; and a delegate to the Democratic National Convention in 1964 and 1968. He is a personal friend of Mayor Daley and, like other lobbyists, can call most legislators by their first names. The lobbyist for the Prudential is Paul N. "Buck" Gordon, former advisor to Warren Wood, Republican speaker of the Illinois House from 1951 to 1959. Dwaine Williams, lobbyist for the Illinois Life Convention and Washington National Life, is Republican precinct captain in Evanston and chairman of the Congressional Action Committee of the Evanston Chamber of Commerce. Dave Brown, lobbyist for the Kemper Group, is a member of the Republican State Central Committee. David Davis of State Farm is a former Republican state senator. The party affiliations of individual lobbyists, however, by no means reflect political allegiances of the companies. One of the directors of the Continental, Perkins' employer, is Robert Stuart, Republican national committeeman from Illinois. Sometimes companies employ a second lobbyist to extend partisan connections. The Prudential frequently calls in a man active in Democratic state politics to assist Gordon. But all lobbyists operate on both sides of the aisle.

The life insurance industry uses various methods to create an atmosphere of receptivity to its proposals. First, companies contribute to the campaigns of incumbent and prospective legislators of both parties. Illinois law forbids insurance companies to make direct political contributions, so the money is donated by individual officers or employees, or through intermediate organizations, such as so-called company political action funds, to which all company employees are urged to contribute. The size and frequency of these contributions cannot be determined, but companies and legislators interviewed conceded that on the scale of Illinois politics it is a large amount, paid out on a regular basis.

Second, the lobbyists perform a variety of material services for legislators in the form of business loans, mortgages, and insurance policies. A special benefit is offered the numerous lawyers in the legislature. If a lawyer has a personal injury or life claim to settle in his private practice the lobbyists use their influence with the companies to obtain a favorable settlement for his client. Scariano recalls telling an insurance lobbyist that he expected a certain legislator to vote with him on a bill and the lobbyist replying: "Oh no, I've helped that one settle too many cases."[37] This last remark points up the artificiality of the distinction between "persuasion" and "service bureau." Legislators incur obligations through acceptance of services as surely as through cash payoffs. On the other hand, while it is impossible to accurately estimate the extent of simple graft in insurance politics, interviews with legislators suggest it is considerable. Several legislators said they personally knew of cases of cash payments for friendly voting on insurance bills, but this practice was more frequently ascribed to casualty rather than life companies and lobbyists.

The life insurance lobby's greatest source of strength, however, is its technical expertise in a policy field which is perceived to be enormously technical. The role of the industry in advising the Insurance Department and drafting legislation has already been discussed; in lobbying the legislature, this expertise is no less important. Most legislators, even those on the insurance committees, have little or no understanding of the insurance industry. Whereas in the case of casualty or fire insurance they may be vaguely indignant at high rates and corrupt practices, their perception of life insurance is limited to unqualified awe at the "gargantuan" complexities involved. This attitude, perhaps engendered by the actuarial mysteries surrounding their own purchases of life insurance policies, is reinforced by the general absence of controversy in life insurance legislation, lending the impression of pure technicality to legislative proceedings.

In these circumstances, a lobbyist explained, "You don't try to persuade anybody. You try to become an expert in your field and get a reputation as being somebody who has honest information. No matter how bad a spot you're in, don't tell your first lie or you're out of business. I operate strictly according to the facts." Similarly, employees

[37]The judicious placement of a company's local law business has already been mentioned (see above, p. 50).

who contribute to the Washington National Political Action Fund are "promised that the company will see that those people get support who take time to listen to our story."

Lobbyists "tell their story" at legislators' desks, at lunches with legislators for which they pick up the check, and they testify at Insurance Committee hearings: "Our strength? It's almost incredible what a man can do by just being there. Strength comes from having a group of people who tell a story that is logical and reasonable to a group of people who don't have the slightest idea what you're talking about."[38]

Bauer, Pool, and Dexter found that the information and expertise of the lobbyists "raised the level of discussion and awareness of public policy."[39] In Illinois insurance politics there is little activity which resembles discussion. Communication flows in one direction from the industry to the legislator. Also, few bills incite controversy within the industry; in the two or three cases in the 75th session where small life insurance companies opposed a bill sponsored by large companies, the smaller companies lacked the staff for preparing convincing technical presentations and relied instead on personal contacts and friends in the legislature—an apparently less successful tactic.[40] As for awareness, legislators who have long benefited from numerous explanations at committee hearings remain strikingly unenlightened about life insurance regulation.

In fact, the life insurance issues which confront legislators are not extraordinarily technical. A perusal of the department's reform package, for example, shows legislation dealing with changes in procedures for filing public notification of mergers, in capitalization requirements, in permissible investments, in the power of the insurance director regarding liquidations and audits, and similar matters that should present no special difficulties to anyone acquainted with business or law. There are a few bills dealing with surplus and reserve requirements which are complicated for the layman, if by no means incomprehensible. But

---

[38] An additional difference between the trade and insurance case is that in the former a member of Congress already has a good idea of the stakes and issues involved and a sense of possible effects on his constituency. The Illinois legislator, however, is usually unaware of the stakes and issues and perceives no clear relationship between them and his noninsurance constituency. Thus the distinction between "service bureau" and "persuasion" is further blurred. To furnish information and statistics to a relatively informed legislator may be simply a service (perhaps much in the nature of the "cover" described by Steiner and Gove, *Legislative Politics*, pp. 77-78). But to furnish information to someone who "hasn't the slightest idea what you're talking about" is more like persuasion.

[39] Bauer et al., *American Business*, p. 346.

[40] Ibid., p. 347, found that among the petroleum lobby the large firms were able to withstand the assaults of the independent producers through their superior information and expertise. A similar effect may be observed in the insurance case, except that the smaller insurers are usually on the defensive, reacting to rather than demanding changes, and they have generally been placated with a compromise amendment or two.

these concepts of relative technicality cannot be credited with having contaminated the entire field with confusion.

The persistence of ignorance and the continued reliance on industry and Insurance Department testimony can only be explained by the absence of any broad policy perspective which would enable the legislator to make sense of the proposals and information that come before him. We have seen how industry-dominated insurance committees have isolated insurance issues from other questions of legislative concern. But even more fundamental is the nonexistence of standards or goals for life insurance legislation, beyond safety and the preservation of state revenue.

Safety is not a policy but rather a pseudopolicy. Like "competition" and "in the public interest," which are pseudopolicies of other types of business regulation, safety is devoid of clear procedural or substantive content. Like the other pseudopolicies mentioned, safety is difficult to identify except in the breach, on an ad hoc basis when an insurance company has failed. Short of this indisputable condition of failure, safety may perhaps be subject to a technical determination based on intricate calculations and details of business operations, but such calculations are especially ill-suited to the processes of the legislature. In this respect, the goal of safety contributes to the place of the Insurance Department as the dominant governmental institution in insurance politics.

Existing enabling laws specify various classes of investments—government bonds, mortgages, real estate, etc.—and limit the percentage of total assets in any one class and in any one investment, an approach based on the principle of diversification of assets. In fact, the percentages enable a company to concentrate its assets in a very few areas; say, first mortgages (up to 60 percent), railroad bonds (up to 33.3 percent), and a home office building (up to 10 percent). In addition there is a "basket clause" under which 10 percent of the assets may be invested at the absolute discretion of the company; and the percentage in any category may be increased with permission of the Director of Insurance. No provisions are made for department approval of individual investments. These statutes have been a restraint for the most part only to the investment in common stocks, and the variable annuities law, providing for "separate accounts" not bound by investment limitations, has provided effective relief.

The problems of defining safety may be seen in the relationship between the pseudopolicy of safety and the industry's own goal of profitability. Superficially, the idea of safety would seem to conflict with the goal of profitability. But it may be argued quite logically—and life companies have consistently done so—that safety is better assured through high profits than through elaborate schemes for asset diversification which are, after all, only a means for cushioning losses. Accordingly, at each session of the legislature bills are proposed, supported by statistical evidence, and passed which expand the investment latitude of the companies. During the 75th session the variable annuities legislation placed a rapidly growing segment of life insurance assets beyond all jurisdiction of the investment laws, as a means of enabling life insurance companies to compete more favorably with mutual funds. The downstream holding company law reinstated investment arrangements that were the scandal of the Armstrong investigations, so that, according to the department's explanation, the companies may "maintain a strong financial position . . . continue to be competitive . . . stay abreast of and to satisfy the increasing needs and demands of stockholders and policyholders."[41] Also, in 1968 the Director on his own authority approved ownership of life insurance companies by other holding companies, another target of the Armstrong investigations, and it is as yet unclear whether this policy will be ratified by law.[42]

The average legislator is unable to decide whether changes in enabling statutes move regulation closer to or farther from absolute safety, for there are simply no standards against which safety can be weighed. Indeed, there is no evidence that investment laws insure against failure. The safety records of English life insurance companies historically have been as good or better than that of American companies, although in England there is relatively little regulation. In the United States there has been no correlation between investment safety (i.e., nonfailure) and the stringency of investment laws. In the nineteenth century failure occurred in those states with very strict investment laws as often as in those with liberal laws.[43] Nor is there evidence that states with mandatory investment laws fared worse than those with enabling laws.[44]

[41]"1967 Legislation Explanation," mimeograph distributed by the Department of Insurance.

[42]The present trend toward holding companies, both those designed to promote insurance ownership of noninsurance subsidiaries and those designed to promote ownership of insurance companies by noninsurance corporations, may be considered a strengthening of the enabling mode, since these arrangements accentuate the goal of profits at the expense of the role of mobilizing capital for economic growth. For the view that holding companies "blur the social purposes which should never be far removed from the concerns of insurance management," see State of New York Insurance Department, *Report of the Special Committee on Insurance Holding Companies*, 1968, p. 18 and passim.

[43]David McCahan, *Investment of Life Insurance Funds* (Homewood, Ill.: Richard D. Irwin, 1953), p. 253. Also see Lester Zartman, *The Investments of Life Insurance Companies* (New York: Henry Holt & Company, 1906), pp. 181–83.

[44]See Winston C. Beard, *The Effects of State Investment Requirements for Life Insurance Companies*. Prepared for the Arkansas Insurance Commissioner by the University of Arkansas College of Business Administration, Industrial Relations and Extension Center in cooperation with the Arkansas Industrial Development Commission, October 1958, mimeographed. In this

Ironically, the successive failures of insurance companies may even serve to buttress the status quo—this in spite of the life insurance industry's palpable distaste for scandal and its desire to ward off any public investigation. It has been pointed out above how a process of administrative natural selection directs attention to the least stable branches of the insurance industry. Similarly, continuous revelations of mismanagement and corruption may work to dramatically reinforce legislative preoccupation with safety, and thus the dependency on technical expertise of the industry and the industry-dominated Insurance Department.

In the previous chapter the enabling mode was associated with the goals of safety and profitability. While profitability of insurance is not an explicit goal of the Insurance Department, it is clearly implied in the aim of preserving insurance as a source of state revenue and the repeated stress on the insurance industry's contributions to the state economy, as well as the department's consistent support of all industry efforts to obtain maximum control over its investment assets. Safety is a pseudopolicy. Preservation of revenue and profitability are genuine ones. In practice the goal of safety, and the privileged position it affords technical expertise, has served as a protection and literally a mystification for the status quo.

---

paper the author, an opponent of "compulsory" or mandatory investment laws, carefully documents the adverse effects of such laws in the past. Nowhere does he suggest that mandatory laws have affected the solvency of life companies. See especially chapters IV and V.

CHAPTER IV

THE
LIFE INSURANCE
ENTERPRISE

Chapter III rather freely ascribed the motive of profitability to much of the life insurance industry's current legislative activity. But within the industry, profits is a word used sparingly and with care. Most life insurance in Illinois and elsewhere is issued by mutual companies which formally make no profits but instead accumulate surplus that the law permits them to distribute among the policyholders. Stock life insurance companies do make profits for their stockholders, but their managers claim that profits are an objective secondary to obligations of prudence and safety to the policyholders. Life insurance investments are usually said to produce a yield, at a certain rate of return, rather than earn profits. While economists for thirty years have argued whether or not the modern corporation maximizes profits, the rhetoric of life insurance has done nothing to intrude its giant industry into the debate.

The freedom of managers to choose among a variety of goals—profit being only one of them—for their enterprise is as important to a consideration of the life insurance industry's role in society as is its autonomous position with respect to the state. It can be argued that the separation of management from the controls of ownership—the arrangement understood as basic to the range of discretion and thus the "mature" character of the modern industrial corporation—was developed first in financial institutions, including life insurance companies, during the second half of the nineteenth century.[1] Aspects of such a

---

[1] See Louis D. Brandeis, *Other People's Money* (New York: Harper & Row, 1967). The classic study of this period on the development of managerial enterprise is Thorstein Veblen, *The Theory of Business Enterprise* (New York: Mentor Books, 1958), especially chapter 6.

recent pattern as an employees' pension fund's ownership of its employer company were long foreshadowed by the mutualization of stock
insurance companies like the Prudential and Metropolitan Life.

To what extent does the life insurance business constrain its managers to follow a particular course in their investment decisions? The
matters to be discussed in this chapter are first, what it is that a life
insurance does: how it comes by its investment funds and the functions
of investment, in theory and practice, for the policyholder and for the
company. Second, there is the question of how much leeway for
choosing investment goals is left the manager by the combination of
fiduciary obligations, relations with policyholders and stockholders, the
dictates of financial prudence, and his responsibilities to society. Third,
what objectives are sought in life insurance investment, and what criteria are applied to achieve them? Finally, is the present direction of
investment likely to be changed in pursuit of wider social responsibilities? (The latter two problems, with their social and public policy implications, are considered further in chapters VI–VII.)

I

All investment decisions are, in a general sense, discretionary. As
already discussed in previous chapters, the allocation of money and
credit to one segment of the economy rather than another, to one
industry or neighborhood rather than another, involves choices that
may have significant social implications. Because of the special character of the life insurance business, however, there exists a wide margin of
discretion beyond the inherent nature of investment activities as such.

To explain, we may begin with a basic model of the life insurance
enterprise. The consumer of life insurance purchases a policy which
promises to pay his beneficiaries a stated amount of dollars in the event
of his death. The company receives periodic payment in the form of
premiums, which are pooled with other premiums and invested. The
accumulated premiums plus the earnings on their investment must be
sufficient to pay the full face value of the policy when any policyholder
dies, even if his death occurs shortly after he has begun paying premiums. Also, earnings must cover the expenses of administering the
business.

This process is made possible by the fact that there are many thousands, sometimes millions, of policyholders in the company. By using
mortality tables, statistics of historical death rates under varying conditions of age, health, and so on, the company can estimate with a high
degree of accuracy at what rate it will have to pay out funds to dying
policyholders' beneficiaries. And by calculating the risk that any given

policyholder will die prematurely, as well as the amount of interest that his premium when pooled can be expected to earn, the company is able to charge a premium rate which, in the aggregate, will ensure that funds are always available to meet its obligations.

In this model, the choices involved in selecting a portfolio are not entirely arbitrary. Accepting as axiomatic here and elsewhere in this discussion that company officers are honest and determined to fulfill their contracts with policyholders, certain constraints on investment policy are readily apparent.[2] First, the company must seek to invest the funds so that, on balance, they earn at least the interest assumed in the calculation of the premium rate. Second, this balance requires that risky investments be compensated for by much safer ones. Third, some portion of the investments should be in convertible securities or other investments which provide liquidity for unforeseen emergencies, the remainder being placed in long-term investments.

This model resembles the public relations image of a life insurance company; it is also the conception upon which public regulation and taxation are based. Even allowing for state investment laws, it admits · considerable discretion: the management might decide, for example, to favor the purchase of bonds from companies whose directors or officers are personal acquaintances; it could give priority in home mortgages to its own policyholders; it could build a luxurious home office building—all familiar practices; as well as any number of other investment choices.[3]

Were the model, as far as it goes, however, fairly close to business reality, life companies would be hemmed in at least to the degree described. But without yet introducing any further complications, actual operations are contrary to the model in several respects. A relatively minor contradiction is the company's demand for liquidity. Cash flows—those monies flowing into the company in the form of premiums and investment income—are predictably higher than necessary to cover various contingencies that may arise. In the two incidents which appear

---

[2] As in chapter III, the illegal and unethical practices of the life insurance industry are underplayed in order that that this analysis may concentrate on the political character of the industry when functioning according to optimum legal and business standards.

In a recent survey members of the insurance industry have shown a higher estimation of their collective honesty than do managers in transportation, public utilities, manufacturing, construction, advertising, and others. See Raymond Baumhart, S. J., *An Honest Profit* (New York: Holt, Rinehart & Winston, 1968), p. 116. "Insurance executives took no personal credit, insisting that ethical behavior was built into their industries." For a somewhat less enthusiastic view of the life insurance industry's morals, see James Gollin, *Pay Now, Die Later* (New York: Penguin Books, 1966).

[3] For an informal view of some of the more imprudent and prodigal allocations of life insurance funds, see Norman F. Dacey, *What's Wrong With Your Life Insurance* (New York: The Crowell-Collier Press, 1962), chapters 3, 4, 5, and 10. Also see Gollin, *Pay Now, Die Later*, passim.

to haunt the public statements of life insurance officials—the influenza epidemic of 1918–19, which was the most serious increase in mortality in recent American history, and the Great Depression of the 1930s— cash inflow more than compensated for funds paid out in death claims, policy surrenders, and policy loans. Failures were confined entirely to flagrantly mismanaged companies and were in no case related to liquidity.[4]

More important discrepancies between the model and reality concern premium rates and investment yields. Illinois, like other states, requires that premiums be calculated according to a legally approved mortality table. But the mortality statistics used lag behind actual conditions of mortality at the time a life insurance policy is issued. For example, all life insurance issued before 1948, which includes the major portion of life insurance currently in force, was priced according to the American Experience Mortality Table, first used in 1861. From 1948 to 1966 policies were sold according to the so-called 1941 Commissioners Standard Ordinary Table, reflecting the mortality experience of the prepenicillin, preantibiotics era of 1931–41. Since 1966 companies have based premium rates on the Commissioners Standard Ordinary Table of 1958, based on death rates of 1950–54. With actual death rates consistently lower than premium costs assume, less money is paid out by the company in the aggregate than anticipated in the charge to the policyholder.[5] Moreover, this advantage to company cash receipts is considerably increased by the fact that mortality tables represent wide cross-sections of the entire population, while insurance companies

---

[4]George Clayton and W. T. Osborn, *Insurance Company Investment* (London, 1965), pp. 65–66. Also Temporary National Economic Committee (TNEC), *Study of Legal Reserve Life Insurance Companies*, Monograph 28 (Washington, 1941), p. 134.

[5]Some idea of the discrepancy between mortality tables and experience may be suggested by the following figures compiled from the *Life Insurance Fact Book 1968* (New York: Institute of Life Insurance, 1968), pp. 108–9.

Deaths Per Thousand

Age	Amer. Exper. Mortality Table	1941 CSO*	1958 CSO	Real U.S. (1959–61) experience
10	7.49	1.97	1.21	0.37
20	7.80	2.43	1.79	1.15
30	8.43	3.56	2.13	1.43
40	9.79	6.18	3.53	3.00
50	13.78	12.32	8.32	7.74
60	26.69	26.59	20.34	17.61
70	61.99	59.30	49.79	38.66
80	144.47	131.85	109.98	92.08
90	454.55	280.99	228.14	227.09
99	(1,000.00)	1,000.00	1,000.00	376.16

*Commissioners Standard Ordinary Table

either will not insure newborns, persons in poor health or hazardous occupations, or else will charge extraordinary rates for such underwriting.[6]

Second, state law prescribes a maximum rate of expected yield on investments which may be figured into the premium charged the policyholder. In Illinois this rate is a 3.5 percent earning before taxes, which is the rate in most other states. This rate, however, is at least a full percentage point below what most life companies earn on their investments *after taxes*.[7] Life insurance companies, as a general practice, do not even assume the state maximum, but instead calculate premiums on an expected yield of around 2.5 or 3 percent. This means, in other words, that life insurance companies are taking in a very sizable increment of interest over what they actually pay out over the years in claims.

It is at this point that the model becomes fundamentally inadequate to describe the range of discretion available to life company managers. The state requires that the company earmark a fund of reserves—so-called because persons usually pay a level or constant premium for their life insurance, and thus pay an overcharge when they are younger, which must be set aside to make up for an undercharge when they are older and more likely to die. The reserve is different from company assets, which comprise the composite wealth of the company. Reserves are entered in accounting books as liabilities owed the policyholder against the assets. Since the minimum amount of reserves required by state law for a company to be solvent is based on the same inaccurate assumptions of investment income and mortality rates, the assets greatly exceed the amount the company must charge against itself as reserves. Most of this difference is allocated to a fund known as the surplus.

None of the constraints of our original model hamper the investment of the surplus. There is no need for a balanced portfolio in terms of risk, nor must investments earn some minimum rate of interest. Should

---

[6] 14.3 percent of ordinary (nongroup) life insurance policies written during 1967 were "extra-risk." A sample of these policies showed the following reasons for extra ratings: heart disease or symptoms, 33%; weight problems, 16%; other medical reasons, 29%; occupation, 12%; other reasons, 10%. *Life Insurance Fact Book 1968*, p. 89. See also Halsey D. Josephson, *Discrimination* (New York: Wesley Press, 1960); and Gollin, *Pay Now, Die Later*, chapter VI.

[7] Here are *net* yields (%) for some Illinois life insurance companies:

	1965	1966	1967
Mutual Trust Life	4.37	4.52	4.57
Franklin Life	4.44	4.51	4.57
Washington National	4.23	4.32	4.44
Continental Assurance	4.74	4.92	5.01
Country Life	4.62	4.71	4.86
North American Life	4.76	4.92	4.99

much of the surplus fund earn no interest whatever, there would be no impairment of the company's ability to pay the claims of the policy-holders. In short, the amount of the surplus provides a significant dimension of company or management discretion beyond the choices already permitted in the business of fulfilling the insurance contract.

The magnitude of the surplus may be indicated in table 7, showing the percent of total assets and reserves in several of Illinois' largest domestic companies during 1967, the year this research was begun. As a result of the Armstrong investigations of 1906, states have passed laws limiting how much surplus an individual company may maintain. Illinois permits domestic life insurers an amount according to a sliding scale, so that the smallest companies are allowed 20 percent of reserves and those with assets over $1,000,000 are allowed 10 percent (or roughly 9 percent of total assets). As table 7 demonstrates, companies

Table 7. Percent of Assets and Reserves Held in Surplus by the Nine Largest
Illinois Life Insurance Companies, 1967

Company	(Assets in $ millions)	Surplus Percent of assets	Percent of reserves
Allstate Life	(115.5)	16.0	19.3
Bankers Life and Casualty	(355.1)	31.9	47.6
Continental Assurance	(1,406.6)	7.6	8.3
Country Life	(364.5)	11.1	12.6
Franklin Life	(1,023.8)	11.8	13.9
Mutual Trust Life	(269.8)	8.2	8.9
North American Life	(121.1)	33.7	51.5
State Farm	(528.5)	11.4	13.0
Washington National	(464.1)	18.2	23.7

do maintain surpluses well above legal limits, for which permission may be obtained from the director "for cause." They may also overcome the legal surplus limits by holding more in their reserves or liabilities than is required by law, purportedly as an extra cushion for possible losses. These excess reserves are frequently 10-15 percent above the requirements, which, as has been explained, are computed conservatively to start with. And, as underwriting practices continue unmodified and surplus funds are invested along with the rest of insurance assets, these excess funds continue to grow. A careful study of the industry's investment income has indicated that this income, on a yearly basis, is 30 percent higher than necessary to simply maintain funds at their present high levels.[8]

The surplus of a life insurance company parallels what in a nonfinancial corporation is called profits—that part of income remaining after all expenditures for operating the business have been deducted. And while the divorcement between stock ownership and management disposition of profits is fast becoming the paradigm of contemporary nonfinancial enterprise, the relationship between management control of the surplus and any institution representing ownership is even more "mature" and tenuous.

A majority of the life insurance in force and an even greater bulk of the industry's total assets are in mutual companies. Mutual companies, as the name implies, have no stockholders, only policyholders who have theoretically purchased a voice in the control of the company and a share in its earnings, along with the face value of their policies.[9] Generalities about the mutual policyholder being both "the insured and the insurer," however, have been elaborated by the courts, which have lately interpreted the policyholders' position as a combination of stockholder and party in a contract, but without the prerogatives or protections of either.[10] The stockholder position has been applied most often to peripheral issues where the role and interest of the policyholder are taken for granted rather than proved.[11] On questions of control or removal of management, or rights to the surplus, policyholder status is dominated by a simple contract theory.[12]

[8] James E. Walter, *The Investment Process* (Boston: Graduate School of Business Administration, Harvard University, 1962), p. 10. On conservative computation of the surplus, see pp. 52–53.

[9] For example, "An insurance company is 'mutual' when there is no group but its policyholders who have an interest in it or power over it," "each [policyholder] taking a proportionate part in the management of its affairs and being at once insurer and insured, contributing to a fund from which all losses are paid and wherein the profits are divided among themselves in proportion to their interest." John Allen Appleman, *Insurance Law and Practice* (Kansas City, Mo.: Vernon Law Book Company, 1941–70), p. 18, Sec. 10041.

[10] For the following discussion the author has benefited greatly from W. H. Boies, "The Legal Status of Mutual Life Insurance Policyholders," mimeo. Also, "Relationship between a Life Insurance Company and a Policyholder," *Yale Law Journal* (March 1939): 839 ff.

[11] For example, prospective jurors in tort cases may be questioned about their mutual insurance policies and thus their "interest" in the profits of the company which is involved in a case they are to hear. Rains v. Schutte, 53 Ill. App. 2d 214, 202 N.E. 2d. 660 (1964). Like a stockholder, a former policyholder of a mutual company is denied any financial interest in the company he has left. Huber v. Martin, 105 N.W. 1031 (1906). But unlike the stockholder, the departing policyholder receives no compensation comparable to the sale of a share of stock.

[12] "The policy provides that it and the application attached thereto constitute the whole contract between the parties. Whatever rights a member of a mutual company has are delineated by the terms of the contract and come from it alone. . . . If the [policyholder] depends

The appropriateness of the contract theory may be seen in the financial relationship between the mutual company and the policyholder. Policies are sold on the premise that the purchaser will receive dividends on his premiums. But despite the resemblance in nomenclature, insurance dividends are not a share in the company's profitable operations. For the privileges of belonging to a mutual company, the policyholder pays a higher price for his policy in the form of a loading fee on his premium; this is later returned to him, less administrative expenses, as the "dividend."[13] All profits remaining over and above this, which in a stock company would—in theory if not in fact—be distributed as genuine dividends to the stockholders, in a mutual company are retained as surplus. The courts have ruled that mutual policyholders have no access to this money as a matter of right, that they may not force management to distribute dividends, nor may they interfere in the amount or manner of apportionment.[14]

The legal limits of company discretion have been set at "arbitrary, unreasonable, or capricious conduct," mismanagement, and fraud; but several actions charging mutual insurers with mishandling surplus funds—for example, by excessive spending on advertising or high agents' commissions—have been unsuccessful.[15] Of particular interest is a series of suits brought as "a policyholder's class action against directors of a mutual company for improvident investments."[16] Gustave B. Garfield, a policyholder in the Equitable Life Assurance Society, charged the corporation and twenty-two of its directors with self-dealing negligence and bad judgment in the purchase and development of the Gateway Center in Pittsburgh. Garfield demanded that the directors restore to the company several million dollars in excess costs. The complaint itself was dismissed, but it appeared that the case at least established the right

---

upon anything but his rights under the contract contained in the policy, he depends on something that does not exist." Andrews v. Equitable Life Assurance Society, 124 F. 2d. 788–90 (7th Cir., 1941), cert. denied, 316 U.S. 682 (1942).

[13] "The word 'dividend' is to some extent a misnomer, the dividend on a participating policy being rather in the nature of a refund and not a return on an investment as the term is generally used in commercial transactions," Joseph M. MacLean, Modern Life Insurance, 9th ed. (New York: McGraw-Hill, 1962), p. 241. See also Dacey, What's Wrong With Your Life Insurance, chapter 21.

[14] Coons v. Home Life Insurance Company, 368 Ill, 231, 236, 13 N.E. 2d., 482, 485; Andrews v. Equitable; Cohen v. Prudential Insurance Company of America, 58 N.J. Super. 37, 155 A. 2d. 304 (1959).

[15] The quotation is from Cohen v. Prudential. One of the major obstacles to litigation is that courts recognize the primary jurisdiction of state insurance departments and require that administrative remedies be exhausted before a court settlement be made. See, for example, Clifford v. Metropolitan Life Insurance Company, 34 N.Y.S. 2d 693 (App. Div. 1942).

[16] Garfield v. Equitable, 205 N.Y.S. 2d. 758 (1960). The story of this litigation, beginning in 1953 and stretching for fifteen years, is told from the company's point of view in R. Carlyle Buley, The Equitable Life Assurance Society of the United States, 1859–1964, vol. 2 (New York: Appleton-Century-Crofts, 1967), p. 421 ff.

of policyholders to sue in a derivative action against the directors on behalf of the company—an important victory because of the small fraction of the mutual company represented by any one policyholder or several policyholders. On appeal, however, the court raised doubts whether the right had in fact been established.[17]

Theoretically, the policyholder's most straightforward check on the discretion of the management is the right to vote for officers at annual meetings, one of the terms of the mutual policy contract. Although policyholders as a group probably possess less sophistication than stockholders, and many are ignorant of their voting rights, the sizes of the surplus funds and the enticements of higher dividends might be expected to encourage occasional insurgent movements. But additional conditions work against proxy fights and in favor of management absolutism. The law requires that an opposition slate be nominated by a certain percentage of policyholders—Illinois requires 0.190 percent— which in a large company is thousands of signatures. There is a limited time in which this must be accomplished; and the company is not required to furnish a list of the policyholders, nor to pay for its preparation. Also, management frequently secures the policyholder's permanent or "automatic" proxy at the time of sale, and the courts have not interfered with this practice, except to impose a limited fiduciary responsibility upon the officers voting. The courts have explicitly denied the use of proxies to oust an incumbent director since "such a departure from ordinary voting is an unfair deprivation of the right of member policyholders to make a real expression of choice."[18]

A perusal of the rosters of officers and directors of mutual companies in Illinois and elsewhere reveals that the self-perpetuation in office of directors of mutual companies, criticized by the report of the TNEC in 1941, remains the pattern today.[19] In one Illinois company with 600,000 policyholders twenty-five ballots were cast—all proxies held by the directors. The largest number of votes cast in 1967 in an Illinois mutual company was two hundred, and even then the vice-president acknowledged in an interview that most of these were cast by employees of the home office. An officer of one of the largest New York mutuals vaguely recalled for the author a case some forty years

---

[17] Garfield v. Equitable, 263 N.Y.S. 2d 922, 924 (1965).

[18] In re Ideal Mutual Insurance Co., 190 N.Y.S. 2d. 895 (1916).

[19] TNEC, *Legal Reserve Life Insurance*, pp. 14–26. Contested elections are very rare. The largest mutual company, Metropolitan Life, has never had a contested election since its mutualization in 1915. In 1967, according to its annual report filed with the Illinois Department of Insurance, every director of the Metropolitan was elected by 50–51 votes cast in person. Another 1,370 ballots were returned by mail. The lowest number of this total received by a director was 1,321. There are over 45,000,000 policyholders insured by the Metropolitan.

ago when some policyholders representing an ethnic group had un-successfully "tried to get their own man."

Mutual company managers indicated in the interviews that they do frequently receive communications from their policyholders regarding company investments. Types mentioned included advice about invest-ment opportunities—one domestic mutual had that week received a clipping file accumulated by a policyholder on real estate in Florida; letters urging the company to extend a small business loan to a friend; notices that some piece of property on which the company has a mort-gage is being neglected; complaints about investments in central city areas. Managers' attitudes ranged from good-humored indulgence, to finding these letters an outright nuisance. In response to a question about policyholder influence on investments, an officer of a large out-of-state company frowned and said:

> Regrettably, they write us all the time, usually without any knowledge of what they're talking about. And one of these letters to the president can cost the com-pany hundreds of dollars to answer. Generally, they'll point out things the com-pany already knows.
> They have absolutely no influence whatsoever and I would hope not. Pre-sumably the companies have professional staffs that do a good job.

In general, then, the policyholders of mutual life insurance compa-nies are ill-situated and unsuited for control. Individually, even the most reasonable appeal represents such a miniscule portion of the com-pany's aggregate responsibilities that legitimacy is difficult to establish. Collectively, policyholders are hampered from forming effective opposi-tion. Once they become members of mutual companies they lack that most basic privilege of the consumer—the option to change product brands: a policy surrender is always a loss to the holder and frequently a gain for the company. With the surpluses of insurance companies providing margins of discretion unusual to industrial corporations, man-agers of mutual companies are to a corresponding degree entrenched and free of policyholder constraints.

Again theoretically, managers in a stock life insurance company are in a more vulnerable position. Stockholders are likely to have greater market sophistication and to be conscious of genuine dividend levels.[20] In practice, however, managers of stock companies are equally secure in their positions and autonomous in their decisions. This is due, first, to the pattern of stockholding in the industry. Increasingly, as will be discussed below, large stock insurance companies are owned by holding

[20]On the general sophistication required to buy and own stock in an insurance company, see remarks on calculating earnings, etc. in "A Red Umbrella in a High Wind," *Fortune* (August 1965): 139 ff.

companies which have overlapping or identical directors with the life company. This is the case with ownership of Continental Assurance and Washington National Life in Illinois. Or stock companies may be owned by nonfinancial corporations, as is Allstate owned by Sears, Roebuck and Company. A third pattern is for the stock to be closely held by the management itself: this was the case of Franklin Life for many years; and Bankers Life and Casualty, a company of $335 million in assets, is owned entirely by its board chairman.

Moreover, stockholders in life insurance companies have a definite interest in *not* receiving large parts of the surplus in the form of cash dividends. Surpluses are a matter of public information, and as the surpluses grow the market price of the stock climbs also; thus the stockholder can capitalize on company profits indirectly by selling his stock. And whereas income tax must be paid on stock dividends, money which stays in the surplus continues earning money for the shareholder which is untaxed. As a result, stock companies seldom pay cash dividends, but instead pay dividends in more stock.[21]

There are still other reasons why attempts by stockholders to control management are unlikely to happen. Life insurance companies operate on an extremely thin ratio of capital stock to total liabilities.[22] Because of the favorable balance of cash coming in and payments flowing out, these companies have no need to turn to the open money market for additional financing. This independence removes a constraint common (if increasingly less so) to most industrial stock companies—the need to operate in such a way as to facilitate future capitalizations. And, finally, should stockholders object too vigorously to management policies, there is the ultimate option of mutualization. Most management of stock insurance companies have either sufficient personal stockholdings or access to cash surpluses, and usually both, to effect a purchase of all stock by the surplus, thereby transforming the company into a mutual. This has been a common practice—usually for other reasons—among life insurance companies: prominent examples are Western and Southern Life, which was the largest stock company at the time of

---

[21] On stock dividends, see Dacey, *What's Wrong With Your Life Insurance*, p. 55. In 1961 Dacey's figures, compiled from *Spectator Life Insurance Year Book*, show Continental Assurance paying a 50 percent stock dividend and Franklin Life a 25 percent stock dividend. Dacey also quotes Raymond T. Smith, vice-president of Best's, writing in Smith's book, *Life Insurance Stocks*: "The true earnings of a life insurance company is understated in the year-end reports. Nearly all companies follow the policy of retaining the greater part of earnings to finance expansion as well as provide an extra margin of protection for shareholders." Ibid.

[22] Here is the percentage of total 1967 liabilities represented by capital stock in seven Illinois stock companies: Bankers Life and Casualty, 1.6 percent; Continental Assurance, 1.8 percent; Country Life, 1.3 percent; Franklin Life, 4.4 percent; North American Life, 1.3 percent; State Farm, 0.6 percent; Washington National, 7 percent. Ratios of major foreign insurers are similar: Aetna Life, 1.8 percent; Travelers, 2.7 percent; Occidental Life, 2.1 percent.

TNEC; Metropolitan Life; and the Prudential, which has only recently completed a mutualization begun in 1911. Managers with sizable stock-holdings can compensate for any future potential gains they may have made in the stock market by allowing for generous purchase prices and by granting themselves the customarily higher executive salaries paid by mutual companies.[23] Since it has generally been the practice of stock companies to pay dividends with stock rather than cash, the managers lose nothing in income and reestablish their control over the assets, now without the bothersome rituals of stockholder control.

II

Life insurance managers cite growth as the primary goal for the companies they control. A sampling of the Illinois interviews may suggest this virtually unanimous preoccupation. In response to a question about the main goals of the company, the president of a medium-sized domestic stock company answered:

We're more interested in growth than in immediate returns. For example, we own a sizable bank in the suburbs. Outside of the Loop, it's the largest bank in Illinois. We let its profits stay in there. If we were interested in immediate yield we could, I guess, invest perhaps in high grade mortgages and debentures. But in these perilous times of inflation, that might be risky and we want to see our assets grow.

Likewise the reply of the treasurer of a domestic mutual company of the same size: "In particular, we're looking for growth. Our investment operation has to earn a sufficient return to support that aim." A similar response came from the president of a smaller Illinois mutual company:

We're wrestling with that one right now in our five-year planning group. We're trying to express goals, and in a plain-words way that any policyholder can understand. Our goal is mainly sound growth as expressed in increasing assets. We never talk profits in this business, and we try to live accordingly. On the other hand, our duty is not to our fellow employees, but to the policyholders and the growth of the company.

Finally, the senior vice-president of one of the largest foreign mutual companies: "Well, you can say we want to keep on growing. Partly it's an individual achievement, a certain pride in your own career, your organization. And growth means fulfilling community needs."

As these remarks indicate, life insurance managers do not see serious conflicts between the goal of growth and various other aims of their enterprise. First, growth is considered necessary to management quality

---

[23] For example, compare the salaries of the top 1967 officers of Continental Assurance with Metropolitan Life, as reported in their annual reports. The chairman of the board of Continental Assurance received $111,545.84, while the chairman of the Metropolitan received $200,000. The president of the Continental received a salary of $76,547.83, and the president of the Metropolitan received $125,000.

and morale. In answering the question of why his company seeks to keep growing, this mutual company treasurer was typical:

That's a tough one. But a mutual insurance company is like any other company. If it didn't grow it would be a liquid trust. But at the later stages, now, it would have difficulty in attracting and holding capable management. These men will feel that they're with a stagnant, dying organization and will go on to another company or out of the industry. You've got to have growth or your company will slowly deteriorate. Any company is only as good as its management. Men in management today—well, you could increase their salaries but it wouldn't help. Salaries aren't that important to them—beyond a certain point, of course. But most people I know want the feeling they're contributing to a successful, growing enterprise. Ego maybe, call it what you will. In the insurance business it's a very real need.

Also, as a mutual vice-president explains, competitive position is measured in terms of asset growth: "We have a certain dedication to this organization and we compete vigorously all across the board. But competing for size isn't size alone, it's competing in accomplishment. We're just about at the top of the industry in assets, but, believe me, we have a simply terrible incentive to be number one."

The relationship between growth and profits is somewhat more complicated. There are officially no profits in mutual companies, and in stock companies profits generally remain undistributed while surpluses expand. On the other hand, there is a homologue to an industrial firm's profits in the surplus, i.e., those funds remaining after the costs of doing business. Except if one insists on the narrow requirement of *distribution* as the definition of profits, the distinction between profits and growth in the insurance industry is entirely superficial. The life insurance industry from its inception has sought asset growth.[24] Stockholders, where they exist, have indeed earned profits, and frequently large ones, but the source of these gains has been largely on stock transactions reflecting the healthy condition of undistributed surpluses.[25]

Perhaps the closest thing to a conflict between growth and profits is the problem of immediate versus longer-term gains. This problem is illustrated in the remark of the stock company president who preferred to let profits sit in the company-owned bank because of the perils of inflation. For all life companies interviewed, the distinction between short-run and long-run gains is subordinated to the broader aim of adjusting investment policy to anticipations of the economic environment. Since cash flows in the short-run are determined by investment decisions long past, the attempt is made to balance present decisions

[24] On the history of asset growth see TNEC, *Legal Reserve Life Insurance*, pp. 5–13.

[25] Dacey has calculated, for example, that a $1,000 investment in 1951 in the stock of Franklin Life was worth $31,830 in 1961 (*What's Wrong With Your Life Insurance*).

against future uncontrollable factors, such as interest rates, inflation, and so on, to achieve maximum asset growth through a system of dollar averaging.

The regularity of management concern with growth raises the question of whether growth should be considered a true goal or policy, rather than a mere response reflecting the nature of life insurance assets. Growth is a phenomenon virtually inherent in the surplus, once it is understood that mutual policyholders are not paid genuine dividends and stockholders have at least as much to gain from the increase of the surplus as from its distribution. With yields on past investments reinvested in new ventures, life insurance conforms to Mortimer's "law of nature" as does no other industry.[26] But the aggressiveness with which managers have recently pursued opportunities for growth belies a mere reflex.

The most ambitious effort at quickening the pace of growth has been in the area of holding company formations already discussed in chapters II and III above.[27] In Illinois, as in other states, large stock companies have already formed or are presently seeking to form holding company structures. This device enables the top management of the life insurance company to control a holding company which owns, in addition to the life company, a mutual fund company or other companies which the life company itself cannot legally own. The purpose of this arrangement is sometimes explained as "providing a full range of financial services for our policyholders." More specifically, it aims in part to increase the share of the savings dollar which is spent for life insurance. Although the number and dollar amount of life insurance sold annually has increased steadily, the percent of savings flowing into the industry has dropped during the last twenty years.[28] Through the holding company device, the insurance industry will use its large sales force to offer the services of a mutual fund while continuing to stress the unique advantages of life insurance.

Mutual companies, which cannot by law be similarly owned, have countered by sponsoring legislation such as S.B. 138 in the 75th Illinois General Assembly. As was explained earlier, this law enables mutual

---

[26] Charles G. Mortimer, *The Purposeful Pursuit of Profits and Growth of Business* (New York: McGraw-Hill, 1965).

[27] See Robert Sheehan, "Life Insurance's Almighty Leap into Equities," *Fortune* (October 1968): 142 ff.

[28] In 1948 life insurance companies accounted for 47.1 percent of the year's growth in savings. In 1967, when institutional savings rose by around $64.1 billion, life insurance got $8.6 billion or only 13.4 percent of the growth.

On the other hand, the ratio of premiums to total disposable income is 4 percent, the same as in 1929. See "Life Insurance Has More Than Held Its Own in the Competitive Marketplace," *Insurance*, January 13, 1968, p. 3.

companies, and stock companies as well, to invest insurance funds in subsidiary or downstream holding companies, which in turn will provide mutual fund services. Mutual companies have also developed the system of variable annuities, backed by "separate accounts" immune to state investment laws, in order to offer consumers some of the features of an equity instrument as a hedge against inflation. Since life insurance companies can provide these supplements to the predetermined fixed amount of the ordinary policy benefit only if they themselves can invest more heavily in equities less vulnerable to the shrinking dollar, an important purpose of both holding company ownership of life companies and life company ownership of holding companies and "separate accounts" is to permit larger investments in common stocks.[29]

Like every aspect of the business, growth is explained and justified by managers in terms of benefits for the policyholder: "This is not a defensive move on our part but a positive approach. We're going to make money for our policyholders."[30] Thus a further question must be raised as to whether growth is part of the fiduciary responsibility of the company and thereby beyond the reach of management discretion. In fact, however, the present policyholder, who has already contracted for his premium payments, has nothing to gain from aggressive growth. As has been shown, reserves are generally more than adequate to cover emergencies. And any policyholder who might entertain proprietary ideas about "his" surplus actually "loses" funds through management's goal. This is especially true in growth-directed sales practices. Because of life insurance accounting methods, the agent's commission and other costs of putting new business on the books is financed by the first year's premium. But in recent years because of the brisk competition for new business and its eventual contribution to asset size, commissions and other costs have come to exceed the first year's premium. These additional costs are paid for by earnings on previously invested assets held in the surplus. Since the rate of new policy lapses and surrenders is at around 80 percent, this involves a loss to the company and—if only in theory—its existing policyholders, as well as to the policyholder who withdraws.[31] Nor can growth be defended on the

[29] On the general questions surrounding life insurance ownership of common stocks see "Life Insurance: $84 Billion Dilemma," *Fortune* (February 1955): 112 ff. Also see "Impact of Investment Regulation on the Life Insurance Industry," *Insurance Law Journal* (July 1965).

[30] Sheehan, "Life Insurance's Almighty Leap into Equities," p. 145.

[31] During the TNEC Hearings Counsel Gerhard A. Gesell asked the chairman of the board of Metropolitan Life, Frederick H. Ecker, if the great growth of the Metropolitan was an advantage or disadvantage to the policyholders. Ecker said he didn't think the question made sense—of course it was an advantage, and there was no reason for a ceiling on size.

Senator O'Mahoney: "To put it another way, the management of the Metropolitan has never come to the conclusion that the company was large enough, and should stop growing?"

grounds that it enhances the competition in the price of insurance to the buying public. Although the retail price of the industry is a subject shrouded in great mystery (not surprisingly, considering the maze of "dividends," "options," "paid-up additions," "band pricing," and the enormous variety of payment plans that attend the average policy purchase), recent studies made with the industry's cooperation have concluded that effective price competition simply does not exist.[32]

Whether or not the holding company device itself will prove detrimental to the surplus is still unclear. Illinois regulatory officials expressed general pessimism about their ability to supervise the business activities of the holding companies and to ensure against their indifference to the fiduciary responsibilities of the life insurance unit. Holding companies have been distinguished in American insurance history for their ability to milk capital from subsidiaries and affiliates. In September 1967, the New York Superintendent of Insurance distributed a questionnaire to other insurance commissioners regarding holding company abuses and regulatory policies in their states. Of thirty-five states responding: "Approximately half . . . reported that they had experienced regulatory problems with domestic insurance companies which arose from intercorporate transactions among affiliated insurance and non-insurance corporations; the control of insurance companies by holding companies; and concern regarding the integrity of holding company management."[33]

Mr. Ecker: "It never has, Mr. Chairman, and that would result in our going out of business. You can't stand still. You either go forward or you go backward."

Thurman Arnold: "Is it correct to say that the existing policyholders would gain if no new business were written . . . [because of the costs of new business]?"

Mr. Ecker: "If, from heaven or some other place all the expense of conducting a business and looking after the affairs of the company were provided, yes."

U.S. Congress, *Hearings Before the Temporary National Economic Committee*, Congress of the United States, 76th Cong., 1st and 2nd Sess., Washington, D.C., 1940.

[32] "Most of the data presented in this book suggest a large amount of price variation in life insurance, not only on similar plans of insurance in different companies but also, in some cases, on different plans in the same company. Indeed, the variation is large enough to suggest that price competition in many areas of life insurance has not been effective. Thus companies that charge prices substantially in excess of the prices charged by some of their competitors for comparable contracts apparently are able to secure customers. Similarly, companies whose price structures raise questions of equity because some of their customers are charged substantially more for protection than others in the same mortality classification apparently do not have to offer any justification for their practices.

"The study further suggests that, except in the case of short-term nonparticipating term policies, premium rates cannot be relied upon when one attempts to determine the price status of a given policy. Since a refined method of price calculation requires detailed policy data and a considerable amount of arithmetic, such a calculation is impractical without the assistance of an electronic computer." Joseph M. Belth, *The Retail Price Structure in American Life Insurance* (Bloomington, Ind.: The Foundation for the School of Business, Indiana University, 1966), pp. 238–39.

[33] State of New York Insurance Department, *Report of the Special Committee on Insurance Holding Companies*, 1968, pp. 50–53.

In the Illinois interviews, life company managers predictably under-played these potential conflicts. When pressed, they ultimately argued that growth and its pursuit are their own best justification. Two presi-dents and one executive vice-president of three of the fastest growing companies in the country have applied an identical word to the indus-try's new mood—"exciting:" "It adds," says one, a characteristic not usually thought of as part of insurance, "excitement." The second com-ments: "It is one more demonstration of our people's willingness to do things a little differently." And the third: "The life insurance business of the future will have vastly extended spheres of influence, and it will offer services and policies far beyond what we have known in the past . . . Never before . . . have we stood on the threshold of such excit-ing times."[34]

The goal of growth, when transposed to the activity of investment, becomes the goal of maximum yield or maximum profitability. All of the life insurance managers interviewed agreed that maximum yield was the primary factor in their portfolio choices. The goal of maximum yield is somewhat contradictory to the practice of estimating premiums on the basis of a rather low assumed maximum, i.e., the minimum yield required to satisfy policy obligations. It is, moreover, at odds with the image in both insurance theory and law that gives the aim of safety an equal or surpassing importance to the goal of yield.

To what extent is the goal of maximum yield compromised by the imperatives of safety? The Illinois interviews indicated that, as in the case of growth versus profits, there is no conflict in practice. The princi-ple prescription for achieving safety has traditionally been portfolio diversification, and life companies do distribute their funds among the various categories of investments. However no manager could recall any instance where a desire for diversification influenced a marginal deci-sion. And even the most aggressive manager must take into account certain risks in his strategy of growth.[35]

The risks facing a life insurance investment officer in allocating avail-able funds are of three types: first, default risk, or the risk that the actually realized yield will turn out to be less than was anticipated; second, market risk, that the market value of securities purchased today will fluctuate downward tomorrow; and third, income risk, which arises

---

[34]The first two statements are in Sheehan, "Life Insurance's Almighty Leap into Equities," p. 145. The third is from *The National Underwriter*, Life edition, March 16, 1968.

[35]"Indeed it would appear from the evidence that the major qualification to use of a simple maximization of expected returns model arises not from a diversification motivation, but from the desire to be fully invested." Lawrence D. Jones, "Portfolio Objectives, External Constraints, and the Postwar Investment Behavior of Life Insurance Companies," Ph.D. dissertation in Economics (Harvard University, September 1959), p. 119.

from the requirement that he invest more funds in the future at unknown interest rates, and that these investments will somehow be in an
unfavorable balance with guaranteed earnings already contracted for. It
should be emphasized that these are not simply, or even primarily, risks
that the company will become insolvent, that bugaboo of insurance
departments; they also present the dangers that the company will not
adequately exploit present opportunities for yield, may fail to secure
protection against future unfavorable economic conditions, or will not
be in the best cash position later on to take full advantage of more
lucrative possibilities should they arise. Life insurance managers reduce
these risks by selecting investments with care and establishing acceptable variations of return on any single parcel; by ordering maturities
according to expected liabilities and the best estimates obtainable of
the economic future; and by hedging their market bets with certain
securities that are readily marketable.

Each category of investment offers a different set of advantages
toward these objectives.[36] Government bonds, since they are always
redeemable, offer the features of flexibility and maneuverability; they
are also available securities when there is little commercial demand for
capital. Industrial bonds enable the insurance investor to adjust interest
rates to the credit standing of the borrower, and they provide a steady
level of return. Mortgages have the advantage of a secure capital base
and often a government-guaranteed yield. Common stocks and certain
types of commercial mortgages provide a degree of protection against
inflation. Other categories, such as preferred stocks, may be attractive
because of their combination of yield and liquidity.

The shift of funds among investment categories is primarily determined by management's appetite for higher yields.[37] The most dramatic movement during the time of the Illinois interviews was away
from residential mortgages, which for many years had been a favored
class because of capital security, FHA and VA guarantees, and high
yields. During 1967 land values were high; the security of government
guarantees was still available; and the guaranteed interest rates (not to
mention the higher paying nonguaranteed or conventional mortgages)
were some three percentage points over the earnings which companies
calculate in their premiums and reserves. The explanation of all managers for the shift was unanimous: higher yields. "We've been completely
out of the residential market for the last two or three years," said the
treasurer of Illinois' largest stock company,

[36]See Clayton and Osborn, *Insurance Company Investment*, chapter VI; and Andrew F.
Brimmer, *Life Insurance Companies in the Capital Market* (East Lansing, Mich.: Michigan State
University Press, 1962), chapters V–IX.

[37]Walter, *The Investment Process*, p. 248 and chapter VI.

mainly because of the ability to get major commercial projects that are simply more attractive from the standpoint of yield. Sure, I know seven per cent sounds pretty good, but we can do better than that today. Also, the savings and loans have taken over a lot of that market. They're more expert at it, it fits in better with their operations. . . . Certainly we could compete if we wanted to. Nothing in this business is final and we may be back in there with both feet someday soon. But today there are many alternatives for greater rewards.

The final balance and distribution among categories is entirely a matter of management discretion. The case of the Illinois stock company with large holdings in a bank as a hedge against inflation is again pertinent. Similarly, the treasurer of a mutual company with over half its current assets in bonds explained that since World War II his company had liquidated its fixed obligations, particularly U.S. government issues, more slowly than the rest of the industry; fearing a recession or worse, the company had shied away from the mortgage market lest it get caught with a glut of foreclosed real estate. While the optimum portfolio is a subject for debate within and among companies, and new techniques of investment are constantly devised, the *criteria* involved— the various portfolio objectives, the advantages and disadvantages of different strategies—are well established and uniform in the minds of the managers making the decisions.[38]

Equally settled are the criteria employed in choosing investment parcels within investment categories. In the home mortgage field, which will be discussed in greater detail in chapter V, there are the traditional underwriting standards of location, occupant's credit standing, and land values. In the area of industrial bonds, investment officers study the quality of the borrowing firm's management, the credit standing of the company, the terms offered. In common stocks, the market performance of the relevant industry group is additionally important. For municipal bonds, managers consider the local political situation, the powers of the issuing government to tax, the earning power of the specific project. And similar criteria apply to other investment categories.[39] As with portfolio diversification, the final decision—regarding, say, how high a credit rating a borrower must have or how well an industry group must perform—is left to management's judgment. But the criteria, the procedures and methods of adhering to the criteria, as well as the goal of company growth through maximum investment yields, are unequivocal.

[38] For a discussion of the investment objectives and techniques of various types of investment, written from a variety of views within the life insurance industry, see David McCahan, ed. *Investment of Life Insurance Funds* (Homewood, Ill.: Richard D. Irwin, 1953). On the development of new methods of investment to meet economic opportunities, see Robert E. Schultz, *Life Insurance Housing Projects* (Homewood, Ill.: Richard D. Irwin, 1957), and H. Wayne Snider, *Life Insurance Investment in Commercial Real Estate* (Homewood, Ill.: Richard D. Irwin, 1956).

[39] See McCahan, ed., *Investment of Life Insurance Funds*, chapters V–X.

III

It would be misleading to separate completely any broader social goals the life insurance industry might pursue from its ordinary business objectives. The life insurance enterprise itself has always been considered by its purveyors to perform a valuable public service. Insurance advertisements and trade literature abound with pronouncements on the importance of protecting one's widow against pauperism and of building a small estate to finance the children's college education. Insurance managers are inclined to characterize themselves, as does the president of an Illinois stock company, as "frustrated social workers": "When you're talking about this business, you've in a way gotten into the area of social work. Two of our senior officers have backgrounds in social work. You feel like you're doing good—someplace. Our company's first policyholders were mainly among blue-collar people and railroad people."

Investment activities in particular are considered an important part of the industry's good works. James F. Oates, the board chairman of the Equitable Life Assurance Society, has reviewed investment history in terms so typical of the industry's self-image that it deserves extensive quotation:

> It is a fact of economic history that the expansion of the railroad system was one of the most significant factors in the growth of the United States. . . . As the transcontinental and Western trunk lines developed and our transportation system spread throughout the land with mounting needs for heavy capital investment, the life insurance companies responded and provided vast funds.
>
> After World War I came the great expansion of the electric utility and telephone industries. . . . By 1940, public utility bond investments of the life insurance industry amounted to some 14 per cent of all assets.
>
> As we look back in these broad sweeps of recent history, another interesting illustration of the relationship of investments to social change arose in U.S. Treasury obligations issued as part of the financing of this country's efforts in World War I.
>
> In the first half of the 1940's, the trend toward U.S. government bonds began a new chapter as history repeated itself. During World War II, the insurance companies invested large sums in Treasury issues—more, in fact, than their net increase in assets during this same period.
>
> A similar pattern of capital responsiveness can be traced for different types of mortgages. Briefly, we might note the upsurge in farm mortgage loans beginning with the outbreak of World War I. . . . as the United States, for the first time, assumed the role of "bread basket of the world."
>
> With the great housing boom which followed World War II, the life companies again directed their reserve assets into this area of financial need. Initially, the surge of funds went into one-to-four family residences as the nation sought to provide adequate housing and as social values became more strongly committed than ever before to individual home ownership.
>
> Later, the flow of mortgage funds emphasized industrial and commercial properties, as shopping centers emerged to serve a growing suburban population and as office buildings dominated urban construction to accommodate industrial and business growth as well as the shift from blue-collar to white-collar employment.

Most recently, apartment house financing has become an important user of life insurance funds as the forces of the real estate marketplace reflect and anticipate the vast housing needs arising out of the wave of new marriages and family formations by the generations born during and after World War II and now entering adulthood. Thus, . . . life insurance funds have been highly mobile both in responding to and, to some extent, in anticipating the needs of a rapidly growing and changing society—sometimes at war, sometimes at peace.[40]

Oil exploration, the development of taconite mining, the jet engine, atomic energy, and the purchase of hospital bonds—all are included by life insurance managers in this saga of service.

Whatever the proportions of ideology and calculation in such accounts, they do make difficult any evaluation of the life insurance industry's commitment to goals other than growth and higher yields on investments. In the Illinois interviews most managers insisted on their determination to be what they frequently called "good corporate citizens." But none were able to clarify this objective beyond cliches: "We have an obvious responsibility to our community. [Probe.] Well, we intend to take an active part in community affairs and encourage our employees to do likewise;" and "Along with our responsibilities to our stockholders and policyholders, we recognize our profound responsibility to the environment. [Probe.] Anything we do must be compatible with that."

Oates has also written on the broader relationship between the life insurance industry and society. Since he was cited often in the interviews as a kind of high priest of social responsibility, his thinking may reflect in a very general way industry's outlook. Amid comments about automation, ethnic integration, lunar weekends, and the physiology of man,[41] Oates identifies "our central problem—as we approach the final third of the twentieth century—how to capture the sense of community which characterized our society until the relatively recent past."[42] And he offers a method toward a solution:

There are many models to choose from, one of which is an approach to urban problems which, appropriately enough, has its home in Athens—an approach with

---

[40]James F. Oates, Jr., *Business and Social Change: Life Insurance Looks to the Future* (New York: McGraw-Hill, 1968), pp. 44-49.

[41]Ibid., pp. 70-71. "Recently Dr. Rene Dubos disclosed some startling evidence that only between five and ten percent of our genes are really at work—the great bulk immobilized by the inhibitions of the environment. He feels sure that a higher percentage will become operative."

[42]Ibid., p. 93. The life industry's conception of the "sense of community," and the good life in general, is closely tied to the idea of the family—a not unexpected emphasis since the life insurance product rests on the value of providing for one's wife, children, even parents. See Oates on "The Family and It's Future," pp. 27 ff. In the Illinois interviews there was a frequent negative reference to dope addiction, divorce rates, and so on, as major threats to American society. For the tenor of these attitudes, see the speech of J. Edward Day, former Postmaster General, former commissioner of insurance in Illinois, and today a vice-president of Prudential, in which he assails the hippies as "nihilists," and contrasts them with life insurance agents who are "solid citizens." *Insurance*, September 23, 1967, p. 30 ff.

which I am sure many of you are familiar. This is known as "ekistics"—taking its name from the Greek word for home. It calls for the closest possible collaboration between the technical and cultural disciplines—engineering and architecture—on the one hand, and behavioral sciences, on the other. If such a science is ever to be evolved and applied, public and private interests must walk hand in hand.[43]

Oates's final vision, of government and business walking hand in hand, is an important aspect in the industry's social purview. So far, however, the precise destination of this prospective ambulation is undecided. There is much talk of cooperation and its being a two-way street, and the general belief that government leaders increasingly recognize the contributions the industry can make to solving what Illinois managers variously saw as "Chicago's disaster," "an apartheid nation of the feared and the fearful," "blights on an otherwise fabulous future." There is sometimes a defensive, yet matter-of-fact, tone, as in the remark of Gilbert Fitzhugh, board chairman of Metropolitan Life and the Life Insurance Association of America: "Government, like nature, abhors a vacuum. If there are legitimate needs that business or some other group does not meet, government will surely move in."[44] But the industry has not yet elaborated on a government-industrial order different from the usual urgings that government follow policies to combat inflation and encourage the growth of private savings. Government, cautions Fitzhugh, must "stick to *promoting* the general welfare, not providing it."[45]

The Urban Investments Program was repeatedly cited by Illinois life insurance managers, many of whose companies were participants, as the most important concrete example of the industry's response to its social responsibilities. Chapter VI will analyze this program in detail and will consider its objectives, its criteria of investment choice, and its impact. Here, however, attention may be called to the vagueness of the program's objectives from the point of view of social responsibility. Directors and participants have simultaneously described the program as an effort to revitalize cities where insurance investments are heavy and where most policyholders live; as a means of reversing the erosion of the urban tax base; as a reward to the growing black insurance market; and as a strategy to preempt governmental initiative.

[43] Oates, *Business and Social Change*, p. 63. Oates has earned his reputation as a leader in the industry's involvement in social responsibility. When he assumed the presidency of the Equitable in 1960, he undertook a search for a director of social research. Finally, on the advice of Robert K. Merton, he engaged John W. Riley of Rutgers University. Appointed a second vice-president, Riley put together a special issue of *The American Behavioral Scientist* (1963) subtitled *Social Research and Life Insurance*, including articles by Kingsley Davis and Talcott Parsons, along with insurance executives. Riley also persuaded the company to declare itself an equal-opportunity employer in its advertising, and in 1965 shocked the industry by running ads in the trade press and in *Ebony* showing a black insurance salesman selling to a white couple.

[44] *Insurance*, December 16, 1967, p. 8.

[45] Ibid.

An early ambiguity of the Urban Investments Program, generally decided in the affirmative, was whether or not companies could expect normal yields on their pledged participation. But there are other less dramatic practices of life companies which, although they may have some residual public relations effects, do represent a diversion of effort and assets from activities either directly profitable or directly promotional and a clear departure from profit-oriented criteria. In the Illinois interviews a wide variety of practices and projects were offered as evidence of social goals. One group of practices involves a socially conscious selection of investments. Most frequently this is the refusal as a matter of company policy to extend credit to certain classes of enterprise: three insurers indicated that no investments are made in liquor or tobacco securities; several others refrain from investing in gambling casinos. Or companies may give preferential treatment to favored borrowers: one loans funds at a slight discount to the suburb where its home office is located, to be used for parking facilities and parks; another company had for several years sought to invest heavily in businesses owned by persons of Scandinavian descent, the national origin of its management.

A second group of projects removes funds from the profit stream and directs them in socially worthy directions. One company interviewed donated a half-million dollars to that year's United Fund campaigns in cities where its offices are located. Another has distributed, free of charge, over twenty-five million full-color reproductions of paintings by contemporary American artists. Several companies make annual contributions to the Life Insurance Medical Research Fund, the Public Health Association, and the National Funds for Medical and Graduate Nursing Education. A large stock insurer cited a $15,000 donation to Georgia State College, in recognition of that institution's program of insurance education. Another has a program which matches any contribution up to $500 which an employee makes to his alma mater. Yet another donated $250,000 to privately supported liberal arts colleges. Several companies participate in the National Merit Scholarship Program.

Unlike the clear-sighted decisions of regular portfolio selection, the criteria used in these practices and projects are often arbitrary and confused in the minds of life insurance investors. A treasurer whose company abstains from tobacco and liquor securities apologized that such a "throwback to the Stone Age" should prevail today. And the vice-president of a company which has turned down loans for Las Vegas casinos confessed that he was unclear about the distinction between gambling and baseball parks or pari-mutual racetracks, which were considered acceptable. Similarly, the only obvious criteria in the second group of allocations appear to be the intrinsic values of charity, higher

education, and contemporary American art. Nor, moreover, were any
managers able to express criteria of acceptable amounts of such contributions beyond assuring the author that the policyholders' funds were
not in danger.

Attitudes toward what constitutes good corporate citizenship are not
unanimous, and some life company managers are rather reluctant social
engineers. The president of a medium-sized Illinois mutual company
said he

once knew of a company in Columbus, Ohio—Nationwide. The head of that company, Mr. Lincoln, wrote a book called *Vice-President in Charge of Revolution.*
Lincoln was once offered a big group, but he wouldn't take it because it was non-
union. Now, I'm not against unions—I've held a few union cards myself—but that
violated his fiduciary responsibility to his policyholders.

Since this manger's company had offered to participate in the Urban
Investments Program, he was asked whether notions of public service
ever influenced investment:

No! It does not effect it. It can't. We're always torn by this thing but our responsibility to the policyholder is first. The only time this has not been true is the case of
the Urban Investments Program. Otherwise our decision is strictly a financial decision. We are simply not authorized to give that money away.

Later in the interview he said that a Methodist church had recently
applied for a loan, but the company, after listening politely to the
presentation, had turned it down because "we can't get into supporting
religious groups."

The diversity, perhaps even glibness and confusion, with which life
insurance managers regard their corporate citizenship is itself evidence
of the high degree of discretion individual managers have in these matters. And the vagueness of purpose and lack of criteria suggest that the
idea of the industry's social involvement is more accurately described as
an impulse than a direction.

IV

A summary of these remarks must return to the problems of profit
maximization and management discretion with which the discussion
began. Setting aside contributions for charity and education which
represent insignificant fractions of a company's assets, do life insurance
managers seek to maximize profits? In the narrow sense of managerial
economics, no. The above analysis has denied the importance of several
reputed obstacles to profit maximization. First, it has rejected the distinction between growth and profits as superficial and inapplicable to
the life insurance enterprise. Second, although there is a desire for asset
diversification and, to a very limited degree perhaps, liquidity, these in
no way conflict with maximum yield but rather support and protect

it against inordinate risks. Third, while managers do strive to extend the power and prestige of their companies, these ends are seen as accomplished through precisely yield and growth. Finally, insurance managers do display an "instinct of workmanship," a search for personal pride in their performance, but these satisfactions are considered to be by-products of a profitable company, not competitors with it.[46]

On the other hand, many of the propositions of a more "realistic" model of the corporation do apply to the life insurance industry. One of them, that information is imperfect and that communications flow through the organization may result in systematic bias or ignorance and thus diminish earnings, is the conclusion of a study of investment search and forecast in several large life companies.[47] Another, that corporations must compromise maximum yield with demands arising from various groups within the organization, is a situation verified in the Illinois interviews: several managers indicated, for example, that they had not withdrawn from the residential mortgage field as quickly as they might have liked so that they could maintain good relations with their mortgage correspondents.[48]

The foregoing analysis has not emphasized these aspects of company decision because they cannot be understood as serious deviations from the goals of maximum yields and asset growth. The modern life insurance corporation is not a runaway horse kicking over its traces and trampling the fields it had yesterday plowed. Nor is it an electronic machine, with perfect information systems and neutral, synchronized operations. But these homely metaphors are probably even less applicable to the classical entrepreneur with whom today's manager is often contrasted. If anything, it may be argued that with refined economic forecasting, operations research, improved accounting methods, and market analysis—all of which the companies eagerly expect will improve returns—the life insurance manager is in a good and steadily improving position to maximize yields. He is aware of changing conditions and does not exploit present investments without an eye to the potential

[46] For alternative positions to the one argued here, see, on growth versus profits, John Kenneth Galbraith, *New Industrial State* (New York: Houghton Mifflin, 1967), pp. 176 ff. On asset preferences besides return, see Kenneth E. Boulding, *A Reconstruction of Economics* (New York: John Wiley and Sons, 1950), pp. 99 ff. On the aims of company power and prestige, see Chester I. Barnard, *The Functions of the Executive* (Cambridge, Mass.: Harvard University Press, 1938), pp. 145 ff.; R. J. Monsen and Anthony Downs, "A Theory of Large Managerial Firms," *Journal of Political Economy* (June 1965): 227 ff.; and Robert A. Gordon, *Business Leadership in the Large Corporation*, 2nd ed. (Berkeley, Calif.: University of California Press, 1961), p. xiii. On personal satisfaction see Thorstein Veblen, *The Instinct of Workmanship and the State of the Industrial Arts* (New York: Viking Press, 1946); and Barnard, *Functions of the Executive*, pp. 146 ff.

[47] On information, communications flows, etc. see R. J. Monsen and Anthony Downs, "Large Managerial Firms," p. 229. The study of the life insurance industry is Walter, *The Investment Process*, chapters VI, VII, and X.

[48] See James G. March, "The Business Firms as a Political Coalition," *Journal of Politics* 24 (1962): 662–78.

gains of the future; he does not carelessly wreck essential parts of the investment organization he may one day require. Nor do the modifications justify a "satisficing" rather than a maximizing description.[49] Mutual managers in particular could satisfy their profit needs by only achieving that yield assumed in their premium rates; but they strive, as do the stock companies, to reach ever higher levels of return and surplus growth.

The insistence on such an abstract and unhistorical standard of profit maximization is peculiar and even nonsensical, except perhaps in terms of the highly specialized interests of economists who have provided these formulations. The notion, however, of a corporation free from the imperatives of the profit motive has had special fascination for modern political thinkers. Although it was recognized early that the triumph of the managers over the stockholders had destroyed a legal order resting on ownership and the responsibilities ownership allegedly entailed, the scholarly attitude toward these developments has been optimistic: released from acquisitiveness, the new managers could use their enormous assets productively and creatively in response to the needs of the wider social community. This enthusiasm climaxed in A. A. Berle's comparison of corporate capitalism with the "City of God," and it has been echoed recently in Galbraith's *New Industrial State*.[50]

The life insurance industry is, indisputably, a model of managerial discretion. Unhindered by policyholders and stockholders, with large unassigned surpluses at their disposal and a steady and predictable cash income, managers make investment decisions in an environment offering returns consistently above business costs. Will these conditions eventually result in a deemphasis of profits and growth in pursuit of wider social responsibilities and objectives? At this juncture two observations may be offered. In the first place, a more socially conscious investment policy need not be less concerned with maximizing yields. For example, not lending to gambling casinos or only to Scandinavians may have no bearing whatsoever on the earnings of the company, depending on the details of the transaction and the availability of other investment opportunities. Similarly, investing in a black ghetto might not be less profitable than investing in a suburb, depending on the interest rates, the costs of servicing, and so on. An important determining factor in the relative profitability of any project are the criteria employed in making specific decisions. While the life insurance industry has demonstrated impulses toward social responsibility, criteria of the extent and

[49] See Herbert A. Simon, "Theories of Decision-Making in Economics and Behavioral Science," *American Economic Review* (June 1969): 262–65.

[50] Adolf A. Berle, *The 20th Century Capitalist Revolution* (New York: Harcourt, Brace & World, 1954), especially chapter V; and Galbraith, *New Industrial State*. Berle, incidentally, in 1967 was a director of three insurance companies, two of them life insurance companies.

substance of these activities are inchoate or nonexistent.[51] (The single somewhat qualified exception is the Urban Investments Program, which will be discussed in chapter VI.)

Second, and more crucial, is the nature of the media of credit, the concept with which this study began. In a fundamental sense, the chief product of a life insurance company is choice itself. In an almost pure credit industry the decision as to which enterprises to facilitate with the funds a company has amassed in its reserves and surplus is exactly analogous to the production of steel and radios in a manufacturing company. Money and mortgages are related as raw materials and use to the product of choice as are iron and skyscrapers to the product of steel. The construction engineer and the shopping center planner may take technical pride in the projects they oversee; life insurance executives find their excitement, as they call it, in deciding to enable these ventures to proceed.

In this light, the profit-oriented decisions which have been described above are perhaps more rational to the life insurance company than to the large corporate manufacturer. Profits from the sale of radios will not necessarily result in the production of more radios (although in the model of the mature corporation something like this happens). But yields on life company investments will virtually always, barring only the short-sighted greed of a company president or bookkeeper, result in the production of more investment choices. Investment procedures, such as the mortgage underwriting discussed in chapter V below, are designed to produce choices more profitably, much as the manufacturing processes are so designed in an industrial company. These procedures are tailored to certain end uses, one set for home mortgages, another for long-term government bonds; but this does not restrict the generalized nature of credit, except as these modifications link discretion more tightly to the goal of profit.

Thus, the idea that the modern corporation will significantly reorder its goals from profits to social betterment, quite apart from the question of its general validity, would seem to be particularly irrelevant to the life insurance industry; this in spite of the fact that it is the prototype of "maturity." In the life company, Galbraith's technocrat, the manager who identifies himself with growth, efficiency, and stability, is an expert in nothing but the techniques of choice. For him, in Galbraith's terms, to attach himself to the goals of the federal bureaucracy, or for that matter, to the strictures of mandatory investment laws, would mean the steady diminution of his own function.

[51] For a different slant on the conflict between profits and social responsibility, see R. G. Garnett, *A Century of Co-Operative Insurance* (London: George Allen and Unwin, 1968), especially pp. 291 ff.

CHAPTER V

HOUSING INVESTMENTS AND SOCIAL CHANGE

The analysis thus far has proceeded to the point where government investment policy, and in particular the *mandatory* mode, may be juxtaposed to life insurance investment behavior under conditions of maximum private autonomy. Chapter II suggested that mandatory policies are characterized by first, coercion, the requirement that life managers invest funds according to prescription; second, purposive reordering of the availability of credit to specific groups or economic sectors; and third, policy directed toward a constituency external to the company. Chapter IV, however, has indicated a role for life insurance executives exactly opposite to these specifications, corresponding to what has been described as the *enabling* mode. Insurance decisions are characterized by a broad range of discretion; in normal business operations there is no purpose except to profit and grow; and the "constituency" for these decisions is "the policyholder"—which turns out to be a euphemism for the company itself. Further, life insurance executives demonstrate a variety of self-consciously social impulses, the content of which, however, is vague and the criteria of satisfying these impulses altogether inchoate. In contrast, the criteria for achieving growth and profits are clear, straightforward, and largely standardized.

The distinction between coercive, socially purposive investment policy through government fiat, and company aggrandizement through executive discretion should be understood before proceeding to the discussion in this chapter, which concerns the life insurance industry's investments in residential mortgages in Chicago during the last three and a half decades. For here the definite social *impact* of these investments must not be confused with the kind of planned change which might be fostered by government. Rather, the pronounced regularities

among companies and their cumulative results is an achievement of a
set of procedures—procedures applied, as it were, "incrementally," for
profit. The significance of the distinction will be evident in chapter VI,
a study of the life insurance industry's Urban Investments Program,
where it will be shown that it is one thing for an industry to affect
social change incidentally, in pursuit of individual company goals, and
quite another to intentionally bring it about. The implications of the
distinction for corporate social responsibility and government social
responsibility is reserved for the conclusions in chapter VII.

Here, then, the subject is the normal business of investing in residential mortgages. While this activity is somewhat less dramatic than certain other credit aspects of the industry, say, its relationship to the
"command posts" of corporate industry and finance, it is quite appropriate to the present analysis. The residential mortgage activities of life
insurance companies place the industry in a special position relative to
society and its needs. Unlike the loan requirements of business and
governments, the demand for residential credit reaches through the
entire spectrum of income and social groups. While housing loans have
some of the reverberations on the economy characteristic of other sectors, the juxtaposition of lender and public consumer—either of housing or of some other expenditure facilitated by the mortgage—is more
immediate. As a result, certain social effects are directly observable.

The attention to mortgages is suited, moreover, to the larger conception of the contemporary ties of corporate business to the government
and society. Among the various forms of investments common to the
life insurance industry, mortgages is the only form dispensed (or more
precisely, dispensable) directly to the black community—a community,
which in our analysis, poses the most serious challenge to the political
status quo. Inadequate housing has been one of the primary and most
aggravating symptoms of inferior social status, and one consistently
singled out for remedy. And in this respect, the Urban Investments
Program may be perceived as the industry's attempt to alleviate the
social consequences of past decisions.

In order to trace life insurance residential lending in Chicago, a random sample of 129 census tracts in Chicago and surrounding Cook
County were chosen for study. Within each tract, approximately 500
lots were selected, and the chain of title for each lot was inspected back
through 1935 for incidence of life company mortgages. This record was
then scrutinized against census characteristics of population and neighborhood.[1] Also, interviews with loan officers and mortgage correspond-

---

[1] The number of lots for which chains of title were finally examined and included in the
data averaged 493 per census tract, or a total of 69,597 lots in the sample of 129 tracts. The
title search was done by hand by the author from July–December 1968, using the records of
the Chicago Title and Trust Company, Chicago, Illinois.

ents helped to reconstruct the reasoning behind these decisions. Particular attention has been directed to the distribution of mortgages between city and suburbs, and between whites and blacks.

An assessment of the life insurance industry's impact on society through its mortgage activities, however, is complicated by the fact that insurance companies are only one of several sources of mortgage credit. Also, the availability of credit is itself only one of a variety of factors influencing the supply of satisfactory housing, the growth of an "inner city," and so on. Nevertheless, as was argued in chapter I, credit is a situational control that enables the working out of other motives and processes, and our methods enable a closer examination of the rationale and structure of mortgage credit by one of its most important suppliers.

I

Before turning to specific social results of investment behavior, some grasp should be had of the general position of the industry in the residential mortgage market.[2] Life insurance companies are ideally suited to mortgage lending. First, and most important, they acquire their funds for a longer term—usually the working or life span of the policyholder—than do the other major institutional lenders, and may benefit from the long maturities of residential mortgages. Second, since they can more accurately forecast when they must pay back funds, life companies need not be deterred by the nonliquid feature of mortgage loans. Third, until very recently at least, they have not had to pay competitive and shifting rates for the funds they acquire; this has enabled them to take full advantage of government insurance programs. Finally, the interstate nature of business operations and more lenient state laws regarding mortgage location have permitted life insurance funds to move from place to place according to demand.

Census data are from the following sources: U.S. Bureau of Census, *Sixteenth Census of the United States: 1940. Population and Housing for Census Tracts and Community Areas, Chicago, Illinois* (Washington, D.C.: Government Printing Office, 1943); Louis Wirth and Eleanor H. Bernet, ed., *Local Community Fact Book of Chicago* (Chicago: University of Chicago Press, 1949); U.S. Bureau of Census, *Seventeenth Census of the United States: 1950. Population,* vol. III, Census Tract Statistics (Washington, D.C.: Government Printing Office, 1953); U.S. Bureau of Census, *Eighteenth Census of the United States: 1960. Population and Housing, Census Tracts.* Final Report PHC (1)-26, Chicago, Illinois (Washington, D.C.: Government Printing Office, 1962); Evelyn M. Kitagawa and Karl E. Tauber, eds., *Local Community Fact Book, Chicago Metropolitan Area, 1960* (Chicago: Chicago Community Inventory, University of Chicago, 1967).

Additional data for the period after 1965 were furnished by the Research and Statistics Division, Hospital Planning Council for Metropolitan Chicago. Mimeo. December 1966; April 1967; and July 1968.

[2] For a general introduction to the legal framework of mortgage lending, methods of company organization, experience with yields, foreclosures, etc., see R. J. Saulnier, *Urban Mortgage Lending by Life Insurance Companies* (New York: National Bureau of Economic Research, 1950).

The suitability of mortgages generally, on farms and commercial properties as well as on homes and apartments—all of which until recently were grouped together as one investment category in the annual reports of life companies—is evidenced in the history of the industry (see table 8). Before World War I, mortgages dominated investment

Table 8. Mortgages Owned by U.S. Life Insurance Companies,
1890-1968 (in Millions)

Year	Farm	Nonfarm	Total	% of assets
1890	a	a	$ 310	40.2
1910	a	a	1,227	31.7
1920	$1,270	$ 1,172	2,442	33.4
1935	1,073	4,284	5,357	23.1
1945	776	5,860	6,636	14.8
1950	1,327	14,775	16,102	25.1
1955	2,273	27,172	29,445	32.6
1960	2,982	38,789	41,771	34.9
1965	4,823	55,190	60,013	37.8
1968	5,801	64,172	69,973	37.2

Source: Life Insurance Fact Book 1969.
aBreakdown not available.

distribution; since then they have been a close second to the combined category of government and privately issued bonds. The relative contribution these mortgages have made to recent housing finance is shown in table 9. In evaluating these figures one must keep in mind that savings and loan associations are largely restricted to housing loans, and that commercial banks control assets much larger—in 1968, two and one-half times larger—than the assets of life insurance companies.[3]

As will be discussed later, the aggregate amount of funds made available for residential lending may affect the competition among different

[3]In 1968 the Federal Reserve Board calculated the assets of commercial banks to be $439.7 billion, compared to $182.6 billion of life insurance companies. U.S. Bureau of the Census, *Statistical Abstract of the U.S.: 1970* (Washington, D.C.: Government Printing Office, 1970), p. 437. This figure is somewhat below the life insurance industry's own estimate of its assets that year of $188.6 billion, *Life Insurance Fact Book 1969* (New York: Institute of Life Insurance, 1969), p. 65.

Table 9. Dollar Amount and Percent of One- to Four-Family Home Mortgages
Held by Life Insurance Companies, Compared to Other Lenders,
1950–68 (in Billions, Except Percent)

	1950		1955		1960		1965		1968	
	$	%	$	%	$	%	$	%	$	%
Life insurance companies	9	19.6	18	20.5	25	17.9	30	13.6	29	11.6
Savings and loan associations	13	28.3	30	34.1	55	39.3	94	44.4	110	43.7
Commercial banks	10	21.7	15	17.5	19	13.6	30	13.6	39	15.5
Mutual savings banks	4	8.7	11	12.5	18	12.9	30	13.6	35	13.9
Individuals and others	8	17.4	11	12.5	16	11.4	22	10.4	25	10.0
Government agencies	2	4.3	3	3.4	7	5.0	6	2.8	13	5.1
Total	46	100.0	88	100.5	140	100.1	212	98.4	251	99.8

Source: Statistical Abstract of the U.S., 1970.

groups of borrowers for loans. Other studies have argued that a pervasive impact of life companies (and other institutional lenders as well) on the distribution of mortgage credit has been to make this aggregate amount steadily more contingent on the overall national market for money.[4] This has occurred with the gradual displacement of the individual as a mortgage lender. His decline—the category "individual and others" comprised 33 percent of the market in 1945, 43 percent in 1920, and 50 percent in 1900—is due to the tendency of financial institutions to absorb an ever greater share of personal savings. But the practical result for the mortgage applicant is to put him at a severe disadvantage during periods of tight money, since he is often unable to outbid businessmen for scarce funds. Moreover, at these times he is left dependent on institutions largely restricted to residential lending, primarily the savings and loan association, which is the very institution most vulnerable to high interest rates.

The readiness of life insurance management to readjust their portfolios for higher yields was discussed in chapter II. And it is this response to tight money which may be observed between 1965 and 1967 on table 10, where new mortgage acquisitions are shown. However, the

Table 10. Nonfarm Mortgage Acquisitions of U.S. Life Insurance Companies, By Type of Mortgage (in Millions) (selected years, 1959–67)

| | 1–4 Family | | Multi-Family | | Commercial | | % Acquisitions |
	Amount	% Assets	Amount	% Assets	Amount	% Assets	residential
1957	3,087	.184	296	.017	1,440	.013	.201
1960	3,423	.168	501	.024	1,695	.014	.192
1963	4,030	.125	1,325	.041	2,951	.021	.166
1965	4,397	.111	2,118	.055	3,473	.022	.166
1967	2,120	.048	2,090	.048	3,423	.019	.096

Source: Institute of Life Insurance, 1968.

Illinois interviews indicate that in the future the homeowner will be disadvantaged not simply with the ebb and flow of money markets but also by the longer-term phenomenon of inflation. The erosion of the position of life insurance in competition for the savings dollar, due to the harm done fixed-amount savings by steady inflation, portends that

[4]Leo Grebler, David M. Blank, and Louis Winnick, *Capital Formation in Residential Real Estate: Trends and Prospects* (Princeton: Princeton University Press, 1956), pp. 206–8.

life companies will be less accessible to the homeowner because of a more or less permanent industry desire for equity investments.

Recent experience suggests that these disadvantages fall more heavily on the prospective and existing homeowner than on the prospective and existing owner of an apartment building. As table 10 shows, while home loans have declined steadily since 1957, apartment loans have increased in proportion to the total holdings. In 1967 the drop in homes was sharp indeed, and quite slight for apartments. This can be explained in terms of the increased aggressiveness toward yield, spurred by the competition of other financial industries. As the head of one of Chicago's largest mortgage banking companies explained: "Life insurance companies for years were in the market for a fairly low rate. Now, all of a sudden, they're looking for these higher yields. We've been able to satisfy their needs in a variety of transactions, especially apartment loans. These pay more and make for easier handling. . . . We don't advertise and sit around waiting for applicants now. We go out and solicit projects." In 1967 and 1968 the interest rate on conventional (non-insured) home loans was between 6¾ and 7¼ percent, while apartment loans brought 8 percent or better. Also, apartment loans acted as a form of compensation by life insurers to their mortgage correspondents for the cutback on homes.

It is difficult to estimate what role apartment loans, as long as they remain fixed-interest investments, will play in an increasingly equity-hungry industry—particularly when, as we have seen, new state provisions for holding companies permit a fuller indulgence of this appetite. There is also the question of whether apartment lending, in whatever volume, will permanently overshadow home lending. Some managers interviewed said that savings and loan associations are better equipped to place and service home mortgages and thus should absorb more of the total. Others insisted that the life insurance industry's obligation to the family hearth was traditional, and that if and when homeowners could compete with other borrowers, the industry would be back in that market, as one put it, "with both feet." In any case, it may be said that for the time being life companies are contributing to the development of a nation of apartment dwellers. Moreover, the interviews, FHA records, and certain aspects of our title data indicate that in Chicago these apartments are primarily high-rise structures for upper-income renters, located along the prestigious shore of Lake Michigan. It must be reemphasized that this cannot be attributed to companies' fiduciary obligations to their policyholders. Home loans have continued to earn well above earnings calculated in premium rates. During 1967, even at 6¾ percent, they brought, after all servicing costs, almost twice the yields assumed in the price of an insurance policy.

It is interesting to contrast life company mortgages with another fixed-interest, long-term credit instrument—industrial and miscellaneous bonds (that is, not government, railroad, or utility bonds). The proportion of industry assets invested in corporate bonds has grown at a steady pace—1.9 percent in 1930, 4.3 percent in 1945, 20.1 percent in 1955, 22.4 percent in 1960, 25.3 percent in 1968—even though yields, until very recently, have been consistently lower than on mortgages, including home mortgages. And the position of the industry in the industrial bond market, in contrast to the mortgage market, has grown until approximately 70 percent of the long-term external debt of American industrial corporations is now held by life companies. This is not to suggest that these funds have been specifically diverted from mortgages, but rather to make the more simple observation that industrial bonds command a stronger borrowing position.

The life insurance industry has been extremely flexible in accommodating the special debt needs of its fellow corporations. One important method has been the so-called direct or private placement, whereby the borrowing company and the participating lenders negotiate the terms of the loan without the mediation of the public market—a technique designed in part to circumvent disclosure requirements of the Securities and Exchange Commission. There is also the forward commitment, the arrangement for financing at an agreed rate for several years in advance, even though in some cases the borrowing company may show no earnings at the time of the contract.[5]

Several executives interviewed spoke about discrepancies in company lending policy between mortgages and bonds. A vice-president of a large New York mutual, when asked whether the bond portfolio was likely to shrink as the company sought more equity investments, mentioned the close relationship between the company and its corporate debtors: "Bonds? I don't think so. Many large corporations have been our customers and have relied on us for some time. And they will be our customers long into the future. We've established a running line to Chrysler, for example, and 100 year loans to some other companies." Another vice-president pointed to the relatively higher price for funds traditionally charged the mortgagee: "A mortgage is influenced by its marketability and the tenant. Really, you ought to get less rate on a mortgage with good credit. The lender has the real estate if the credit

---

[5] A study by the Life Insurance Association of America of the eighteen largest companies and ten others in the direct placement field, accounting for 83 percent of the total bond holdings of the industry, indicated that in 1966, 92 percent of the bonds were acquired in this manner, the *lowest* proportion since 1958. See Kenneth M. Wright and Robert H. Parks, *1967 Economic and Investment Report* (New York: Life Insurance Association of America, 1967), pp. 32–35 (pamphlet). On foreword commitments, see David McCahan, ed., *Investment of Life Insurance Funds* (Homewood, Ill.: Richard D. Irwin, 1953), chapter VIII.

fails. Yet the workings of the system are such that you pay more on the mortgage. Even the same company has to pay more for its mortgage—even a company like Sears, Roebuck."

In fact, however, life insurance companies have been quite obliging to their corporate borrowers in the area of mortgages, too: commercial mortgage loans have tripled in importance over the last decade, also cutting into funds which may have been available for home borrowing. Here, insurers have overcome the 75 percent state statutory limit on their participation in a first mortgage by providing the borrowing company with a second mortgage, whereas the homeowner is traditionally left to turn elsewhere, usually to a finance company, for his second mortgage.[6] In no sense does this service to corporate business require a sacrifice of yield. On the contrary, second mortgages bring higher yields, and the larger life companies have further adjusted to a period of tight money by demanding a percentage of the profits of the project financed—the so-called kicker to the mortgage that adds some of the advantages of an equity instrument.

The degree of flexibility and inventiveness which life companies have shown in their bond dealings and not in their home lending is due in part to the structure of the two markets. The consumer of housing is not organized or situated for direct placements or other large-scale negotiations. The discrepancy may also be a result of the life insurance industry's commanding role among holders of corporate debt—to a degree, as A. A. Berle and others have argued, that they are virtually able to dictate interest rates. Finally, it is probably a consequence of that business phenomenon so often perceived but seldom analyzed for its implications, the interlocking directorate—in this case between insurance lenders and corporate borrowers.[7]

In light of these last remarks, it is necessary to reconsider whether indeed industrial corporations do not comprise an external constituency in response to which decisions are made—an element that had been described as missing in the parochial, autonomous, and profit-oriented world of life company investing. While there is certainly something to be said for such an interpretation, the conception preferred here is that of a favored clientele. For one thing, director interlocks between life insurance and industrial corporations were as numerous at

---

[6] Among the largest suppliers of money to these finance companies is the life insurance industry itself. In 1965 the industry's holdings in finance companies amounted to $8.3 billion or nearly one-half of the nonmanufacturing bond investment total. *Life Insurance Fact Book 1969*, p. 79.

[7] For a summary of director interlocks between life insurance and industrial and commercial companies, see "Interlocks in Corporate Management," a Staff Report to the Antitrust Subcommittee of the Committee on the Judiciary, 89th Cong., 1st Sess., *House*, March 12, 1965, pp. 190 ff. The TNEC study by Gesell and Howe cited earlier provides similar information for 1935.

the time of the TNEC investigations as today, but the bond portfolio of the life companies was quite small. Second, the strong position of the large insurance companies in the bond market would appear to direct the flow of influence in the opposite direction; interlocks have certainly not inhibited life companies from an aggressive and ingenious pursuit of yields from their corporate loans.

Moreover, the nature of the private lending transaction is such that the aggregate shifts of capital among economic sectors do not have the same political content as would government laws to purposely channel assets. Private investment is an incremental process, guided by goals and criteria of profit and growth rather than of social change. While it lends itself to an analysis of the various groups which are indulged and deprived over an extended period of time, these results are a byproduct of discrete and autonomous decisions. Industrial companies compete for available insurance funds; once a loan is committed, it is not later diverted elsewhere or renegotiated at higher rates. Instead *new* money flows into life company coffers, some of which will continue to be allocated to specific companies or parcels within one sector—say, corporate bonds—while a greater portion of the inflow may go elsewhere—to housing, or the stock market. Life insurance companies generally make a preliminary allocation of funds to be distributed within each investment area on an annual basis, but this is continually reviewed and readjusted according to market conditions. Chrylser will not use its directors on the board of a life insurer to secure similar favored treatment for a fellow corporation like American Motors, anymore than one homeowner will be particularly concerned with the bargain of his neighbor. American Motors will use its own friends in life companies to negotiate the best terms available in the market at the time. But barring the description of direct constituency pressure, what does seem to be the case is that industrial corporations as a group have been able to better withstand certain monetary pressures and have enjoyed favorable treatment on a regular basis to the mutual advantage of lender and borrower.

The industry's deemphasis of residential lending in recent years is reflected in the Chicago sample. Table 11 summarizes new and renewed loans by time period, company type, place of domicile, and size. Rising to a peak in the decade following World War II, mortgage loans declined sharply during 1955-59 and 1960-64, and have tapered off since. A few points should be noted. First of all, because this tabulation is not sensitive to distinctions between single- and multifamily loans, the decrease shown is somewhat less than the actual decrease in single-family homes, particularly in recent years. Second, the change from 1965 to 1967 is slight, considering the tightness of the money market; this may

Table 11. Number of Life Insurance Company Residential Mortgages
in Chicago Sample, By Type, Domicile, and Size of Company, 1935-68

	1935-44	1945-54	1955-59	1960-64	1965-66	1967-68
Total						
No.	4160	5451	1937	1165	415	345
Aver. per year	416.0	545.1	387.4	233.0	207.5	172.5
Percent	100.0	100.0	100.0	100.0	100.0	100.0
Mutual companies						
No.	a	3367	1204	761	275	255
Aver. per year		336.7	240.8	152.2	137.5	127.5
Percent		61.8	62.2	65.3	66.3	73.1
Stock companies						
No.	a	2084	733	404	140	90
Aver. per year		208.4	146.6	80.8	70.0	45.0
Percent		38.2	37.8	34.7	33.7	26.9
Foreign companies						
No.	a	4418	1518	882	336	300
Aver. per year		441.8	303.6	176.4	168.0	15.0
Percent		81.1	78.3	75.7	80.9	86.9
Domestic companies						
No.	a	1033	419	283	79	45
Aver. per year		103.3	83.8	56.6	39.5	22.5
Percent		18.9	21.7	24.3	19.1	13.1
Large companies[b]						
No.	a	2907	1069	631	224	237
Aver. per year		290.7	213.8	126.2	11.2	118.5
Percent		53.4	56.2	54.2	53.9	68.7

[a]Breakdown not available.
[b]Company classified as large if assets for median years (1940, 1950, 1960) totaled over
$750,000,000 in 1935-44; or $1,000,000,000 in later periods.

be due to the Urban Investments Program, as well as to the step-up in
apartment lending—an interpretation supported by the slight increase
among the largest companies which are both the most active apartment
lenders and participants in the program. Third, stock companies have
withdrawn credit from the Chicago housing market more rapidly than
mutual companies, and it is tempting to surmise that this reflects a
more aggressive policy regarding yields than the mutuals. However, a
control for size (not shown) destroys this pattern, indicating that the
large mutuals and the smaller stock companies shifted out of residential
lending faster than the smaller mutuals and the larger stock companies.
During the tight money of 1965-66, both large stock companies and
large mutuals moved out in greater force than their smaller counter-

parts, perhaps reflecting their greater flexibility of market response. In 1967 the disparity is probably due to the more extensive participation of the large mutuals in the Chicago phase of the Urban Investments Program. While a few large stock companies also participated, this represented a much smaller percentage of company assets than for the large mutuals. These movements are reflected in the recent distribution between foreign and domestic company loans, the foreign industry dominated by mutuals, the domestic by stock companies.

Finally, it must be recognized that the decline in new mortgages in our sample cannot be attributed to the deemphasis of residential credit only, as if Chicago was the entire investment universe. An important feature of life insurance lending, as was stressed in chapter II, is its mobility. The fewer number of loans in recent years in Chicago is partially the result of more mortgages elsewhere. Thus between 1962 and 1967 the East North Central region, of which Illinois is a part, increased its dollar amount of mortgages by 31 percent, compared, for example, to a 52 percent increase in the Pacific and 60 percent in the South Atlantic states. (See table 12. These increases are in mortgage holdings, not acquisitions, as shown in table 11.)

That these differences in mortgage increases do not correspond to actual increases in life insurance held by the populations of these regions is also demonstrated in table 12. Moreover, on a cumulative,

Table 12. Percent Increase in Mortgages, 1962-67 and Percent Increase
in Life Insurance in Force, 1957-67 (by Region)

Region	Percent increase	
	Mortgages	Insurance in force
East North Central (incl. Illinois)	31%	123%
New England	39	123
Middle Atlantic	31	101
West North Central	43	140
South Atlantic	60	162
East South Central	44	162
West South Central	37	150
Mountain	44	183
Pacific	52	182

Sources: Life Insurance Fact Book 1968 and *Life Insurance Fact Book 1969.*

state-by-state basis Illinois citizens have paid for approximately 6.5 percent of the total life insurance in force and account for 4.5 percent of the nonfarm mortgage holdings, or an approximate 30 percent negative disparity. As a contrast, citizens of Virginia, a state chosen at random from the South Atlantic area, have paid for 2.3 percent of the total life insurance in force and benefited from 3.8 percent of the nonfarm mortgages, or a 65 percent advantage.[8] In other words, with regard to mortgages, Illinois suffers from precisely the outflow of funds that compulsory investment statutes are designed to prevent.

Life executives explain that the movement is due to increased demand in, say, Richmond or Atlanta or Los Angeles. While this is true, it partakes of circular reasoning. Certainly one of the inducements of those cities is the availability of jobs and housing, and these conditions are themselves in part a product of available credit. Nor is there any question of a demand for housing funds in the city of Chicago, were such funds made available at workable interest rates. In the meantime, life insurance purchases in Illinois subsidize growth elsewhere. This is not to question the long-range economic advantages of a mobile mortgage market, but rather to illustrate one more facet of investment decision.

II

The extension of mortgage credit provides numerous benefits beyond the straightforward capability of home or apartment ownership. Traditionally, home ownership has been associated with the values of independence, higher social status, and family security in addition to the more practical advantages of financial investment, hedge against inflation, and enhancement of one's credit standing. Moreover, one-fifth of mortgage loans are made sometime after purchase, thus enabling repairs and remodeling and such nonreal estate expenditures as education, travel, automobiles, and home appliances. The benefits to apartment owners are similar, while at the same time mortgages permit them to furnish housing for their tenants. For the neighborhood, the availability of mortgage credit allows persons to move in and out, buy and sell at will, improve their property and maintain its value—differences between a stable and desirable community and a stagnant or decaying one.[9]

As mortgage lenders, life company executives decide to whom they will distribute these benefits and who must seek funds elsewhere or do

[8] Computed from data in the *Life Insurance Fact Book 1969*, pp. 21 and 83.

[9] On the uses of mortgage funds and on residential finance in general, see Glenn H. Beyer, *Housing and Society* (New York: The Macmillan Company, 1965), chapter 5. A good case study in the results of (among other things) the unavailability of mortgage credit is Gilbert Osofsky, *Harlem: The Making of a Ghetto* (New York: Harper and Row, 1966).

without them. At this point in the investment process, the goal of yield (which has already influenced the amount of funds allocated in advance for residential mortgages) must be translated into a set of criteria for evaluating and discriminating among credit applicants. In the interviews, the criteria generally cited were three: (1) the borrower's ability and willingness to repay the loan; (2) the value of the property on which the mortgage is made and which is the physical security for the loan; and (3) the location of the security and its desirability. The vagueness, however, of these criteria as stated is apparent. Take location, for example: location may be considered in terms of the physical position of the area, its proximity to downtown; or its situation among a particular class of neighbors; or, alternately, amidst a certain type of housing structures. In other words, underwriting remains, despite the various risk-rating systems devised by the FHA and others, an inexact science, one which permits a sizable margin of choice within the parameters of sound appraisal practices. That the mortgage decisions made by the life insurance industry are highly patterned is observable from their end distribution; but it is the association of this end distribution with certain social characteristics that indicates the subtleties of the industry's lending criteria, rather than an a priori investigation of the criteria alone.

In order to introduce our method of analysis, we may begin with the broad relationships between mortgage lending and the borrowers income and between mortgage lending and the property on which the loan is made. Tables 13 and 14 indicate the incidence of life company mortgages in the sample, controlled for median family income and median value of owner-occupied (nonrental) structures of the corresponding census tracts. Since the sample is based on census tracts rather than on loans pulled at random from throughout the Chicago area, and since these tracts contain an unequal number of lots upon which a mortgage might be made, a standard unit of lending frequency has been computed—mortgage density. Mortgage density is a ratio of the number of life insurance mortgages to the number of lots picked at random and examined in the tract, which we attempted to standardize at 500. These densities were then arranged on a scale of one to five: one equals a density of zero; two, a density of 0.01 to 0.05; three, 0.06 to 0.10; four, 0.10 to 0.25; five, over 0.25, or one loan for every four lots during the time span indicated. A density of five does not mean that 25 percent of the lots carried life insurance mortgages at the time of their examination; rather it signifies that among the several thousand transactions recorded for 500 lots over the designated period, an average of one-quarter of the lots at some time held a life insurance mortgage. This measure is sensitive to the greater amount of capital invested in apartment mortgages even though there is no clue in the tables to distinguish

Table 13. Mortgage Density in Tracts, Controlled for Median Family Income, 1935–66[a] (Percent)

	Median family income					
Mortgage density	Under $750	$750– 1,000	$1,001– 1,300	$1,301– 1,600	$1,601– 2,000	Over $2,000
1935–44[b]						
1	33.3	34.8	3.4	5.3	0.0	0.0
2	60.0	47.8	44.8	21.1	16.7	0.0
3	6.7	8.7	13.8	15.8	16.7	0.0
4	0.0	8.7	37.9	52.6	16.7	100.0
5	0.0	0.0	0.0	5.3	50.0	0.0
	(100.0)	(100.0)	(99.9)	(100.1)	(100.1)	(100.0)
N=	(15)	(23)	(29)	(19)	(6)	(1)
	Under $2,500	$2,500– 3,000	$3,001– 4,000	$4,001– 5,000	$5,001– 7,500	Over $7,500
1945–54[c]						
1	69.2	21.4	22.0	0.0	0.0	0.0
2	30.8	64.3	46.3	29.4	0.0	25.0
3	0.0	7.1	22.0	26.5	21.4	25.0
4	0.0	7.1	7.3	38.2	50.0	25.0
5	0.0	0.0	2.4	5.9	28.6	25.0
	(100.0)	(99.9)	(100.0)	(100.0)	(100.0)	(100.0)
N=	(13)	(14)	(42)	(33)	(14)	(4)
	Under $4,000	$4,000– 5,500	$5,501– 8,000	$ 8,001– 10,000	$10,001– 14,000	Over $14,000
1955–64						
1	89.9	88.9	22.6	6.3	0.0	0.0
2	11.1	5.6	56.6	46.9	50.0	42.9
3	0.0	0.0	15.1	21.9	20.0	28.6
4	0.0	5.6	5.7	18.8	20.0	14.3
5	0.0	0.0	0.0	6.2	10.0	14.3
	(100.0)	(100.1)	(100.0)	(100.1)	(100.0)	(100.1)
N=	(9)	(18)	(53)	(32)	(10)	(7)
	Under $5,000	$5,000– 7,000	$7,001– 9,000	$ 9,001– 11,000	$11,001– 15,000	Over $15,000
1965–66						
1	100.0	90.6	63.3	34.2	29.4	0.0
2	0.0	6.3	23.3	39.5	47.1	25.0
3	0.0	3.1	6.7	7.9	11.8	50.0
4	0.0	0.0	6.7	15.8	11.8	0.0
5	0.0	0.0	0.0	2.6	0.0	25.0
	(100.0)	(100.0)	(100.0)	(100.0)	(100.1)	(100.0)
N=	(8)	(32)	(30)	(38)	(7)	(4)

[a]White-owned and managed companies only, on this and all tables hereafter (tables 13-38).
[b]Because of changes in census boundaries, only urban tracts are included in 1935–44.
[c]1950 census shows 9 missing values for income.

them from individual homes: since apartment buildings commonly span several lots, this is recorded in multiple tabulations for the transaction and reflected in higher densities. For a given census characteristic, then, the allocation of mortgage funds at various values may be compared. Thus, in table 13 for 1935–44, 33 percent of the tracts with a median family income under $750 show a density of zero—no mortgages—and no tract shows a density above three; at incomes between $1,600 and $2,000 no tracts have density zero, and 50 percent reach a density of five. This method enables an analysis of the social attributes of those tracts—and by extrapolation, those borrowers—favored with life company credit and those denied it.

Finally, although table 11 includes investments made in the sample by all legal-reserve life insurers doing business in Illinois, tables 13–32 exclude mortgages written by black-owned and managed companies. This is because a large portion of the mortgages these companies finance are for land contract transactions, described in section VI below, and there is no way reliably to distinguish these from ordinary mortgages.[10] Thus, the life insurance industry behavior described in the rest of the chapter is the behavior of the white industry, which is not, to our knowledge, involved to any significant extent in land contracts in the Chicago area.

This chapter will concentrate on the relationship of life insurance lending to certain aspects of the so-called urban crisis rather than on the overall pattern on mortgage distribution, but tables 13 and 14 point to the basic bones of the total process. Table 13 shows that for the entire period of study the variable of income is the best single indicator of the level of life insurance lending. The ramifications of this fact will become clearer as we proceed; here, however, it should be noted that life company lending increases upward along the income scale. Moreover, the difference in mortgage ratios for low-income and high-income tracts sharpens through time; and we may speculate, in light of the statements of mortgage officers interviewed, that this is related, among other things, to the smaller amount of funds available for mortgage investment, rather than to an appreciably increased relative demand by higher-income groups. Table 14 indicates that, to a lesser degree than income, but still pronounced, this same gravitational pull is at work for property values. Life insurance companies have consistently lent more heavily on more expensive homes. In recent years, however, the increased investment in apartments has somewhat masked the pattern,

[10]This fact was discovered in a study of the records of the Contract Buyer's League of Chicago, and confirmed in interviews with executives of the two largest black companies domiciled in Illinois. For insight into the lending practices and difficulties of such companies, see Robert C. Puth, "Supreme Life: A History of a Negro Life Insurance Company," Ph.D. dissertation (Department of Economics, Northwestern University, 1967).

Table 14. Mortgage Density in Tracts, Controlled for Median Value of Owner-
Occupied Homes, 1935–66 (Percent)

Mortgage density	Median value of homes					
	Under $2,500	$2,500–3,000	$3,001–4,000	$4,001–6,000	$6,001–10,000	Over $10,000
1935–44[a]						
1	23.5	33.3	16.7	0.0	0.0	0.0
2	47.1	50.0	61.1	21.4	25.0	0.0
3	5.9	8.3	11.1	28.6	25.0	0.0
4	20.6	8.3	11.1	50.0	37.5	71.5
5	2.9	0.0	0.0	0.0	12.5	28.6
	(100.0)	(99.9)	(100.0)	(100.0)	(100.0)	(100.1)
N=	(34)	(12)	(18)	(14)	(8)	(7)
	Under $10,000	$10,000–12,000	$12,001–14,000	$14,001–16,000	$16,001–19,000	Over $19,000
1945–54[b]						
1	28.6	6.7	0.0	0.0	0.0	0.0
2	42.9	60.0	31.6	40.0	14.3	18.8
3	14.3	6.7	31.6	20.0	0.0	31.3
4	14.3	26.7	31.6	20.0	42.9	37.5
5	0.0	0.0	5.3	20.0	42.9	12.5
	(100.1)	(100.1)	(100.1)	(100.0)	(100.1)	(100.1)
N=	(14)	(15)	(19)	(5)	(7)	(16)
	Under $13,000	$13,000–16,000	$16,001–19,000	$19,001–21,000	$21,001–25,000	Over $25,000
1955–64						
1	75.9	27.8	20.6	20.0	4.2	0.0
2	17.2	50.0	52.9	46.7	54.2	33.3
3	3.4	0.0	17.6	26.7	20.8	33.3
4	3.4	11.1	8.8	6.7	16.7	22.2
5	0.0	11.1	0.0	0.0	4.2	11.1
	(99.9)	(100.0)	(99.9)	(100.1)	(100.1)	(99.9)
N=	(29)	(18)	(34)	(15)	(24)	(9)
	Under $15,000	$15,000–17,000	$17,001–20,000	$20,001–25,000	$25,001–28,000	Over $28,000
1965–66						
1	87.2	33.3	64.7	34.5	25.0	0.0
2	2.6	44.4	20.6	41.4	50.0	60.0
3	5.1	5.6	2.9	13.8	0.0	40.0
4	5.1	16.7	8.8	6.9	25.0	0.0
5	0.0	0.0	2.9	3.4	0.0	0.0
	(100.0)	(100.0)	(99.9)	(100.0)	(100.0)	(100.0)
N=	(39)	(18)	(34)	(29)	(4)	(5)

[a]Because of changes in census boundaries, only urban tracts are included in 1935–44.
[b]1950 census shows 53 missing values for value of owner–occupied homes.

since upper-income apartments are not generally located in communities with expensive homes on which the census property values are based. Life company mortgage officers generally explain this in terms of "finding the safest possible properties for our policyholder's money," or "I always think what I would have if I had to foreclose." Considering, however, that the activity of appraising is nothing else but the careful adjustment of the terms and size of the loan to the individual borrower's income and property value, it is evident that "willingness and ability to pay," and "the value of the property" implies more than meets the eye. Although any conclusion that the rich get richer would be premature, it would not be entirely misleading as a guiding maxim to what follows.

The channeling of credit to the suburbs, an integral part of the social and economic depletion of the inner city, is indicated early in our sample. Table 15 shows the industry's unit distribution of mortgage loans among tracts in Chicago and surrounding suburbs of Cook County. During 1935–44, the movement was well under way with 29.5

Table 15. Distribution of Residential Mortgage Loans between
Urban and Suburban Tracts, 1935–66

	No. loans	% of total	No. loans per tract per yr.	No. of tracts
1935–44				
Urban	2,885	70.5	3.0	(93)
Suburban	1,205	29.5	3.4	(36)
	(4,090)	(100.0)		
1945–54				
Urban	2,829	55.9	3.0	(93)
Suburban	2,228	44.1	6.2	(36)
	(5,057)	(100.0)		
1955–59				
Urban	743	44.5	1.6	(93)
Suburban	926	55.5	5.1	(36)
	(1,669)	(100.0)		
1960–64				
Urban	459	46.6	1.0	(93)
Suburban	524	53.4	2.9	(36)
	(983)	(100.0)		
1965–66				
Urban	221	62.4	1.2	(93)
Suburban	133	37.6	1.8	(36)
	(354)	(100.0)		

percent of the mortgage loans, but not far ahead of the population itself, which in 1940 was 26 percent suburban. Even in this period, however, the average number of loans for individual suburban tracts exceeded the city average. With the surge in homebuilding which occurred in the decade following World War II, life insurance companies greatly increased their suburban allocations, while the cities barely held their own in absolute numbers and slipped in percentage of the total. By the late fifties, the average number of loans in suburban tracts was over three times the urban figure, and the suburbs now received 55.4 percent of the mortgages, a position consolidated and held into the next decade, although in 1960 only 43 percent of Chicago's population lived in the suburbs.

During 1965–66 life companies still provided more mortgages for the individual suburban tract than its counterpart in the city, but the total distribution between city and suburbs is reversed. Some of this is due to the fact that in this period there was less new construction in close-in Cook County as builders, lenders, and choice suburbanites moved farther out. But another important factor in drawing funds back to the cities has been the life insurance industry's increased investments in multiunit, particularly high-rise, apartments, to which suburban zoning is uncongenial.

Table 16 shows the mortgage densities for urban and suburban tracts, giving a clearer impression of life insurance credit's departure from the city.[11] In the period of 1945–54, 22.6 percent of the city tracts received no loans at all, and another 37.6 percent very few; by 1955–64, 37.6 percent none and 43.1 percent very few; and by 1965–66, 67.7 percent of the city tracts were completely cut off from the industry's mortgage funds. Suburban mortgages also reflect the steady cutback in mortgages evident in the city, but they continue to show a greater percentage of tracts in the higher densities.

When asked about their apparent favoritism to the suburbs, mortgage officers answered in generalities, thus drawing attention for the first time in our discussion to a recurring phenomenon in life insurance investment—the total absence of social design, of planning beyond rather parochial business considerations: "I can't explain it. It didn't happen in Europe. Maybe it only goes to a point, then convenience becomes important. My own son wants to move back to Chicago. . . . Take the old shore—they have attracted people who can afford it. And they say we'll be a nation of apartment dwellers anyway." Another said simply, "it's the trend." A third gave a more precise, somewhat ques-

---

[11] Census data on Cook County suburbs available for 1940 is not broken down by tracts, and thus cannot be analyzed in terms of mortgage density.

Table 16. Mortgage Density in Urban and Suburban Tracts, 1945–66 (Percent)

	Mortgage density	Tracts	
		Urban	Suburban
1945–54			
	1	22.6	5.6
	2	37.6	27.8
	3	18.3	22.2
	4	18.3	27.8
	5	3.3	16.7
		(100.1)	(100.1)
	N=	(93)	N= (36)
1955–64			
	1	37.6	8.3
	2	43.1	41.7
	3	10.7	25.0
	4	6.4	19.5
	5	2.2	5.6
		(100.0)	(100.1)
	N=	(93)	N= (36)
1965–66			
	1	67.7	30.6
	2	18.3	44.4
	3	5.4	13.9
	4	6.5	11.1
	5	2.2	0.0
		(100.1)	(100.0)
	N=	(93)	N= (36)

tion-begging, explanation: "our reputation is involved, I suppose. It's more prestigious to invest there." This, of course, raises the question of the influence of the two all-important factors in life company mortgage decisions—income and property values—as major components of prestige (see tables 17 and 18). In fact, the difference between suburb and city is now considerably diminished, particularly at the highest levels of income and property values. There remains, however, a residual suburban bias which calls for further investigation.

Mortgage officers commonly speak of the "economic life of a neighborhood," explaining their penchant for suburban loans in terms of a desire for property that will retain its value for the life of a twenty- or thirty-year mortgage. Table 19 compares the loan experience of urban and suburban tracts which are older—less than 15 percent of the homes built in the last decade—with newer communities—over 60 percent of

Table 17. Mortgage Density in Urban and Suburban Tracts, Controlled For
Median Family Income, 1945–66 (Percent)

Mortgage density	Median family income[a]					
	Low		Medium		High	
	Urban	Suburban	Urban	Suburban	Urban	Suburban
1945–54						
1	44.0	50.0	15.1	4.5	0.0	0.0
2	48.0	50.0	39.6	36.4	0.0	9.1
3	4.0	0.0	24.5	22.7	28.6	18.2
4	4.0	0.0	18.9	27.3	57.1	36.4
5	0.0	0.0	1.9	9.1	14.3	36.4
	(100.0)	(100.0)	(100.0)	(100.0)	(99.9)	(100.1)
N=	(25)	(2)	(53)	(22)	(7)	(11)
1955–64						
1	88.9	—	18.0	12.5	0.0	0.0
2	7.4	—	57.4	41.7	60.0	41.7
3	3.7	—	16.4	20.8	0.0	33.3
4	0.0	—	6.6	20.8	20.0	16.7
5	0.0	—	1.6	4.2	20.0	8.3
	(100.0)	(—)	(100.0)	(100.0)	(100.0)	(100.0)
N=	(27)	(0)	(61)	(24)	(5)	(12)
1965–66						
1	92.3	100.0	52.0	33.3	25.0	23.5
2	5.1	0.0	26.0	50.0	50.0	41.2
3	2.6	0.0	8.0	5.6	0.0	23.5
4	0.0	0.0	12.0	11.1	0.0	11.8
5	0.0	0.0	2.0	0.0	25.0	0.0
	(100.0)	(100.0)	(100.0)	(100.0)	(100.0)	(100.0)
N=	(39)	(1)	(50)	(18)	(4)	(17)

[a]Income categories:

	1945–54	1955–64	1965–66
Low:	Under $3,000	Under $5,500	Under $7,000
Medium:	$3,000–5,000	$5,500–10,000	$7,000–$11,000
High:	Over $5,000	Over $10,000	Over $11,000

the homes less than ten years old. Evidently age plays some role, with
new tracts in the city and suburbs receiving more mortgages than the
older city and suburban tracts. But since 1955, at least, and disregard-
ing the older urban neighborhoods where apartment mortgages have
influenced densities, the newer suburbs have outdistanced the two city
tracts of the same age.

That age in itself is of little importance was suggested by the remarks
of a mortgage correspondent who invests for one of the largest foreign
insurers in Illinois:

Let's start at the beginning of a suburb. Take Highland Park. The original homes
were built in the 1880's, around the business district. Those homes are still pretty

Table 18. Mortgage Density in Urban and Suburban Tracts, Controlled for
Median Value of Owner-Occupied Homes, 1945–66 (Percent)

Mortgage density	Median value of homes[a]					
	Low		Medium		High	
	Urban	Suburban	Urban	Suburban	Urban	Suburban
1945–54						
1	17.6	16.7	0.0	0.0	0.0	0.0
2	70.6	25.0	26.6	44.4	11.1	21.4
3	5.9	16.7	26.6	33.3	22.2	21.4
4	5.9	41.6	40.0	11.1	55.5	28.6
5	0.0	0.0	6.7	11.1	11.1	28.6
	(100.0)	(100.0)	(100.0)	(99.9)	(99.9)	(100.0)
N=	(17)	(12)	(15)	(9)	(9)	(14)
1955–64						
1	63.4	16.7	22.9	14.3	5.9	0.0
2	29.3	33.3	54.3	42.9	52.9	43.8
3	2.4	0.0	17.1	28.6	17.6	31.3
4	2.4	33.3	5.7	14.3	17.6	18.8
5	2.4	16.7	0.0	0.0	5.9	6.3
	(99.9)	(100.0)	(100.0)	(100.1)	(99.9)	(100.2)
N=	(41)	(6)	(35)	(14)	(17)	(16)
1965–66						
1	88.1	66.7	58.1	27.8	12.5	16.7
2	7.1	16.7	25.6	55.6	37.5	41.7
3	2.4	16.7	7.0	0.0	12.5	33.3
4	2.4	0.0	7.0	16.7	25.0	8.3
5	0.0	0.0	2.3	0.0	12.5	0.0
	(100.0)	(100.1)	(100.0)	(100.1)	(100.0)	(100.0)
N=	(42)	(6)	(43)	(18)	(8)	(12)

[a]Value categories:	1945–54	1955–64	1965–66
Low:	Under $12,000	Under $16,000	Under $17,000
Medium:	$12,000–16,000	$16,000–21,000	$17,000–25,000
High:	Over $16,000	Over $21,000	Over $25,000

good, well maintained. Why? It's the people who live there. Highland Park has
continued to renew itself, and is destined to have a long economic life on the
average. There are still areas to build new homes. The yards are maintained, the
dutch elms sprayed. There's a good school system—that's one of the most important items. And, very important, young people still want to live there.

Take, as a contrast, Norwood Park. It was built in the 1920's. Right after the
war the homes were good, every home occupied by a professional or a minor
executive. But come back 10 years later. The original builders are dying off. The
neighborhood's not renewing itself. The people who are moving in are of a different
class; now they're blue collar people. The homes continue to increase in value
because of inflation. But the people—young executives—are no longer interested.

We wouldn't ordinarily make a mortgage in Norwood Park. Highland Park has a
continual flow of executives making $20,000 a year. They can afford to maintain
those homes.

Table 19. Mortgage Density in Urban and Suburban Tracts, Controlled for Percent
of Homes Built in Last Decade, 1945–66 (Percent)

| Mortgage density | Percent built in last decade | | | |
| | Under 15% | | Over 60% | |
	Urban	Suburban	Urban	Suburban
1945–54				
1	25.3	0.0	0.0	0.0
2	40.0	41.7	25.0	40.0
3	17.3	25.0	50.0	20.0
4	14.7	25.0	25.0	20.0
5	2.7	8.3	0.0	20.0
	(100.0)	(100.0)	(100.0)	(100.0)
N=	(75)	(12)	(4)	(5)
1955–64				
1	43.5	14.3	0.0	7.7
2	43.5	57.1	50.0	30.8
3	12.9	28.6	50.0	23.1
4	0.0	0.0	0.0	23.1
5	0.0	0.0	0.0	15.4
	(99.9)	(100.0)	(100.0)	(100.1)
N=	(69)	(7)	(2)	(13)
1965–66				
1	72.5	71.4	50.0	23.1
2	14.5	14.3	50.0	38.5
3	5.8	14.3	0.0	15.4
4	5.8	0.0	0.0	23.1
5	1.4	0.0	0.0	0.0
	(100.0)	(100.0)	(100.0)	(100.1)
N=	(69)	(7)	(2)	(13)

In other words, the "economic life of a neighborhood" is less a matter of buildings and age than the financial success stories of its occupants. Notice here that while lenders seek to minimize risks on each individual mortgage, this is computed with reference to the prospective borrower's neighbors. Notice also the vicious circle of credit: neighborhood maintenance is employed as a basis for extending mortgage credit which, in turn, may contribute significantly to a neighborhood's maintenance. Unfortunately, the small number of cases forbids additional cross-tabulation. But table 20, showing older urban and suburban tracts, is offered as slight corroborating evidence for the leveling influence of income.

With income, property value, and age of property failing to account satisfactorily for the insurance industry's suburban emphasis, a final variable may be tried—the extent to which tracts in the city and suburbs are characterized by homogeneous neighborhoods of single-family

Table 20. Mortgage Density in Urban and Suburban Tracts with under 15 Percent
of Homes Built in Last Decade, Controlled for Median Family Income,
1945–64 (Percent)

| Mortgage density | Median family income[a] | | | | | |
| | Low | | Medium | | High | |
	Urban	Suburban	Urban	Suburban	Urban	Suburban
1945–54						
1	39.3	0.0	18.2	0.0	0.0	0.0
2	42.9	0.0	40.9	66.7	0.0	20.0
3	3.6	100.0	25.0	33.3	33.3	0.0
4	10.7	0.0	13.6	0.0	67.7	60.0
5	3.6	0.0	2.3	0.0	0.0	20.0
	(100.1)	(100.0)	(100.0)	(100.0)	(100.0)	(100.0)
N=	(28)	(1)	(44)	(6)	(3)	(5)
1955–64						
1	68.6	–	21.7	25.0	–	0.0
2	28.6	–	60.9	50.0	–	66.7
3	2.9	–	15.2	25.0	–	33.3
4	0.0	–	2.2	0.0	–	0.0
5	0.0	–	0.0	0.0	–	0.0
	100.1	(–)	(100.0)	(100.0)	(–)	(100.0)
N=	(23)	(0)	(46)	(4)	(0)	(3)

[a]For value categories, see table 17.

homes. Table 21 gives the mortgage densities for urban and suburban tracts with 60–85 percent single-family homes, and with 86–100 percent. The importance of this neighborhood homogeneity factor is reflected in the fact that the urban tracts in areas of more single-family homes received somewhat more mortgages than the suburban tracts with fewer single-family homes. On the other hand, the suburbs continue to out-borrow the city at each given level. Again, the small number of cases resists further analysis, but table 22 provides a control for medium and high income. The results, while sketchy, nevertheless contribute to the cumulative evidence of a preference for the suburbs which is not accounted for by the most frequently cited underwriting criteria, perhaps lending credence to the vagaries of trend and prestige. But there is yet a broader influence to be considered, to which we may now turn.

III

The diversion of mortgages to the suburbs cannot be understood merely in terms of buildings and incomes, anymore than the residue known as the inner city can be understood solely in those terms. Mortgage lenders openly acknowledge the role of other social indicators in

Table 21. Mortgage Density in Urban and Suburban Tracts, Controlled for
Percent Owner-occupied, 1945–64 (Percent)

| Mortgage density | Percent owner-occupied | | | |
| | 60–85% | | 86–100% | |
	Urban	Suburban	Urban	Suburban
1945–54				
1	8.3	8.0	0.0	0.0
2	58.3	16.0	12.5	0.0
3	8.3	32.0	25.0	33.3
4	25.0	32.0	37.5	33.3
5	0.0	12.0	25.0	33.3
	(99.9)	(100.0)	(100.0)	(99.9)
N=	(37)	(25)	(8)	(6)
1955–64				
1	9.1	9.1	0.0	0.0
2	72.7	63.6	75.0	33.0
3	9.1	13.6	12.5	41.7
4	9.1	13.6	12.5	8.3
5	0.0	0.0	0.0	16.7
	(100.0)	(99.9)	(100.0)	(99.7)
N=	(11)	(22)	(8)	(12)

Table 22. Mortgage Density in Urban and Suburban Tracts with over 60 Percent
Owner-occupancy, Controlled for Median Family Income, 1945–64,
(Low Income Not Shown) (Percent)

| Mortgage density | Median family income[a] | | | |
| | Medium | | High | |
	Urban	Suburban	Urban	Suburban
1945–54				
1	7.7	5.6	0.0	0.0
2	53.9	22.4	0.0	10.0
3	7.7	28.0	25.0	20.0
4	30.8	33.6	50.0	40.0
5	0.0	11.2	25.0	30.0
	(100.1)	(100.8)	(100.0)	(100.0)
N=	(13)	(18)	(4)	(10)
1955–64				
1	5.9	4.5	0.0	0.0
2	70.8	59.0	100.0	45.5
3	11.8	18.2	0.0	36.4
4	11.8	13.6	0.0	9.1
5	0.0	4.5	0.0	9.1
	(100.3)	(99.8)	(100.0)	(100.1)
N=	(17)	(22)	(2)	(11)

[a]For income categories, see table 17.

their loan appraisals. An article in a recent and a widely used mortgage banking text, which includes contributions of several notables in the life insurance business, comments on "family and social relationships":

> One who has had a harmonious domestic life, who associates with a good class of people in his own social and economic group and who is generally adaptable is to be preferred to one whose home life has not been harmonious, whose wife is known as a social climber, or whose reputation for honesty has not been established. Such a man is like to live beyond his means and prove to be an unsatisfactory borrower.

After these caveats regarding the borrower, the text moves on to the location of the security and the "appeal" of the neighborhood. "The appeal rests on many things such as . . . the economic level of its inhabitants, the class and age of the house on which a loan is sought, and the race and nationality of the individual families who live there."[12]

The Chicago data provide no information on social-climbing wives, but table 23 indicates the importance of race in the question of the suburban bias. A comparison of the mortgage densities in tracts that contain less than 10 percent blacks shows considerable shrinkage of the lending gap observed earlier between city and suburbs. Observe that at the higher density levels the factor of race increases in importance after 1955. This might have been predicted from the fact that after a consolidation in the 1930s, in the mid-1950s began an extensive residential expansion of the black population.[13] In particular, this expansion was into higher-grade residential areas which, when white, had been attractive to life companies and now were cut off, depressing the urban average. The regional supervisor for mortgages for one of the largest New York mutuals was succinct in his explanation of his company's suburban preferences: "There is one big fear—that the city of Chicago will be controlled by minorities."

Moreover, a mortgage correspondent who operates in Chicago for another New York mutual suggested that even the prestige of suburban lending has its limits:

> We've made very few loans in Robbins. [A black suburb represented by one tract in the sample.] We've had better results with our Chicago loans to Negroes than our suburban loans. It's a problem of status. It seems as though when a Negro family gets into trouble they rent a room. In the suburbs they lose the home.
>
> Take Terrytown in Gary. We've had nothing but trouble. The amount of equity has no relation to foreclosure rates. With whites, there's a direct relationship.
>
> It's the comparative instability of the Negro family. He doesn't appreciate what he's got. In Terrytown, he moves out.

---

[12] Robert H. Pease, ed., *Mortgage Banking*, 2nd ed. (New York: McGraw-Hill, 1965), pp. 220, 224. Pease is vice-president of Draper and Kramer, Inc., a Chicago mortgage banking firm which acts as mortgage correspondent for many large life insurance companies. The book also contains contributions by several life company officials—New York Life, Connecticut General, Northwestern Mutual, Pacific Mutual, and others.

[13] See Pierre de Vise, *Chicago's Widening Color Gap* (Chicago: Interuniversity Social Research Committee, 1967), pp. 30 ff.

Table 23. Mortgage Density in Urban and Suburban Tracts with
under 10 Percent Black Population, 1945-66 (Percent)

Mortgage	Tracts			
density	Urban		Suburban	
1945-54				
1	13.6	(22.6)[a]	3.0	(5.6)[b]
2	31.9	(37.6)	27.3	(27.8)
3	25.8	(18.3)	24.2	(22.2)
4	24.2	(18.3)	27.3	(27.8)
5	4.6	(3.3)	18.2	(16.7)
	(100.1)		(100.0)	
	N=(66)		N=(33)	
1955-64				
1	10.0	(37.6)	6.1	(8.3)
2	57.5	(43.1)	54.5	(41.7)
3	17.5	(10.7)	24.2	(25.0)
4	10.0	(6.4)	9.9	(19.5)
5	5.0	(2.2)	6.1	(5.6)
	(100.0)		(99.8)	
	N=(40)		N=(33)	
1965-66				
1	57.6	(67.7)	25.9	(30.6)
2	19.2	(18.3)	48.1	(44.4)
3	6.4	(5.4)	11.1	(13.9)
4	16.0	(6.5)	14.8	(11.1)
5	0.0	(2.?)	0.0	(0.0)
	(99.2)		(99.9)	
	N=(31)		N=(27)	

[a]Mortgage density, all urban tracts.
[b]Mortgage density, all suburban tracts.

Here the implications of reviewing the borrower's application in the context of his membership in a social group—in this case a particularly deprived one—are immediately apparent, providing a possible corollary to the maxim of the rich get richer.

The question of life insurance mortgage lending to blacks raises the issue of "institutional racism" and whether this lending ought to be designated as such. The idea of institutional racism is that the principal promulgators of racism are institutions, including business institutions, rather than individuals. Unfortunately, however, the term does not always clearly distinguish between racism resulting from attitudes of individuals who are powerful within institutions and make racist policy, and racial biases built into various and seemingly neutral institutional procedures of operation.[14] A clearer conception is made possible by dividing the matter into procedural and attitudinal bias. Procedural bias refers to racial results produced by standards, criteria, or methods applied routinely to achieve a goal which itself has nothing to do with race. Thus, to cite a familiar example from outside the business world, a university selecting its students to achieve a high academic level, and therefore limiting its choices to students from academically prestigious high schools, is likely to produce an entirely different racial composition from procedures designed to maximize another goal, such as a socially representative student body or enriched education for financially needy students. Contrariwise, a school enrolling white students and excluding blacks as a straightforward matter of policy and tradition illustrates attitudinal bias. Clearly, the two types reinforce one another. Life insurance companies, for example, may seek out suburban investments from the purest of profit motives and in the process underwrite zoning codes dictated by the crudest racial prejudices of suburbanites. But the simple distinction between procedural and attitudinal bias is helpful in understanding the life insurance industry's relationship to the black population.[15]

There are, however, certain methodological difficulties in applying these concepts backward in time, since the procedures have remained relatively stable since the introduction of FHA insurance and appraisal methods in the early 1930s. The goals of yield and growth; the stress on "neighborhood economic life" and other group references; the computation of risk on individual parcels rather than the total portfolio; certain exclusions from family income—for example, the earnings of a wife until she is past child-bearing age; all these and others may be assumed to have run through the lending history examined and to have had an impact on the racial distribution of loans. On the other hand, the content of attitudinal bias has undoubtedly changed considerably, say, from simple aversion to, as it was expressed above, fear of minority "control." Racial attitudes as they exist today will be discussed to some extent in chapter VI, with respect to the Urban Investments Program. But even in the most candid of interviews life insurance executives do not say: "Look, underwriting works in this direction. But on top of

[14] For an application of the term "institutional racism" to everything from health standards and intelligence testing to the denial to voting rights, see Louis L. Knowles and Kenneth Prewitt, eds. *Institutional Racism in America* (Englewood Cliffs, N.J.: Prentice-Hall, 1969).

[15] Anthony Downs makes a distinction between "overt racism" and "institutional subordination," the latter term including "perceptual distortion" and attitudes not explicitly linked to race. See Anthony Downs, *Urban Problems and Prospects* (Chicago: Markham Publishing Company, 1970), pp. 78 ff. While this is closer to the mark, we wish to distinguish between such appraisal items as income and property values and others like "Are the people clannish?" and "Do they respect law and order?" (Pease, *Mortgage Banking*, p. 159) which, despite their identical bureaucratic setting, reflect certain social attitudes and stereotypes.

that we here at Illinois Life dislike blacks and are afraid of them." On the contrary, they consistently justify prejudice—"He doesn't appreciate what he's got"—by an appeal to the relentless requirements of underwriting. Our historical analysis is necessarily limited to controlling for certain prominent procedural variables and, at least provisionally, ascribing the discriminatory residues to racial attitudes. Also, an attempt is made to examine certain assumptions of the procedures in the light of other facts.

Table 24 summarizes the relative extent of residential lending in

Table 24. Mortgage Density in Tracts, Controlled for Percent Black Population, 1935-66 (Percent)

Mortgage density	Percent black				
	0	1-10	11-50	51-90	91-99
1935-44[a]					
1	13.8	0.0	40.0	0.0	44.4
2	35.4	36.4	60.0	100.0	55.6
3	13.8	18.2	0.0	0.0	0.0
4	30.8	45.5	0.0	0.0	0.0
5	6.2	0.0	0.0	0.0	0.0
	(100.0)	(100.1)	(100.0)	(100.0)	(100.0)
N=	(65)	(11)	(5)	(3)	(9)
1945-54					
1	10.2	9.1	20.0	55.6	54.5
2	28.4	45.5	60.0	44.4	45.5
3	25.0	27.3	0.0	0.0	0.0
4	27.3	9.1	20.0	0.0	0.0
5	9.1	9.1	0.0	0.0	0.0
	(100.0)	(100.1)	(100.0)	(100.0)	(100.0)
N=	(88)	(11)	(10)	(9)	(11)
1955-64					
1	8.4	0.0	33.3	52.7	72.0
2	50.7	100.0	50.0	36.8	16.0
3	21.2	0.0	8.3	5.3	8.0
4	14.1	0.0	8.3	5.3	4.0
5	5.6	0.0	0.0	0.0	0.0
	(100.0)	(100.0)	(99.9)	(100.1)	(100.0)
N=	(71)	(2)	(12)	(19)	(25)
1965-66					
1	36.4	52.0	40.7	78.3	95.2
2	42.4	20.0	33.3	17.4	4.8
3	6.1	12.0	14.8	4.3	0.0
4	15.2	16.0	3.7	0.0	0.0
5	0.0	0.0	7.4	0.0	0.0
	(100.1)	(100.0)	(99.9)	(100.0)	(100.0)
N=	(33)	(25)	(27)	(23)	(21)

[a]Urban tracts only.

white and black census tracts. The data are blunt. Until 1955 black tracts were virtually cut off from life insurance mortgage funds. Although the situation improved somewhat after that, they continued to lag far behind the white tracts in obtaining significant levels of mortgage density. A sense of the absolute preponderance of loans to white communities may be had by taking account of the numbers of tracts among which the various densities are distributed. Thus in 1955–64, four all-white and no black tracts reached densities of five or over. In the density of four, 4 percent represents one black tract and 14.1 percent ten white tracts.

As has been already suggested, industry mortgage officers and their correspondents universally insist that the sharp discrepancy is a result of the criteria applied in underwriting mortgage loans. "The Negro market?," went the typical explanation: "We've been in it for many years. [The company] always said, it makes no difference what race, but the loan must meet minimum standards. And the FHA's and ours are not the same and never have been." And another: "Historically, this thing has little to do with race. We've always sought choice suburban areas, better city areas, and better Negro ones too. No, we're not in Lawndale and Woodlawn. We want better areas, with less hazardous investments."

This is not to say that race is naively and completely disavowed as a factor in underwriting. Most persons interviewed admitted to heeding the text book warning against neighborhoods in the beginning stages of racial transition. One acknowledged that "the climate had changed quite a bit," that "time was when a Negro family moved onto a block, that was it as far as the lender was concerned, and for the surrounding blocks maybe too." Others had deeper interpretations of the Negro mortgage market: "It's a problem of status. . . . He doesn't appreciate what he's got." But, again, the psychosociology was generally tied by the respondents to the impersonal demands of good lending practice.[16]

It is interesting to compare this perspective with that of Chicago's leading black mortgage banker, a man who has demonstrated his procedural realism in his career—in 1966 he was the first black man to be admitted to the Mortgage Bankers Association, a national trade association of mortgage banking and life insurance—and in his role, which will be discussed later, in the Urban Investments Program. He reacted briskly to the suggestion that economic factors were the major obstacles to equal lending treatment:

[16]The tenet of the impersonality of lending procedures, which neither discriminate against nor provide special advantages to particular individuals, is a complement to the businessman's tenet of the impersonality of profits themselves, defended not as a source of income but as symbols of accountability and rational economic calculation. See Francis X. Sutton, Seymour E. Harris, Carl Kaysen, and James Tobin, *The American Business Creed* (New York: Schocken Books, 1962), pp. 71 ff.

Economic factors, hell. Look at all those Polish neighborhoods along the Dan Ryan. They're ready for urban renewal. But the money pours in. Or look at the Back of the Yards. That's an old area. But then look at Douglas Park, or Garfield Park. If they had had the flow of mortgage money they wouldn't be gutted as they are today. When these neighborhoods changed there was money available alright, but to speculators who milked the persons who wanted to buy homes there.

Within the system there is a willingness to lend all you need to buy a car. A car can't appreciate and be put on a balance sheet. When you want to buy a house, however, you get only a big frown. Now, they'll lend you a 100 per cent loan on an eight thousand dollar Cadillac and they won't give you a ninety percent FHA insured loan on a house. The house represents a method of capital appreciation in the ghetto community. And a strong capital base is a threat to the white community.

The real estate manager of a black-owned and managed life insurance company expressed a similar view:

Racism. . . . There was a time, and there still is, when one's race had much to do with whether or not a person could get a mortgage. Just today a [large foreign mutual company] agent applied here for a home mortgage loan. We give our employees loans when they need them. Why can't this man get financing from the company for whom he works? For years [the company] has been saying, "we'll be glad to have your life insurance—or certain segments of your life insurance—but we won't give you a loan."

Little effort need be expended here on the grosser effects of procedural bias. The pronounced preference of life insurance companies for higher-income borrowers and suburban properties has been demonstrated above. In 1960, following the pattern of earlier years, blacks in Chicago had a median family income of $4,800, compared to a white median family income of $7,700; and they lived overwhelmingly in the city. On the other hand, there is considerable evidence in the data of the aggravating factor of racial prejudice. Tables 25 through 28 show the distribution of mortgage densities among white and black tracts, controlling for four characteristics of borrower and property which are of primary importance in underwriting; the purpose here is to pare away the effects of these procedural factors and observe the influence, if any, of attitudes. Table 25 indicates that throughout the years studied, at the same levels of family income blacks consistently fail to attain the same levels of mortgage lending as whites. The period 1955–64 suggests that as black tracts move from the low- to the medium-income category the factor of race is somewhat less determining, but the gap persists. In other words, meeting the procedural bias toward higher income mitigates but does not overcome the disparity. Table 26 reveals a similar pattern. In the same price range of owner-occupied dwellings, white tracts are regularly favored by life insurance companies over black ones. And, again, the influence of race is evident in the medium-priced homes as it is in the low-priced, but it is less severe.

Many blacks in Chicago live in areas characterized by multi-unit apartment buildings rather than individual homes. To adjust for the life

Table 25. Mortgage Density in All-White and Predominantly Black (over 50 Percent) Tracts, Controlled for Median Family Income 1935–66[a] (Upper Income Not Shown) (Percent)

| Mortgage density | Median family income[b] | | | |
| | Low Percent black | | Medium Percent black | |
	0	51–99	0	51–99
1935–44[b]				
1	36.4	37.5	2.8	25.0
2	50.0	62.5	30.6	75.0
3	4.5	0.0	19.4	0.0
4	9.1	0.0	44.4	0.0
5	0.0	0.0	2.8	0.0
	(100.0)	(100.0)	(100.0)	(100.0)
N=	(22)	(8)	(36)	(4)
1945–54				
1	0.0	57.9	12.7	0.0
2	50.0	42.0	34.9	100.0
3	0.0	0.0	25.4	0.0
4	50.0	0.0	22.2	0.0
5	0.0	0.0	4.8	0.0
	(100.0)	(100.0)	(100.0)	(100.0)
N=	(2)	(19)	(63)	(1)
1955–64				
1	—	88.0	11.1	31.6
2	—	8.0	51.9	47.3
3	—	0.0	20.4	15.8
4	—	4.0	13.0	5.3
5	—	0.0	3.8	0.0
	(—)	(100.0)	(100.2)	(100.0)
N=	(0)	(25)	(54)	(19)
1965–66				
1	—	92.1	40.0	50.0
2	—	5.3	40.0	50.0
3	—	2.6	0.0	0.0
4	—	0.0	20.0	0.0
5	—	0.0	0.0	0.0
	—	(100.0)	(100.0)	(100.0)
N=	(0)	(38)	(20)	(6)

[a]Urban tracts only.
[b]For income categories, see above, table 17.

Table 26. Mortgage Density in All-White and Predominantly
Black (over 50 Percent) Tracts Controlled for Value of Owner-occupied Homes,
1935-66[a] (High-priced Not Shown) (Percent)

Mortgage density	Low-priced homes		Medium-priced homes	
	Percent black		Percent black	
	0	51-99	0	51-99
1935-44				
1	8.3	16.6		
2	33.3	83.3		
3	20.8	0.0		
4	37.5	0.0		
5	0.0	0.0		
	(99.9)	(99.9)		
N=	(24)	(6)		
1945-54				
1	20.0	55.0		
2	50.0	45.0		
3	10.0	0.0		
4	20.0	0.0		
5	0.0	0.0		
	(100.0)	(100.0)		
N=	(20)	(20)		
1955-64				
1	15.4	84.0	14.3	37.5
2	53.2	12.0	46.4	50.0
3	7.7	0.0	28.6	6.3
4	7.7	4.0	10.7	6.3
5	15.4	0.0	0.0	0.0
	(100.0)	(100.0)	(100.0)	(100.1)
N=	(13)	(25)	(28)	(16)
1965-66				
1	60.0	92.6	38.9	76.7
2	20.0	7.4	44.4	17.7
3	0.0	0.0	0.0	5.9
4	20.0	0.0	16.7	0.0
5	0.0	0.0	0.0	0.0
	(100.0)	(100.0)	(100.0)	(100.3)
N=	(5)	(27)	(18)	(17)

[a]Value categories:

	1935-44	1945-54	1955-64	1965-66
Low:	Under $3,000	Under $12,000	Under $16,000	Under $17,000
Medium:	$3,000-6,000	$12,000-16,000	$16,000-21,000	$17,000-25,000

Table 27. Mortgage Density in Tracts with under 25 Percent
Owner-occupied Homes, Controlled for Percent Black, 1935–66 (Percent)

Mortgage	Percent black				
density	0	1–10	11–50	51–90	91–99
1935–44					
1	9.4	0.0	25.0	0.0	42.9
2	28.1	33.3	75.0	100.0	57.1
3	18.8	22.2	0.0	0.0	0.0
4	37.5	44.4	0.0	0.0	0.0
5	6.3	0.0	0.0	0.0	0.0
	(100.0)	(99.9)	(100.0)	(100.0)	(100.0)
N=	(32)	(9)	(4)	(1)	(7)
1945–54					
1	9.1	0.0	25.0	57.1	75.0
2	13.6	60.0	75.0	42.9	25.0
3	31.8	40.0	0.0	0.0	0.0
4	36.4	0.0	0.0	0.0	0.0
5	9.0	0.0	0.0	0.0	0.0
	(99.9)	(100.0)	(100.0)	(100.0)	(100.0)
N=	(22)	(5)	(4)	(7)	(8)
1955–64					
1	0.0	0.0	40.0	58.3	86.7
2	46.2	100.0	60.0	25.0	13.3
3	30.8	0.0	0.0	8.3	0.0
4	15.4	0.0	0.0	8.3	0.0
5	7.7	0.0	0.0	0.0	0.0
	(100.1)	(100.0)	(100.0)	(99.9)	(100.0)
N=	(13)	(1)	(5)	(12)	(15)
1965–66					
1	100.0	100.0	40.0	60.0	100.0
2	0.0	0.0	20.0	40.0	0.0
3	0.0	0.0	20.0	0.0	0.0
4	0.0	0.0	0.0	0.0	0.0
5	0.0	0.0	20.0	0.0	0.0
	(100.0)	(100.0)	(100.0)	(100.0)	(100.0)
N=	(2)	(5)	(5)	(5)	(6)

insurance industry's preference until 1965 for single-family home loans
and for neighborhood homogeneity, table 27 gives the lending history
of black and white tracts which have less than 25 percent of the inhabitants living in single-family homes. By comparing table 27 with table 24
it becomes clear that apartment structures in the near vicinity have had
little negative effect on credit for white neighborhoods, but (though
here the extrapolation must be from a very few cases) this circumstance
has tended to adversely affect black tracts. Moreover, the deviant cases

support rather than upset the racial pattern. The two tracts with densities over two in 1955–64 contain sizable white communities housed in
luxury apartments bordering the southern shore of Lake Michigan, thus
accounting for the concentration of funds. Likewise, the tract with
density five in 1965–66 is a fashionable high-income, high-rise community on the near north lakefront, whose minority population is separated from whites by certain boulevards but is nevertheless included in
the area's statistics.

Finally, tables 28 and 29 compare white and black tracts according
to the housing condition. During 1935–45 blacks lived predominantly

Table 28. Mortgage Density in Dilapidated Tracts (over 20 Percent
Substandard Housing), Controlled for Percent Black, 1935–54 (Percent)

Mortgage density	Percent black				
	0	1–10	11–50	51–90	91–99
1935–44					
1	36.8	0.0	40.0	0.0	37.5
2	26.3	37.5	60.0	100.0	62.5
3	5.3	25.0	0.0	0.0	0.0
4	26.3	37.5	0.0	0.0	0.0
5	5.3	0.0	0.0	0.0	0.0
	(100.0)	(100.0)	(100.0)	(100.0)	(100.0)
N=	(19)	(8)	(5)	(3)	(8)
1945–54					
1	30.0	0.0	40.0	55.5	54.5
2	20.0	40.0	60.0	44.4	45.5
3	40.0	40.0	0.0	0.0	0.0
4	10.0	20.0	0.0	0.0	0.0
5	0.0	0.0	0.0	0.0	0.0
	(100.0)	(100.0)	(100.0)	(99.9)	(99.9)
N=	(10)	(5)	(5)	(9)	(11)

in older, run-down neighborhoods, as did many whites. In this period,
however, in those tracts with over 20 percent of the buildings in dilapidated condition whites, and only whites, continued to receive mortgage
money—albeit smaller rations than neighborhoods in better condition.
The continued flow of mortgage loans undoubtedly contributed, along
with population movements, to the fact that by 1955–64 only two
all-white tracts were in such dilapidation, contrasted with eleven all-
black tracts. By 1955–64, however, some blacks had inherited residential areas which were structurally sound. Table 29 shows tracts with less
than 5 percent dilapidated, and with 6–10 percent. Those black tracts in

Table 29. Mortgage Density in Tracts with under 5 Percent Substandard
Housing and 6-10 Percent Substandard Housing, Controlled for Percent
Black, 1955-64 (Percent)

	Percent black				
	0	1-10	11-50	51-90	91-99
Under 5 percent substandard					
1	5.2	—	0.0	25.0	0.0
2	51.7	—	80.0	75.0	25.0
3	22.4	—	20.0	0.0	50.0
4	13.8	—	0.0	0.0	25.0
5	6.9	—	0.0	0.0	0.0
	(100.0)	(—)	(100.0)	(100.0)	(100.0)
N=	(58)	(—)	(5)	(4)	(4)
6-10 percent substandard					
1	14.3	0.0	50.0	33.3	100.0
2	42.9	100.0	0.0	50.0	0.0
3	14.3	0.0	0.0	16.7	0.0
4	28.6	0.0	50.0	0.0	0.0
5	0.0	0.0	0.0	0.0	0.0
	(100.1)	(100.0)	(100.0)	(100.0)	(100.0)
N=	(7)	(1)	(2)	(6)	(4)

best condition are able to compete with some success for funds. At the
6-10 percent level of dilapidation, though, the racial effect reasserts
itself dramatically.

The question of dilapidation brings up once more the matter of the
neighborhood as a reference point in evaluating prospective mortgage
loans. Because of residential segregation, black neighborhoods tend to
be less homogeneous than white neighborhoods in income and other
social characteristics. This fact is reflected in our sample, which in
1955-64 finds 42 percent of medium-income predominantly black
tracts housed in the lowest value homes, compared with 24 percent of
the medium-income white tracts. The lack of neighborhood homogeneity means that a well-kept house will be situated next to a decrepit one.
Partly because of lending patterns, newly black neighborhoods are prey
to deliberate overcrowding by landlords who divide up formerly spa-
cious apartments for their new lower-income tenants. Those persons
who are able to afford better housing are prevented by the artificial
scarcities of segregation from moving elsewhere. Because of the empha-

sis put on neighborhood in underwriting, then, it might be argued that it is not race itself which inhibits lenders, but rather the motley social pattern of black neighborhoods.

Tables 30 and 31 address this argument. Table 30 compares middle-income tracts, controlling for the value of the housing. Because of the

Table 30. Mortgage Density in All-White and Predominantly Black (Over 50 Percent) Medium Income ($5,500-10,000) Tracts, Controlled for Value of Owner-occupied Homes, 1955-64 (Percent)

Value of owner-occupied homes	Mortgage density	All-white	Tracts predominantly black
Under $16,000	1	15.4	62.5
	2	53.8	37.5
	3	7.7	0.0
	4	7.7	0.0
	5	15.4	0.0
		(100.0)	(100.0)
	N=	(13)	(8)
$16,000-21,000	1	14.3	0.0
	2	46.4	75.0
	3	28.6	12.5
	4	10.7	12.5
	5	0.0	0.0
		(100.0)	(100.0)
	N=	(28)	(8)
Over $21,000	1	0.0	33.3
	2	61.5	0.0
	3	15.4	66.6
	4	23.1	0.0
	5	0.0	0.0
		(100.0)	(99.9)
	N=	(13)	(3)

cases lost in cross-tabulating more than two variables, tracts with over 50 percent black inhabitants have been combined and compared to all-white tracts. Table 30 suggests that middle-income whites living in neighborhoods of less valuable housing continue to have access to mortgage funds, while blacks in similar circumstances are cut off. As in the other tables, the discrepancy narrows at the next level of income.

Still, however, it might be asserted that our analysis so far has been based on averages, and averages do not accurately reflect the enormous social diversity within ghetto neighborhoods. Accordingly, table 31 controls for the condition of the neighborhood by considering only

Table 31. Mortgage Density in All-White and Predominantly Black
(Over 50 Percent) Medium-Income ($5,500–$10,000) Tracts with under 5 Percent
Substandard Housing, Controlled for Value of Owner-occupied Homes,
1955–64 (Percent)

Value of owner-occupied homes	Mortgage density	All-white	Tracts predominantly black
Under $16,000	1	10.0	33.3
	2	50.0	66.6
	3	10.0	0.0
	4	10.0	0.0
	5	20.0	0.0
		(100.0)	(99.9)
	N=	(10)	(3)
$16,000–21,000	1	8.3	0.0
	2	50.0	50.0
	3	33.3	25.0
	4	8.3	25.0
	5	0.0	0.0
		(99.9)	(100.0)
	N=	(24)	(4)
Over $21,000	1	0.0	0.0
	2	66.6	0.0
	3	0.0	100.0
	4	33.3	0.0
	5	0.0	0.0
		(99.9)	(100.0)
	N=	(9)	(1)

those tracts with less than 5 percent substandard housing—an absolute, rather than an average, figure. Because of the still smaller number of cases, the findings can only be suggestive, but they are consistent with the overall pattern: the life insurance industry is willing to underwrite mortgages for middle-income whites living in cheap but well-maintained housing in greater proportions than for blacks in similar circumstances. In the neighborhoods of higher-priced housing, black tracts have fared somewhat better. This last statement, however, must be strongly qualified by the lending experience of 1965–66 (table 24). In the general shortage of mortgage funds, black neighborhoods as a group, including those previously favored, were relegated to very low levels of lending, resuming a position relative to whites reminiscent of the periods before 1955. In fact, the 95 percent of tracts having received no money at all is higher than at any time before 1955.

IV

A frequent comment in the interviews on the subject of racial discrimination in life insurance lending was: "Well, we'll approve just about any loan the FHA will insure"—the implication being that the ultimate responsibility for any unsatisfying social results must be laid at that agency. Since many critics of the housing industry also blame the FHA, and since the FHA represents the most direct and pervasive of the many laws, ordinances, and programs which encircle residential mortgage investment, it must be considered whether the decisions ascribed to the life industry are indeed in large measure a result of credit manipulations by government.[17]

The most important contribution of the FHA to the underwriting practices of mortgage lenders has been the emphasis on the neighborhood as a reference unit in determining the quality of a potential loan—the effects of which have been discussed above. Although this emphasis is somewhat ironic considering that one of the purposes of the National Housing Act of 1933, which created the FHA, was to make home ownership and improvements available to persons cut off from normal and existing mortgage funds, it is perhaps understandable in view of the specific mechanisms the FHA employed. Instead of lending money directly to worthy borrowers, the FHA operates on the principles of insurance, charging a small percentage fee in exchange for guaranteeing a long-term loan in case of foreclosure, with debentures backed by the credit of the United States. Unlike standard insurance procedures, which adjust rates to the amount of risk assumed in order to maintain an overall solvency, rates on FHA loans are set by statute. As a consequence, it is not surprising that FHA protected its solvency through a preoccupation with the appraisal of risk, and refined its measures of risk to include the "soundness of the neighborhood."

FHA underwriting, then, involved the standard evaluations of borrower's income and the condition of the property. But government manuals went on to warn appraisers against neighborhoods blighted by "smoke, fog, unpleasant odors, or inharmonious racial groups," and to recommend such neighborhood selling points as restrictive covenants, protection by high-speed traffic arteries and other barriers against "instability." Any lender seeking FHA insurance was likewise obligated to abide by these underwriting standards.

[17] For criticisms of the policies and practices of the Federal Housing Administration, see Robert Tebbel, *The Slum Makers* (New York: Dial Press, 1963), especially chapters 5 and 8; Charles Abrams, "Segregation Housing and the Horne Case," *The Reporter*, vol. 13, no. 5 (October 6, 1955), p. 30; on Chicago, see de Vise, *Chicago's Widening Color Gap*, pp. 113 ff. A good compendium of information on FHA practices is Congressional Quarterly's publication, *Housing a Nation* (Washington, D.C.: Congressional Quarterly Service, 1966).

The neighborhood concept culminated in a system of "red-lining," whereby large sections of the city—predictably those housing minority groups and the oldest, most dilapidated supply of housing—were declared out-of-bounds for purposes of mortgage insurance. This is the system tacitly acknowledged in a memorandum to FHA regional directors from commissioner Philip K. Brownstein at the beginning of a government reassessment which would culminate in the policy reversal of 1967, discussed in chapter VI. Brownstein cautioned that the "automatic exclusion" of neighborhoods from FHA programs "can result in shutting off capital government in these neighborhoods" which "in turn accelerates decline."[18] Although no red-lined map was made available to the author for inspection, after the policy reversal the FHA did another map which specified 'A' and 'B' "riot prone" areas—those community areas within the city of Chicago in extreme social and economic decay and those in a deteriorating condition, respectively. Several mortgage officers, moreover, indicated that these areas represented the mirror image of FHA's previous readiness to extend insurance.

It is useful to examine life insurance lending in 1955–64 in the predominantly (over 50 percent) black tracts in our sample in light of these FHA designations (see table 32). Among those attaining mortgage

Table 32. Mortgage Density in Predominantly Black (Over 50 Percent) Tracts, Controlled for 1968 FHA Designations of Community Areas, 1955–64 (Percent)

| Mortgage density | FHA designation | | Not designated |
	'A' (Dilapidated)	'B' (Deteriorating)	
1	94.7	50.0	0.0
2	5.3	33.3	66.6
3	0.0	11.1	16.7
4	0.0	5.6	16.7
5	0.0 (100.0)	0.0 (100.0)	0.0 (100.0)
N=	(19)	(18)	(6)

densities in the 'B' group is one tract bordered with luxury high-rise apartments on the lakefront. Another is a tract in the vicinity of the University of Chicago which was designated by the FHA in 1960 as a

[18] *FHA Commissioner Letter No. 38,* 1965, addressed to insuring officers. This was provided the author by John McKnight who in 1968 was director of the Midwest Field Office of the U.S. Civil Rights Commission.

conservation area. In 1960 this tract was inhabited by over 25 percent whites with middle to upper-middle incomes, and on the basis of the data it cannot be said with certainty who actually received the loans. The third 'B' area with considerable mortgage lending is in the Chicago community of Greater Grand Crossing which, in 1960, was in rather good economic condition and, it may be assumed, has achieved the status of a FHA 'B' area since then.

More significant perhaps are those tracts left out of the designations. While hardly indulged lavishly with insurance company loans, they did not find themselves totally cut off as did the majority of 'A' and 'B' areas. These tracts fall in four community areas: South Shore, Chatham, Roseland, and Morgan Park. Along with Greater Grand Crossing, they form an "S"—extending westward from the south lake shore to central Chicago's thoroughfare of State Street, then due south for some forty blocks to 118th Street, and westward to Western Avenue, another thoroughfare. All of them are solidly middle and upper-middle income.

The contiguity of these community areas is fundamental. Although not all of the tracts they encompass were black in 1960, they form the outlines of the expansion of the black community which began in the late 1950s and extended through the 1960s.[19] This contiguity signifies the restrictions placed on blacks by the FHA, mortgage lenders, and real estate brokers. Except for the roadblocks of housing discrimination, one would expect to find black residents located in various sections of the city. Instead, the FHA, lenders, and realtors have maintained a hands-off policy toward black migration into all-white communities until somehow—and our interviews indicate it is frequently when a black life insurance company supplies the money for a land contract—the dam is broken.

The extreme unlikelihood that loans would have been extended to neighborhoods in the early stages of racial transition, even in the absence of the FHA, however, is suggested by the mortgage banking textbook cited earlier: "If minority groups in any neighborhood are homogeneous, the problem of the experienced underwriter is not so difficult, but during a period of transition when there is fluidity of movement of racial and national groups within a neighborhood, the underwriter must proceed with caution."[20] This stricture was amply supported in the interviews. Also, our data show that upper-income suburbs, almost all above FHA price limits and thus ineligible for government insurance, did not suffer from want of investment money. Between red-lining practices, public and private, and the refusal to grant mortgages to

[19] A useful history of Chicago's racial transition and its social and economic components is in de Vise, *Chicago's Widening Color Gap.*

[20] Pease, *Mortgage Banking*, p. 224.

persons moving into white neighborhoods, the black homeowner was virtually squeezed out of the market.

Moreover, the black areas receiving life insurance money are several miles from the dilapidated, geographical "inner city." Placing the issue of racial transition aside, the question still remains as to whether, in the absence of the FHA red-lining, life insurance companies may not have been willing to *selectively* extend mortgages to credit-worthy black borrowers within the older ghetto. How much capital did the FHA itself actually shut off? Unfortunately, the entire period of study is under the FHA program, so that comparisons of lending in dilapidated areas at other periods is impossible. The question might be answered at its most simple level, however, in terms of the life companies' determination to underwrite the best possible loans: as long as demand outside rundown areas remained strong, it may be assumed that life companies themselves would take cognizance of the relative risks and invest elsewhere. This simple answer leads to a further question: one of the purposes of FHA was to broaden the demand for mortgages by reducing the amount of the down payment and monthly mortgage payments for prospective occupants of single-family homes and investors in multiunit apartments. Did the FHA, then, have the effect of so broadening the demand for properties outside these areas and so successfully sweetening the bait with mortgage insurance that capital was no longer available for more risky investments?

The National Bureau of Economic Research studied the effects of FHA mortgage insurance on stimulating housing demand for the periods 1934–41 and 1948–50 and concluded that the effects before the war were at most "modest," and after the war insignificant:"The somewhat greater relative increase in mortgage debt in the post-World War II boom than in the expansion of the twenties. . . . suggests that the primary manifestation of the credit liberalization program must be found in construction costs and housing prices."[21] As for the advantages of mortgage insurance, our data indicate that those tracts with the most expensive houses requiring conventional mortgages consistently reached higher levels of mortgage density than the insured, medium-income tracts. Nor is there evidence that the life insurance companies committed money to mortgages at higher levels than they would have in the absence of mortgage insurance.

Another criticism frequently leveled at the FHA is that in concentrating on mortgages for single-family homes rather than apartment houses the FHA skewed the private market in favor of the middle-income borrower and away from the dense inner city toward the sub-

[21] R. J. Saulnier, Harold G. Halcrow, and Neil H. Jacoby, *Federal Lending and Loan Insurance* (Princeton: Princeton University Press, 1958), p. 344.

urbs. The rejoinder here must be again the FHA's feeble role in stimulating demand above what it had been in earlier boom periods without mortgage insurance. But a perusal of FHA files suggests additional relevant facts. First, under Sec. 608, WWII housing and veteran's rental housing, between 1946–51 FHA insurance commitments were made directly to life companies for twenty-nine apartment buildings. The average rent for these apartments was $110.70, considerably higher than the $44 median rent for the city of Chicago in 1950. Second, under Sec. 207, FHA insurance for rental housing, between 1960 and 1966 six commitments were made to life insurance companies. Five of the six were located on the luxury lake-front streets of Sheridan Road and South Shore Drive. Finally, during approximately this last period, six FHA commitments were made to life insurance lenders under Sec. 220, FHA insurance for new and rehabilitated housing in urban renewal and conservation areas. Five of them were for high-rise apartments in the urban renewal district near Michael Reese Hospital, the University of Illinois, and Illinois Institute of Technology, located on the near-south side; two were on the south lake shore; and one was in the Hyde Park 'B' renewal district near the University of Chicago. The rents for these buildings ranged from two to three times the average rent for the city. This listing does not include FHA commitments made to life insurance companies through mortgage correspondents, but our examination of FHA records of loans to the latter showed the same high-rent luxury characteristics.

In other words, whatever role may be credited the FHA in neighborhood uplift, it corresponds comfortably to established private underwriting procedures. The procedures did not result in absolute racial discrimination: Prairie Shores, the project eventually built on the near-south side of Chicago, was soon occupied by 20 percent blacks, and the Hyde Park project by 5 percent blacks. But they were the same white-collar, professional and middle-income group serviced by life company mortgages in the single-family market. The emphasis on homes, per se, cannot be said to have produced special results.

Whether another federal program less tied to the underwriting criteria and conventions of private lending might have produced a different configuration of private finance will be deferred to the conclusions in chapter VII. But before prematurely ascribing the same admixture of attitudinal and procedural bias to both industry and government there is a last consideration. Ultimately, the amount of risk assumed on a property is the marketability of the property in the eventuality of foreclosure. Thus, to confront the argument of the life companies and the FHA on their own ground, the question must be raised whether, in fact, from the standpoint of their respective goals of profitability and solvency of the federal insurance fund, the investments shunned were unacceptable because of the lack of a market in case of default.

Part of the answer to this question is in the manner of the self-ful-filling prophecy. As the Brownstein memo suggests, "infusion of capi-tal" has the effect of "stabilizing, and upgrading" property;[22] the mar-ketability of a property is not enhanced when neither conventional nor insured mortgages are available at reasonable rates. But in the case of Chicago, for the period of the late 1950s and 1960s at least, more concrete evidence of the existence of a market may be offered. This is the flourishing institution of land contracts, discussed below. In addi-tion to giving lie to procedural "neutrality," land contracts are also an important result of the lending decisions described.

V

A full consideration of the broader effects of the mortgage patterns we have analyzed is best left to such studies as those undertaken by the Kerner Commission.[23] Here, however, some of the more immediate social conditions to which life insurance has contributed may be men-tioned. The first is the shortage and inadequacy of housing available to blacks. One point which was raised frequently in the interviews, and one implicit in the social service concept of life insurance investment held by many persons in the industry, is that whatever its biases, mort-gage investment benefits the housing needs of all American society. As upper-income families move to the suburbs, so the argument goes, lower-income persons inherit their vacated structures, and thus enjoy a generally improved housing supply. A study, however, of the chain of residential moves in seventeen metropolitan areas, including Chicago, indicates that, like so many other hard-headed perspectives of life insur-ance lenders, this too has a selective impact. Poor people do indeed benefit: persons under $3,000 represent 13 percent of the population, and represent 14 percent of the movers in the residential chain. But blacks do not move to new homes in proportion to their income: as occupants, they comprise only 60 percent of the figure which would be expected on the basis of income. These fewer black occupants, more-over, themselves move only 70 percent of what would be predicted on the basis of their income.[24] In other words, not simply income, but its combination with other social factors—not the least of which is discrim-

---

[22] Brownstein, *FHA Commissioner Letter No. 38.*

[23] See U.S. National Advisory Commission on Civil Disorders, *Report* (New York: Bantom Books, 1968).

[24] John B. Lansing, Charles Wade Clifton, and James H. Morgan, *New Homes and Poor People: A Study of Chains of Moves* (Ann Arbor: Institute for Social Research, University of Michigan, 1967).

ination in lending—creates a kind of racial inheritance tax, subtracting significantly from the presumed benefits.

Second, a direct result of racially biased lending practices has been the system of land contracts. The land contract is the credit vehicle by which poorer black families cut off from normal mortgages have been forced to purchase their homes, paying considerably more at less favorable terms than their white counterparts. While life insurance companies, banks, and savings and loan associations have been unwilling to extend funds, certain other lenders have been willing to loan money to real estate speculators at large discounts, commonly ten points, along with sizable down payments;[25] in Chicago, as we have mentioned, black insurance companies have been among the most active in this area. The speculator in turn sells the mortgage to the black buyer on contract: that is, the parties sign a contract agreeing that after an initial down payment and a stipulated number of monthly payments of a given amount, the ownership will be turned over to the inhabitants of the home. After greatly inflating the price and charging a large down payment, the lender also regularly receives 7 percent interest, the maximum under Illinois law, on the unpaid principal.

A study of fifteen properties purchased on contract during the 1960s in the Englewood section of Chicago, indicated the following: first, that thirteen of the fifteen Negro purchasers made down payments of 65 percent to 500 percent higher than what would have been required for an FHA loan; that fourteen paid on the average of $63.50 more per month than would have been required for a conventional loan obtained through regular lenders; and all paid a price (not including interest) from 35 percent to 115 percent more for the property than did the contracting speculator who obtained the loan.[26] Nor is the viciousness of contracts limited to high prices: until the property is completely paid for it can be repossessed by the speculator upon the default of a single payment. In the meantime, although the purchaser builds up no equity in his propective property he is legally responsible for its condition and for all damage by fire, vandalism, and so on.

[25] Discounts are a method by which the financial community overcomes FHA limits on interest, usury laws (which apply to the contract speculator), etc. A percent of a loan ("points") is deducted and kept by the lender, although the borrower pays interest on the full amount of the loan *before* anything was deducted. Although in the case of FHA transactions, law forbids that the borrower pay such discounts, this is circumvented by raising the seller's price to compensate for this amount. During the tight money of 1966, for example, lenders were charging up to 6 and 7 points on FHA loans. Information on discount rates is published regularly in *The Mortgage Banker* and in government publications by the FHA and the Federal Reserve Board.

[26] "Mortgage Availability in Racially Transitional Areas," prepared by the Chicago Commission on Human Rights, presented at a public hearing of the Commission on August 9, 1967. Mimeo.

How pervasive this practice is can only be estimated. During 1968 in the Lawndale community alone the Contract Buyers League, an organization to find refinancing for victimized families, enlisted over 1,000 members and claimed that over half of the approximately 5,500 homes in the community were purchased on contract. The League has described the personal costs of this "impersonal" lending:

> For the black contract buyer, the present state of affairs spells hardship, suffering, exhaustion, and despair. It means that husbands must work two and sometimes three jobs in order to make ends meet. It means that wives must work, that family life is all but destroyed, and that children must be left unsupervised, and then people ask why there is a high crime rate in black areas. It means that widows beyond retirement age must scrub floors. Contract buying also means for many that they have chosen the lesser of two evils. Couples were faced with the choice of continuing to pay exorbitant rents comparable to their current monthly installments or buying on contract with the hope that someday they might own their own homes. It also means that they must stand under the criticism of the white community for not maintaining their buildings and living in squalor. And it hurts all the more because they are only too well aware that they cannot do much in the line of repairs after having put all their money into the pockets of speculators through their outrageous monthly installments. It means, too, that they must face embarrassment in admitting that they entered into bad deals, especially when many of them sought out the advice of attorneys when they made their purchases. Contract buying means only one thing: frustration or the impossibility of escaping from living in a slum.[27]

And the Negro mortgage banker quoted above also spoke of the problems of this generation of buyers saddled with inflated land contracts:

> The very fact of a liquidity position is very important. I once planned to write a book called "Going to California." That's what white people would say as they moved out of changing neighborhoods. They're not going anywhere but across town, you see, but that's what they said. Anyway, we too would like to move to California. With the knowledge that you can do that if you want to, there's a different attitude. But in the core areas there's no financing, no buyers, and no way out.

The land contract system, then, stands as direct refutation of the argument that black homes had no marketability during the earlier period of racial transition. The qualification of *during this earlier period* must be added; for it is an additional hardship of lending procedures that inequities get frozen into the process until these procedures, even if fairly administered, are then no longer adequate as a remedy. Thus, in chapter VI it will be shown that after so many years of life insurance lenders' denying that there was a viable market for black-owned homes, in 1967, because of the inflated costs brought by contracts, there indeed was no market. Here, as elsewhere, credit acts to fulfill its own prophecies.

[27]"The Contract Buyers League Demands Justice," p. 5. Prepared by the Contract Buyers League of Chicago and distributed December, 1968. Mimeo.

Finally, in light of these systematic results, the question must be reconsidered as to whether the insurance industry should not be charged with the coercive and purposive reordering of credit away from the city, particularly the black inner city; and, indeed, whether, given the presence of the FHA, this might not be seen in part as a government-induced process. But once again, the incremental, profit-oriented, socially unplanned nature of the mortgage lending which has been described must be insisted upon. To be sure, one of the FHA's initial purposes was to attract more funds to housing and in this sense it played a role in the social results. The FHA, however, was part of a general shoring up of economic sectors by the New Deal, along with agencies like the National Recovery Administration, the Reconstruction Finance Corporation, and the Securities and Exchange Commission. Reordering was not the aim; the philosophy, rather, to the extent that there was one, was to get money being withheld in personal savings back to the job of irrigating the economy; and housing, particularly low-income housing, was one of the dry gulches. That the FHA became so preoccupied with its underwriting standards was so little a matter of racial plan that during the first years of the Johnson administration these standards flourished under a black Secretary of Housing and Urban Development, who bragged in public about his agencies' suburban projects.[28] Moreover, whatever its biases, the FHA remained entirely voluntary: some of the largest life insurers had largely or entirely declined its services.

Life insurance companies, for their part, seek only investment yield and asset growth. Although underwriting procedures incorporate such vagaries as prestige and mask racial prejudice, these are in no way investment goals. Indeed, what is striking is that despite the high-level executive rhetoric about the deep social involvements of the life insurance industry, mortgage officers are only dimly aware, at best, of the cumulative external effects of their decisions, and nothing could be farther from their minds than a social plan.

From the point of view of the companies, they operate to *supply* funds not to deny them. In the interviews any suggestion of favoritism to the suburbs over the city, say, was brushed aside by the argument that a savings and loan or some other lender would supply the funds. And this was, in a sense, true, although as we have seen in the case of the blacks, it has meant steep carrying charges. But if blacks have not been favored by the life insurance lenders, neither have other Chicago residents been protected from the rigors of profit. When money became scarce in 1965–66, and life insurance companies moved out of the

[28] See Martin Nolan, "A Belated Effort to Save Our Cities," *The Reporter*, vol. 37, no. 11, December 28, 1967, p. 16 ff.

single-family housing market, some suburbanites were cut off from mortgage funds as surely as city dwellers; others paid higher interest rates to compete with corporations.

None of this is to deny the social effect of life insurance lending; on the contrary, it is to stress that the incremental, workaday exigencies of autonomous private credit provide the industry with a sense of social impulses and accomplishments, but not of social engineering. That dramatic impacts are produced nonetheless is what makes the matter so politically important and, as chapters VI and VII will show, so problematic for the direction of social change.

CHAPTER VI

THE
URBAN INVESTMENTS
PROGRAM

This chapter will describe the Life Insurance Urban Investments Program as it operated in Chicago. Figures available on program allocations by state show Illinois in third place behind California and Texas; and within Illinois, Chicago received the lion's share. Moreover, since Chicago is an investment city for all of the major national companies as well as for locally domiciled insurers, and since the social conditions of the Chicago ghetto are common to most large northern cities, the experience there is representative of the larger program.

Our analysis focuses on the purposes of the program, its procedures of implementation, and the social contents of the inner city. In a sense, an epitaph for the chapter might be the scriptural injunction against the left hand's knowing about the right hand's good works, for the program's double aspect—one, a project to aid the inner city, and two, a politically-inspired public demonstration of the life insurance industry's willingness to help—largely prefigured the results. Of equal interest, however, is the manner in which the essentially unplanned regularities of the procedures discussed in chapter V marked the social outcome and how, in the absence of effective industry coordination, this was bound to happen.

Because the Urban Investments Program raises a great many problems peripheral to the concerns of our discussion, a few subjects which will not be discussed below might be mentioned. The first is the question of whether any program can be successfully executed in the inner city with the expectation of even small money returns to the investor. In this chapter the subject is the specific shortcomings of the life insurance industry's effort. Another problem not discussed is that of scale. The two billion dollars eventually committed and dispersed is dramatically small in scale compared to the need and, in this respect, the program may be seen as deficient from the start. Our analysis, however, perceives the results of the program as a consequence of a particular set of political and social conditions and industry motives and organization, and is interested only secondarily in size, on the presumption that a commitment several times larger would have compounded the actual outcome, not improved it. Third is the matter of whether credit is, by its very nature, a mechanism of the status quo. Each of these topics will be touched on in the concluding chapter, along with a general discussion of the meaning and viability of corporate social responsibility.

I

There are many precedents for the Urban Investments Program, and they are pertinent for the light they shed on the purposes of such enterprises. Take, for example, the Metropolitan Life Insurance Company and the several residential projects which may be identified as deviations from normal investment in response to social problems. In 1911, a period of acute shortage of workingmen's homes, Metropolitan Life undertook the financing of Mapleton, its first experiment in small mortgage loans for new construction. In 1921, this time at the urging of the New York State Lockwood Committee which was investigating the scarcity of mortgage funds, the company constructed and assumed management of an apartment project in Long Island City, offering rents much lower than those prevailing in similar new buildings. In 1938, reflecting the management's opinion that the FHA was stimulating a desire for home ownership in people who couldn't afford it, the company began its series of "Parks" with Parkchester, almost a city in itself, in the Bronx, housing over 12,000 lower-middle-income families. In 1943 and 1944 Metropolitan Life built its first slum clearance projects, Stuyvesant Town, in Manhattan, for white residents and Riverton, in Harlem, for blacks. In each case, necessary enabling and inducing statutes were passed by the New York legislature.[1] Each event was heralded as evidence of the Metropolitan's social responsibility, and managers then, as in 1967, took great pride in the effectiveness of their trusteeship. For example, when Dr. Lee Frankel, a former professional sociologist, assumed the office of vice-president that he was to hold during much of this period, it was announced that "Insurance, not merely as a business proposition but as a social programme, will be the future policy of the Company."[2]

[1] Marquis James, *The Metropolitan Life: A Study in Business Growth* (New York: Viking Press, 1947), chapters XV and XIX. Also see Robert E. Schultz, *Life Insurance Housing Projects* (Homewood, Ill.: Richard D. Irwin, 1956).

[2] James, *The Metropolitan Life*, p. 273.

Also interesting is the political climate at the time of each of these investments. Nineteen hundred and eleven was a period of sharp public criticism of security capitalism. Metropolitan Life's biographer tells, perhaps apocryphally, of the company's treasurer being deeply shaken upon hearing of a workman who, after losing his home in a foreclosure, became a soap-box anarchist; and that the company undertook Mapleton after considering that several European governments were providing mortgage loans for their citizens at very low interest rates.[3] Nineteen hundred and twenty-one, the second date, was in the wake of postwar rumors of the impending nationalization of the industry, and the year of William Randolph Hearst's personal crusade for the nationalization of insurance in order that "a public business might be managed for service rather than profit."[4] Nineteen hundred and thirty-eight was filled with general anxieties about New Deal plots and the specific terrors of the TNEC hearings. Finally, the slum-clearance projects coincided with the prosecution and decision of the South-Eastern Underwriters' case—although in these there is perhaps no reason to find a climate other than the freeze by New York City on the assessed valuation of land and buildings for twenty-five years at the level before development.

None of this is to suggest elements of hypocrisy in Metropolitan Life's credo of responsibility; on the contrary. What the political background does indicate, however, is that social impulses are more likely to materialize into money and bricks when industry officials perceive a threat to their autonomous control over life company assets, and that this links social responsibility to other, political purposes.

In the case of the Urban Investments Program, the collective industry conscience found its embodiment in Orville Beal, president of the Prudential Insurance Company. Nineteen hundred and sixty-seven was Mr. Beal's last year before retirement, and one might speculate that such an undertaking would have special appeal to a man at the end of a long career in business statesmanship. Moreover, Beal was president of the Institute of Life Insurance, the main political, public relations, and educational organ of the industry, and was, no doubt, a man keenly aware of the political environment. Beal was present at the press conference in the White House Fish Room where Gilbert Fitzhugh, president of Metropolitan Life—and, incidentally, a close friend of President Lyndon Johnson's—gave him major credit for reminding his fellows that "we are pretty much involved in the life of the country—we should do

[3] Ibid., p. 246.
[4] R. Carlyle Buley, *The American Life Convention 1906–1952: A Study in the History of Life Insurance* (New York: Appleton-Century-Crofts, 1963), vol. I, p. 574.

something as far as our share in trying to alleviate the problems in these inner cities."[5]

In 1967 there were certainly favorable conditions for the actualization of social impulses. First of all, there was the troublesome relationship of the industry to American blacks. For the last several years there had been sporadic criticism of life insurance underwriting and personnel policies as being radically discriminatory—indeed, one unpleasant exchange had occurred at a recent Prudential stockholders meeting with Mr. Beal presiding.[6] In 1966 twenty national organizations, in collaboration with Martin Luther King, had staged a boycott against Metropolitan Life, the largest single insurer of blacks, in an effort to bring the industry's investment practices into harmony "with the demands of a democratic America and the goals of a great society."[7] The Negro market, referred to by the speaker as "pre-sold individuals," seeking entrance into "white clubs, white stores and white insurance companies," with thirty billion dollars to spend annually, was the subject of an address in 1967 to a convention of small stock companies: "When you go to this Negro market, you've got hundreds and hundreds of little nests. . . . This is a group that has learned to love their families.

"And if they buy our products it is only reasonable to help finance their projects at reasonable rates and using the same business judgments as we would use to judge a white loan on a similar project."[8]

Second, the steady deterioration of the inner city was of direct business concern to the life insurance industry. Life companies have heavy investments in home office buildings, real estate, commercial and residential mortgages, and public utilities in the cities.[9] Executives interviewed in Illinois mentioned a variety of related liabilities, such as the erosion of the urban tax base, the unavailability of trained stenographers, and threats to the health and safety of city dwellers who were their policyholders.

Both of these conditions were dramatized for the industry by the urban riots of 1965 and 1966. Amid the general shock suffered by the American business community as a whole, the life insurance industry was wounded by the financial losses of its brother and subsidiary companies in the field of casualty insurance, as well as by the destruction of

[5] *Weekly Compilation of Presidential Documents*, vol. 3, no. 37, September 18, 1967, p. 1284.

[6] Reported in James Gollin, *Pay Now, Die Later* (New York: Penguin Books, 1966), pp. 175 ff.

[7] See Dempsey Travis, "Boycott," *Focus/Midwest*, vol. III, nos. 8 and 9, pp. 16–17.

[8] *The National Underwriter* (Life edition), December 9, 1967, p. 6.

[9] See the address of John S. Pillsbury, chairman of the Life Insurance Association of America and president of Northwestern Mutual Life at the annual meeting of the Mortgage Bankers Association of America in Dallas, Texas, October 1967. Reprinted in *The Mortgage Banker* (November 1967).

commercial properties on which it held mortgages. More important, the riots created a series of governmental responses which related specifically to the industry's investment activities. Repeated testimony before the Kerner Commission stressed the serious shortage of capital and credit in the ghettos as having contributed to the crisis. Several agencies, including the Office of the Vice-President, the Departments of Labor and Housing and Urban Development, and the Federal Reserve Board had likewise commented on the shortages and proposed tax incentives, government-backed financial institutions, cooperative and development banks, and legal requirements to draw public funds to the task of urban reconstruction.[10]

Just how seriously the life insurance industry regarded these particular proposals is impossible to gauge. But several of the Illinois executives interviewed specifically mentioned the political situation as a catalyst for the companies' social zeal. One said, for example: "I think men like Beal and Oates [president of the Equitable quoted at length in Chapter IV] have a higher motive. But as far as the industry—they say, 'Government's going to do it, we'd better beat 'em to the punch.' But these things [i.e., higher motives] don't come from the first generation, who may have made their money partly as a protest against society." And there is a good deal of supporting evidence of a generally more defensive posture toward the federal government. Henry Root Stern, former New York superintendent of insurance and counsel to several large companies, had declared that federal regulation was a certainty, in large part because of the financial power of the industry.[11] Robert E. Bowles, chairman of the Life Underwriters Political Action Committee, reported to the industry that a leading economist had proposed to the government that it absorb the insurance industry and its assets into the Social Security system.[12] James L. Bentley of Georgia, president of the National Association of Insurance Commissioners—perhaps with an eye to proposals in Congress to nationalize auto insurance and thereby endanger the private status of the entire industry—warned that 1967-68 was "the last time around" for the settlement of problems "on a voluntary basis"; Bentley suggested that the urban pledge would demonstrate a "heavy role of public service [which] couldn't be ignored by public officials."[13]

A few months after the program was announced, the Institute of Life Insurance, led by Orville Beal, released its *Future Outlook Study*, which

[10] See for an overview, U.S. Congress, Senate, Subcommittee on Financial Institutions of the Committee on Banking and Currency, *Hearings, Financial Institutions and the Urban Crisis,* 90th Cong., 2nd Sess., 1968.

[11] *Insurance,* June 17, 1967, p. 12.

[12] Ibid., September 23, 1967, p. 36.

[13] Ibid., January 6, 1968, pp. 19 ff.

questioned how deeply the government might move into the activities of the private sector.[14] A "distant early warning line" was established to provide "feedback" of relevant events in government and public opinion. Some executives predicted a "battleground." Norman C. Buck, vice-president of Lincoln National Life, lamented:

> Our business deals with some of life's most intimate problems. . . . We extend the helping hand in time of need.
>
> Yet, we are told, the public suspects our motives, regards us as legalistic, rather than humanitarian, and thinks of us as being rich, powerful and aloof from the public interest. How can we convince the public that ours is a very personal business and that we do care about the public welfare?

Buck's answer—the Life Insurance Urban Investments Program.[15]

II

If the double purposes of the program—to aid the inner cities and to protect the industry's investment autonomy from political interference—were to stir cross-currents, there was yet another set of circumstances which would act as a powerful undertow. This was the state of the insurance business in 1967. As earlier chapters have discussed, the industry feared itself to be losing ground to other financial institutions and had embarked on a campaign of aggressive growth and yields through larger investments in equities and diversification of financial services. Interest rates were at extraordinarily high levels, a strategically important time for companies that lend large amounts on long and fixed terms. Related to the high interest rates was rampant inflation, the condition which had caused the industry's competitive fears for the future, now coupled with signs of a business recession which could cut into cash flows.

It is perhaps evidence of the reality of the industry's social impulses that the program was undertaken at all under these circumstances, since, presumably, other political defenses, say, massive campaign contributions, might have been adequate for the interim and would not have compromised the goals of growth and yields even to the very small degree of the program. On the other hand, having decided to go ahead, it was "understood from the beginning," in the words of one trade official, "that we weren't going to hand this money out on street corners." Acting on the proposal of the Institute of Life Insurance, in early 1967 the Life Insurance Association of America (LIAA) appointed a Committee on Urban Problems under Fitzhugh, one of the chief tasks of which was to consult with government officials and secure guarantees and loan insurance for possible inner-city investments. Only after

[14] Quoted in *The National Underwriter* (Life edition), January 27, 1968, p. 10.
[15] Ibid., p. 10.

several pledges of government cooperation and the extraction of a new policy from the FHA to provide loan insurance for mortgages in formerly "red-lined" districts, were the committee's recommendations presented to the executive committees of the LIAA and the American Life Convention (ALC), where they were unanimously adopted.

Unfortunately for the course of inner-city investment, the committee erected a rather frail vessel. Although the program was sponsored by the two major trade associations, participation was entirely voluntary. Companies joined in for a percentage of the billion dollars based on their assets and maintained full control over the details of allocating their pledge. After fifty-nine companies had agreed to subscribe and the public announcement had been made, the public relations and political aspects returned to the Institute of Life Insurance, and the job of coordinating the investment side of the program was assigned to a group of staff from the trade associations, which was designated as the Urban Clearinghouse, operating out of the offices of the LIAA in New York. In addition, the committee was reconstituted as the ALC-LIAA Joint Committee on Urban Problems, made up of nine executives of large companies (later a black vice-president of a smaller company was added), which would meet every few months to guide the staff.

The Clearinghouse functioned as its name implies, putting companies in touch with groups who might assist in placing loans, such as the American Hospital Association, the International Council of Shopping Centers, the National Housing Partnership. It furnished participants with a monthly *Urban Investment Report* containing program statistics and a description of innovative or otherwise noteworthy investments.[16] But the staff's most important function, at least on paper, was to approve or disallow individual investments made by the companies in fulfillment of their pledges, according to a set of criteria implementing the objectives of the program.

Shortly after the program was announced the staff issued "Eligibility Standards for Investments Under the Urban Problems Program of the Life Insurance Business." This two-page mimeographed document is notable for its vagueness and flexibility, reflecting at once the inexperience of the industry in inner-city investing and the general receptiveness to company initiative. Any city, large or small, might qualify. In the area of housing, the standards allow for moderate- or low-income, single-family or apartments, new or rehabilitated, insured or conven-

[16]Unless otherwise indicated, all information on the details of the program, its administration, and finance comes from *Urban Investment Report*, nos. 1–14 (April 1970–March 1971), mimeos., and various progress reports and tabulations issued jointly by the American Life Convention and the Life Insurance Association of America. The author wishes to thank Dale Gustafson of the American Life Convention in Chicago for his assistance in following the program, although he is, of course, totally without responsibility for the analysis here.

tional, in the urban core or outside, provided that it be for persons moving from the core. In the area of commercial loans, the standards are even less specific, endorsing any project "which will benefit those residing in the core areas," and suggesting—"though not necessarily limited to"—factories and other industrial facilities, medical and educational facilities, a wholesale bakery, a laundry processing plant. Projects to "retain" jobs are eligible as well as those to provide them. No mention is made of race, and the fact that the inner city is inhabited mainly by blacks is betrayed only by the stated eligibility of housing for persons moving from the inner core—a provision not likely intended to conjure up the picture of whites fleeing the ghetto. Nor is mention made of racial transition, or of white or black ownership.

The standards define the constituency of the program in terms of residency within the urban core, which is in turn designated by the presence of "blight or near-blight conditions." This, too, is not a rigid formula, since other stated criteria include persons moving outside the core and, by inference, factory owners who might live outside. Nevertheless, the thrust, if such a word may be used for these essentially flabby provisions, is toward benefits for the dilapidated and poor areas, rather than those in better condition.

Finally, the standards provide that "the interest rate should be no higher than the regular market rate for investments coming within normal operations." Since the companies' demand for market rates will be shown to have been a major stumbling block in inner-city investing, it is necessary to speculate on the importance of this factor in the original formulations of the program. To be sure, "handing the money out on street corners" was never contemplated; but significant distance stretches between street corners and upper-middle-income apartments, and there is evidence that market rates were not always the preoccupation they later became. The original recommendations of the Committee on Urban Problems had noted that "it would be understood that yields *near* the market rate would be expected" (emphasis added).[17] Moreover, shortly after the public announcement, the Joint Committee notified President Johnson that in response to his request for immediate action the staff would undertake the placement of eight federal rent supplement (221)(d)(3) projects, and was proceeding with further reviews of the total FNMA backlog amounting to $38,000,000. While the yield of 6 percent, plus the minimum ceiling on discounts, was far beyond the rate assumed in the premium rates to the policyholder, it was also below yields available on, say, FHA 203(b)—insured mortgages

[17]"Report of the Urban Problems Committee to the Board of Directors of the Life Insurance Association of America (as revised and adopted by the Board at its meeting on August 18, 1967)," mimeo.

on single-family homes, which carried no discount limitations, and even further below noninsured apartment and commercial loans. This is not to suggest a surfeit of altruism on the part of the Joint Committee. Indeed, this commitment, solicited by the government, was definitely compatible with the political as well as social objectives of the program. What is indicated, however, is that these original purposes of the program had not yet been totally submerged by the pull of market rates.

Throughout the program the staff endeavored to clarify its social objectives and impose relevant boundaries. For example, their monthly reports suggested price guidelines for low- and moderate-income housing; argued the advantages of lending to black over white entrepreneurs; explained that an available pool of GNMA securities which yielded 8 5/8 percent was unacceptable on the grounds that a fully insured government bond at these rates was a "normal" investment, rather than one suited to the program. But equally apparent in successive issues of the *Urban Investment Report* is the staff's consistent modification of the criteria to accommodate the companies. This was done in the name of what was called the "spirit of the Program." For example, loans were approved for black colleges, institutions not generally associated with conditions of blight, and even black colleges in small towns, provided that a "significant percentage" of its students came from urban centers and would be returning there. Also in the spirit of the program, as interpreted by the staff, were apartment buildings with relatively high rents—one in question had been $165 for three rooms—if they provided "housing opportunities . . . for moderate-income minority groups in an area where there was a lack of such opportunities."

Ultimately, of course, a posture of flexibility and accommodation was the only one possible for the Clearinghouse. For, despite its paper duties, it had little effective power over company decisions. Often companies simply failed to submit dispersal reports: at one point well into the program the staff notified the companies that it had received reports from only one-third of those participating. Frequently, company reports that were submitted did not include the detailed breakdowns of borrower and loan characteristics necessary for perusal by the staff. Information on the number of loans actually disqualified by the staff after they were committed is not available, but it may be surmised that the number was negligible.

That the Clearinghouse lacked the administrative teeth to insure adherence to the original social ends of the program is largely due to its status as an agency of the trade associations, which were in turn accountable to the company members. However, since participation in the program was entirely voluntary and was initiated by certain executives of large companies, many of whom were on the Joint Committee which had direct control over staff policy, the question may be asked why these companies were not amenable to a more closely controlled program—one where the market rates, once the difficulties of investing in the blighted core became evident, would have given way to the social objectives, rather than the other way around. One answer, of course, is that businessmen are generally reluctant to divest themselves of any autonomy, even to an organization under their own control. While this explanation would apply to the program—a great emphasis was put on the desirability of "each company doing what it can do best"—it begs the question. A supplementary explanation is in the specific nature of the commitment. Conceived by a very few companies, the one-billion dollars was proposed as a fixed amount, to be distributed on a pro rata basis according to assets. Consequently, unlike a situation where the founding companies might pledge a set percentage of their own assets, the number of companies who could be persuaded to participate in the program reduced the shares of those already pledged. Also, initiators of the program conceived of it as a continuing effort which depended on enthusiastic participant support.[18] As a trade official reported, "many of the larger companies never liked the program to begin with," and a recalcitrant administration of its details could only reduce its palatability.

The question of participation, moreover, is related to the political purpose which, in our interpretation, galvanized the industry into social action. Certainly several heads of the largest companies with a long-standing public commitment to social responsibility and billions of dollars in their control—say Beal of the Prudential, Oates of the Equitable, and Fitzhugh of Metropolitan Life—separately or as a group could have set up an investment pool and closely and expertly directed its investments, exploiting the favorable publicity in each company's own behalf. But as a technique for blocking government intrusion into private investment, a united industry front was more effective.[19] In May 1969 the Institute of Life Insurance notified its members of an impending nationwide advertising campaign describing "the concern of the life insurance business for the quality of American life": "This campaign should go a long way toward informing the public—and even its most skeptical components—that the life insurance business has clearly seen its urban responsibility and has moved to meet it swiftly."[20]

---

[18] See Beal's testimony in *Hearings, Financial Institutions and the Urban Crisis*, p. 161.

[19] In fact, some individual companies did stress their joint participation with others in the program in their advertising. But an overemphasis on one's own generosity entailed the danger of backfiring in the form of customer protest. The strategy adopted maximized political benefit while smoothing the competitive edge.

[20] During 1968 and 1969 the Institute of Life Insurance carried out an extensive publicity campaign for the program. This included sponsorship of three one-hour television documentaries on "The Urban Crisis," and repeated full-page advertisements in 156 newspapers and 21 weekly and monthly magazines. Advertisements emphasized the racial aspects of the program:

The staff complied with this political objective. Although the fostering of a competitive spirit could have been useful to step up the pace and amount of commitments—much as is done in other types of fund raising, through the publication of each company's contribution—the Clearinghouse scrupulously maintained an industry persona. No names of individual companies appeared with descriptions of new projects. A mimeographed list of participants was circulated from time to time, but there was no indication of which companies had actually fulfilled their pledges. There was one exception: when a company completed its pledge, a notification was sent to interested organizations and agencies within the company's home state.

It is useful to view this aspect of the program in the light of some of Mancur Olson's propositions about organizational incentives. The strengthened political position of the industry against government intervention may be considered a "collective good," from which the entire industry would necessarily benefit, just as the deprivation of investment autonomy would be a deprivation for every company. Thus, in contrast to certain business benefits which the program might have provided through favorable publicity, there was no political purpose in specifying which companies had contributed and which had not. On the other hand, state insurance regulation, as was seen in chapter III, is very often directed in favor of specific companies and segments of the life insurance industry. As a consequence, the enhancement of an individual company's reputation for social responsibility, through the local announcement of its having fulfilled its pledge, might have political importance in the manner of "selective goods."[21]

Olson's ideas may also be applied to the extent and structure of company participation. Of the 353 members of the ALC and the LIAA, only 154 participated in the first billion dollar pledge. Virtually all of the large companies joined, but a far smaller proportion of the smaller companies, even though all pledges were according to asset size. This can be understood simply as a reflection of the higher sense of social involvement among large companies.[22] But, again, such an explanation

in one appearing in November 1968 a black social worker discusses "second-class citizenship"; in May 1968 a black construction worker is pictured at the site of a social services center in Bedford-Stuyvesant; in July 1969 a discussion of "backlash" and "blacklash" is illustrated by a young black executive type and the caption, "White's don't want me to succeed." While it is difficult to know how much emphasis may be placed on these obviously carefully and expensively prepared advertisements, it is interesting to note that the question of "blacklash" reappears in two of the three advertisements announcing the commitment of a second billion dollars, perhaps reflecting a growing awareness of industry's problematic relations with the ghetto community. This accords with our own analysis on pp. 174 ff.

[21]Mancur Olson, *Logic of Collective Action* (New York: Schoken Books, 1968), chapter I.

[22]On the importance of size of firm as a structural variable determining knowledge and action in respect to the external environment, see Raymond Bauer, Ithiel de Sola Pool, and Lewis Anthony Dexter, *American Business and Public Policy: The Politics of Foreign Trade* (New York: Atherton Press, 1963), p. 476 and passim.

begs the question, and Olson's propositions offer additional clarification. It is in the nature of a collective good that those who do not participate in the group benefit in spite of their inaction. In the case of the Urban Investments Program, there were actually two "collective goods"—the reinforcement of the life insurance industry's political position and the improvement of the inner cities. Our interviews suggested that a company's willingness to "pay" for the former hinged at least in part on the perceptibility of its impact on the latter.[23]

The leadership of the larger companies that supplied the bulk of the funds speaks for their sense of social efficacy. Moreover, the Illinois companies that failed to participate suggested that they did so not out of a lack of social consciousness as such, but rather from a feeling of unimportance in such a grand undertaking. A typical explanation, this one by the president of a small stock company, was: "Well, we thought of it. But we're such a small company compared to the Prud and the Metropolitan. We're just not set up to develop projects of that kind. A few mortgages, yes, but we didn't think we ought to go in with our policyholders' money just for that." And the general counsel for a medium-sized Illinois mutual that was participating in the first billion but doubted whether they would resubscribe for the second, told of his misgivings about the role of "small potatoes":

> The smaller companies were supposed to be able to get in a pool. We notified New York we were certainly willing. But we never even had an expression of interest. I don't know if one has been set up. We get these mimeos, but they're kind of general and not to the point.
>
> Some companies are heavily in the residential field and are all tooled up for that sort of thing. We're just not adequately staffed.
>
> Frankly, I thought there would be more interest. Prudential's commitment, of course, is larger than our whole surplus. Maybe they don't want small potatoes, it's not worth bothering with. Or maybe they don't need us in the act.[24]

III

Several echelons of personnel were involved in the actual implementation of the program in Chicago. They ranged from the vice-president of a large New York mutual who sat on a Black Business Steering Committee and on the Lawndale People's Planning Counsel, to the loan officer of a mortgage banking company arranging shopping center loans for a large stock company, to the black mortgage banker with $2,000,000 to loan on home mortgages for another large company.

[23] Olson, *Logic of Collective Action*, pp. 53–57.

[24] In the second billion-dollar commitment some effort was made by the staff to arrange for smaller companies to participate in individual projects with larger ones. In the *Urban Investment Report* of November 16, 1970, the staff announced one such arrangement, commenting more generally that these efforts "have not been successful because the arrangements are seldom acceptable to both larger and smaller companies."

Their opinions on the merits of the program varied. For example, the regional supervisor for one of the largest and earliest participants said that their experience had been "entirely successful," and he was certain "there will always be some money for this program." A loan representative in the regional office of a midwestern company—whose president, incidentally had been very active on the Joint Committee—disagreed:

We never would have gone into it without LIAA prodding. I've reviewed some of the credit reports and they're atrocious. Everyone's talking about a second billion, but not another billion after that.

We're not too happy. And we have indications that the policyholders are not too happy.

While enthusiasm was found in unequal strength at various levels, the Illinois interviews confirmed the common impression of a broader social perspective as one moved up the executive ladder. But presidents, for the most part, do not decide on credit applications; and this section will hereafter confine its observations to the officers and correspondents responsible for actually finding and reviewing loans.

The extremely vague nature of the criteria furnished by the Joint Committee was reflected in a variety of social perspectives concerning the program. One of the most striking aspects of the interviews was the total absence of any plan or even forecast of social trends into which individual projects might fit. On one occasion a respondent insisted: "Look! There's no master plan here. There's no conspiracy. Ours is a very competitive business, a very technical business!"—a reply unusual only in its vehemence. When asked directly about subjects so commonly and publicly debated that loan officials could not claim total aloofness without appearing ignorant, they generally adopted a position compatible with passivity. This comment on racial integration is illustrative: "Integration is meaningless. The white talks integration more than the black. The black wants separate but equal. He's happiest with his own. This general theme has been repeated everyplace." In those rare instances where an official did perceive a glimmer of policy, particularly one favoring specific action, it was inevitably neutralized by the claim of helplessness: "Well, I suppose the Program is committed to integration, spurring integration. But the companies rely on the correspondent for programs, and historically we've had no such role, and no experience in this area."

Nonetheless, there were similarities enough to shape an industry pattern and to enable our consideration of the program as a whole. The first, and most important of these, was the strict adherence to a market rate of interest on all investments, a rate comparable to a similar investment made under nonprogram conditions. "This is a competitive program," went a typical explanation:

It would be grossly unfair to the policyholders of insurance companies to say we are going to lend one billion of your money on unrealistic terms. Insurance companies are already hurting in competing for the savings dollar. And in housing they did give up some return. Over in commercial loans they're getting 7 3/4 and 8 per cent.

As for discount points . . . we had to. We tried to remain competitive in the market. We didn't want to break the market or overcharge. In the beginning we got 4 1/2 points. That was too low. We increased it to 5 1/2, now we will probably reduce to 5.

Among the indefiniteness of the other criteria to implement decision—actually more a list of suggestions than criteria—the rule of market rates had the effect of dominating the program, delimiting the parameters of choice. For example, the commitments to the 221(d)(3) rent supplement program were mentioned above as evidence of the sincerity of purpose. But it is also signficant that among the many government-subsidized housing programs, this was the only one at market rates; and because of the government's specifications for per unit costs, there was not a single 221(d)(3) project in Chicago, a city of high construction costs. Several other projects were mentioned during the interviews as being unfeasible at market rates—for example, the refinancing of land contracts; and others as unfeasible because they were specifically designed to provide below-market loans—for example, a business development corporation for direct equity funding of new ghetto businesses.

Certain allowances in underwriting procedures were indeed made. Before the program some companies had refused to include as family income the earnings of a woman until she was past child-bearing age; others would now count a wife's earnings, even though she had not been on a job longer than six months—although given the nature of these provisions one might be inclined to consider them corrections rather than allowances. And, to be sure, the companies were now lending in areas where, as one officer said, "the age and condition of the property just doesn't warrant this treatment." But the unanimous judgment—in reality a judgment more significant on past lending practices than on the program itself—was that all investments had been safe and sound. "How risky?" answered the regional mortgage manager of a company which had made over 1,500 home loans in the first year of the program:

It's hard to say. I had the feeling at the beginning that they would involve a lot more risk. Even with government insurance, especially VA. And remember, they only guarantee a portion of the loan.

But now I don't think there is any more risk involved; they're no worse than any group of conventional loans. And there's a reason. A lot of these loans are to people who have never owned homes before. They have a real desire, and it shows in the way they maintain their mortgage payments.

In the Midwest, we've had only one foreclosure. When one loan was delinquent—it was delinquent before the company took it—the correspondent took it
back when he found out.

Even the loan representative who had seen the "atrocious" credit
ratings boasted that the investments he had placed for his company
were "very good real estate."

Considering the interest rate and quality of the loans, the question
arises of the source for the industry's sense of public service, of the
"real romance," as one mortgage officer put it, in the Urban Investments Program. One answer is simply that money was invested where
none was available before; but that in itself would seem to constitute
nothing romantic. The more probable answer lies in the program's complex relationship to American blacks. We have already mentioned that
the original criteria specified the residents of blighted or near-blighted
areas as the beneficiaries of the program and that this was modified by
the staff to accommodate company commitments. At the stage of implementation the nature of this modification may be observed more
closely.

What was evident to veteran mortgage men in Chicago, and what
quickly became evident to anyone more naive, was that in 1967—at
least in the field of housing, which was the first emphasis of the program and, for most companies, the administrative path of least resistance—there was no way to invest in blighted neighborhoods at market
rates. The unsuitability of rent supplement housing has already been
discussed; and there were similar obstacles to lending on one- to four-
family homes, even with the FHA's new willingness to insure these
loans. In light of the analysis in chapter V, we must here refer to the
Humpty-Dumpty asymmetry of the process of neighborhood decay and
reconstruction. In chapter V the impossibility of obtaining normal
mortgage loans from life insurers and other lenders during periods of
racial transition was shown to have created a grossly inflated ghetto
price structure, saddling homeowners with long-term land contracts for
exorbitant amounts of money. By the time of the program many of
these persons were anxious to sell—many had already moved to new
transitional areas, renting their houses to the welfare recipients they left
behind. But their welfare-recipient neighbors and renters were unable to
buy these homes, especially at the artificially high prices. In other
words, while there had been a lively market in 1955 and 1960, there
was virtually none at all a decade later. With the prospect of providing
insured loans to new buyers ruled out, the option of refinancing existing contracts with life insurance money was likewise of limited use,
since the overcharges made refinancing at market rates impossible.

A similar deadlock existed in multiunit apartment buildings. Costs of construction and land exceeded the level at which apartments might be furnished profitably for low-income residents of blighted areas. FHA cost ceilings per unit made government subsidies unavailable, except perhaps in high rise structures, which loan officers deemed unsuitable because of the social problems they might create—"God knows we don't want another Robert Taylor Homes," or another "mile-high slum." The only remaining use for market-rate insurance money was in the rehabilitation of older existing structures. But it is in the nature of building rehabilitation that cost estimates tend to be unreliable. This, coupled with continually rising labor costs, had made it difficult for nonprofit foundations to recoup even 3 percent on their investment. At market rates, the program could not rehabilitate without pegging rents at a range outside the core communities' ability to pay.

In short, while neighborhoods may be built, maintained, and even allowed to decay at market rates, it takes something more—or, more precisely, something less in the way of private profits—to put them back together again.[25] "The only thing that can help Woodlawn," went the typical loan officer's prognosis, "is for the University of Chicago to finish clearing it out"; "Redevelopment south of the Loop? People mentally don't think of going south—it's so bad. It may take a New Yorker."

At the time of the interviews, which took place several months into the program, the working definitions of the "core" were various, but generally no longer tied to the standard of blight: "where we weren't making loans before, low or moderate income, white or black;" " 'A' or 'B' areas, and those not yet quite over the hill." One large company issued a widely circulated map which extended the bounds of the "core" considerably to the southwest, and north of the FHA 'A' and 'B' designations, following the current outlines of racial transition. Perhaps the reluctance to be more explicit about the racial components of the program was a legal as well as a public relations inhibition. In any case, the musings of the president of the Chicago mortgage banking company most active as correspondent for participants in the program were closer to the mark: "If you're white, you can forget it."

To ascribe a kind of "romance" to lending to blacks is, of course, to imply that the industry was in the process of overcoming certain racial attitudes: it is difficult to imagine that investments to low- or, more particularly, moderate-income whites would be much of an adventure.

---

[25] On this point and a concise evaluation of a variety of public and private programs, see Lawrence M. Friedman, "Government and Slum Housing," *Law and Contemporary Problems* 32, no. 2 (Spring 1967): 357–70.

And, indeed, the interviews presented a good deal of evidence of attitudes the industry might be anxious to overcome. This is not to say
anything about the relative extent or virulence of race prejudice among
life insurance managers. Rather, the language and views they expressed
are undoubtedly familiar in great sections of white America: "We find
these people still living in the jungle. Why, there are people on
welfare—three, four, five kids, and the husband leaves home. Talk to
the welfare people if you want to find out. . . . And if I took those
people and put them along the Lake Shore, the Lake Shore would
become a jungle"; and: "There's no doubt that a Negro moving into
that area has an effect on the value of that property."

Some of the attitudes pertained specifically to lending. One remark
quoted in chapter V bears repeating: "It's the comparative instability of
the Negro family. . . . He doesn't appreciate what he's got. In Terry-
town he moves out." Also: "They need guidance. The average black
businessman hasn't been oriented. But if he will just stay sober, and out
of politics, keep out of trouble with women . . . ." Again, what is
important is not the attitudes themselves, but the self-conscious attempt of an industry to invest money in an urban program in spite of
such attitudes. The last remark quoted, it may be mentioned, was made
in the office of a mortgage banker working in the program for a large
eastern stock insurer, and in the presence of a visitor from the life
company's home office, a black man hired to develop programs for
black businessmen.

Furthermore, it must be reemphasized that the demand for market
rates itself was not a racial subterfuge for avoiding business with ghetto
blacks. Several of the largest companies made a point of allocating large
shares of their pledges to black mortgage correspondents as a means of
boring closer to the "inner core." But this strategy was likewise unsuccessful. The President of the largest black mortgage banking company
in Chicago explained:

> [The New York mutual] had committed a million dollars for strictly 'A' and 'B'
> areas in the inner core. *But I recommended that the funds also be given to persons
> who were moving out of these areas.* The money shouldn't be used to reinforce the
> ghetto. So on the second million allocated, it was for persons in the core area or
> moving out. But they must have lived in or near the core area at the time of the
> move, such as Douglas Park.
> The really hard core areas? They need a subsidy. Either a decrease in the cost of
> a home, like mobile homes, or a subsidized interest rate, say a point or two, or
> subsidized equity money. We've subsidized wheat farmers and cotton farmers, why
> not people? And here the initiative will still have to be from the federal government
> (emphasis added).

The expansion of the concept of core to include all blacks, considering the troubled social conditions which foreshadowed the pro-

gram, must have seemed quite logical to company officials. But, linked to the iron rule of market rates, this change produced some rather paradoxical results.

IV

Chapter V used the concepts of attitudinal and procedural bias to distinguish two sources of racial effects in life insurance lending. By the time the Urban Investments Program was underway in Chicago, the force of procedures acted within a racially predefined sphere. Again, by procedures is meant the adherence to market rates and the methods for securing requisite safety, prestige, property values, and so on, at those rates. In the program the procedures might be described from the industry's point of view as underwriting the best in a bad situation.

Like so many other criteria in the program, the new one of aiding blacks did not serve to order the social complexities confronting the industry. Blacks were, first of all, quite diversified in skills, occupation, income, family size, and general living conditions. Second, nothing in the general goal of providing housing, jobs, and services eliminated the traditional role of whites in the inner city as landlords, businessmen, and employers. In Chicago the effects of the procedures may be summarized bluntly: if a loan was to a black, it more than likely was located outside the blighted core; and if the loan was inside the core, it was probably not to a black.

The results of the program may be considered in two areas: first, housing—both home loans and apartments—which was emphasized in the first billion dollar pledge and for which the method of title deed analysis provides direct evidence; second, commercial loans—to provide jobs and services—emphasized in the second billion, and discussed in the interviews which were then supplemented with industry data. Let us turn directly to the data on housing. As an overview, tables 33 and 34 continue the analysis of chapter V and show the distribution of mortgage densities by race, and race controlled for income, for 1965–66 and 1967–68. Compared to the two preceding years, during the program fewer all-black and predominantly black tracts were entirely cut off from life insurance funds; and three black tracts, compared with the previous one, reached a density above two. In contrast, a greater proportion of white tracts received no mortgages and less than half the previous proportion reached densities above two. Among medium-income tracts whites have generally lost ground, while medium-income blacks have, on the average, maintained their position; and the low-income black and predominantly black tracts have made considerable gains. In other words, the program did turn racial attitudes in favor of the black tracts.

Table 33. Mortgage Density in Tracts, Controlled for Percent Black Population, 1965-68 (Percent)

Mortgage density	Percent black				
	0	1-10	11-50	51-90	91-99
1965-66					
1	36.4	52.0	40.7	78.3	95.2
2	42.4	20.0	33.3	17.4	4.8
3	6.1	12.0	14.8	4.3	0.0
4	15.2	16.0	3.7	0.0	0.0
5	0.0	0.0	7.4	0.0	0.0
	(100.1)	(100.0)	(99.9)	(100.0)	(100.0)
N=	(33)	(25)	(27)	(23)	(21)
1967-68					
1	57.6	52.0	37.0	65.2	76.2
2	33.3	24.0	44.4	26.1	19.0
3	6.1	12.0	3.7	4.3	4.8
4	0.0	12.0	14.8	0.0	0.0
5	3.0	0.0	0.0	4.3	0.0
	(100.0)	(100.0)	(99.9)	(99.9)	(100.0)
N=	(33)	(25)	(27)	(23)	(21)

For the effects of procedures, however, one must look deeper inside the data. In order to see the investment pattern in greater detail, from the original sample of 129 we selected 62 urban tracts that had some fraction of black population and thus fell within the redefined scope of the program. Table 35 classifies these tracts according to a poverty index of community areas in Chicago that heavily weighs median family income and includes values for percent unemployed and on public assistance. It is evident from the data that very little of the program's funds went for housing in the tracts located in the community areas most desperately in need. It is also worth noting that a classification of tracts according to the length of time the community area has been poor (not shown) charts an identical distribution, and those least favored by life insurance funds are probably also the most dilapidated.

The difficulty in maintaining the criterion of blight and still earning the going market rate is reflected in table 36. Here mortgages made during the program are compared against the FHA's designations of 'A,' blighted areas; 'B,' not blighted but deteriorating; those areas in good condition and therefore not designated. Seventy-six percent of the 'A' tracts, 45.8 percent of the 'B' tracts, and only 23 percent of the tracts not designated were cut off from program funds, and no tract in the blighted area reached a mortgage density above two. This is somewhat

Table 34. Mortgage Density in Tracts, Controlled for Percent-Black Population and Income (Upper Income Not Shown), 1965–68 (Percent)

Mortgage density	Low income/Percent black					Middle income/Percent black[a]				
	0	1–10	11–50	51–90	91–99	0	1–10	11–50	51–90	91–99
1965–66										
1	—	—	100.0	84.2	100.0	40.0	61.9	38.1	50.0	50.0
2	—	—	0.0	10.5	0.0	40.0	14.3	38.1	50.0	50.0
3	—	—	0.0	5.3	0.0	0.0	9.5	14.3	0.0	0.0
4	—	—	0.0	0.0	0.0	20.0	14.3	4.8	0.0	0.0
5	—	—	0.0	0.0	0.0	0.0	0.0	4.8	0.0	0.0
N=	— (0)	— (0)	(100.0) (2)	(100.1) (14)	(100.0) (19)	(100.0) (20)	(100.0) (21)	(100.1) (21)	(100.0) (4)	(100.0) (2)
1967–68										
1	—	—	100.0	63.2	78.9	65.0	57.1	23.8	75.0	50.0
2	—	—	0.0	26.3	21.1	25.0	23.8	57.1	25.0	0.0
3	—	—	0.0	5.3	0.0	5.0	9.5	4.8	0.0	50.0
4	—	—	0.0	0.0	0.0	0.0	9.5	14.3	0.0	0.0
5	—	—	0.0	5.3	0.0	5.0	0.0	0.0	0.0	0.0
N=	— (0)	— (0)	(100.0) (2)	(100.1) (19)	(100.0) (19)	(100.0) (20)	(99.9) (21)	(100.0) (21)	(100.0) (4)	(100.0) (2)

[a]For income categories see table 13 on 1965–66.

Table 35. Mortgage Density in Tracts Located in the Ten
Poorest Community Areas, 1967–68 (Percent)[a]

Mortgage density	Poorest 5	Other 5	Total 10
1	87.5	64.2	76.6
2	12.5	35.7	23.3
3	0.0	0.0	0.0
4	0.0	0.0	0.0
5	0.0	0.0	0.0
	(100.0)	(99.9)	(99.9)
N=	(16)	(14)	(30)

[a]Rank from Chicago Hospital Planning Council.

ironic, since the FHA designations were in large part a response to the insurance industry's expressed desire to obtain insurance for mortgages in precisely such areas.

The problems of investing at market rates in the poorest and most blighted neighborhoods have already been discussed. However, the deviant cases, those tracts listed in the FHA 'B' areas in table 36, which show densities of three or higher, illustrate additional aspects of inner city lending. All of them are within, or border directly upon, the Urban Renewal Area of "Englewood," the single most intensively planned and

Table 36. Mortgage Density in Tracts, 1967–68, by 1968 FHA-Designated
Community Areas, (Percent)

Mortgage density	'A' (dilapidated)	'B' (deteriorating)	Not designated
1	76.0	45.8	23.1
2	24.0	33.3	53.9
3	0.0	8.3	15.4
4	0.0	8.3	7.7
5	0.0	4.1	0.0
	(100.0)	(99.8)	(100.1)
N=	(25)	(24)	(13)

financed urban renewal area in Chicago. During the previous decade the city had provided ten new public schools, a site for a junior college campus, a large public housing structure for the elderly; and had re-routed traffic arteries for a landscaped commercial mall. Not-for-profit corporations had financed two large, federally subsidized luxury apart-ment complexes; community businessmen had raised funds to expand the two local hospitals; and a local, white-owned bank had contributed to the building of over 200 single-family homes, with 200 more planned. In fact, it was this same white-owned bank which acted as the program correspondent for a major company and had placed many of the loans reflected in the data. In other words, in the case of these 'B' areas, the insurance industry was providing funds to a community already in the process of revitalization, one which underwriting proce-dures for "economic life" would designate among the best property in Chicago that by any stretch of the standard could be called "deteriora-ting."

Two of these tracts, moreover, were still in the process of racial transition, as were most of those designated 'B.' Table 37 compares the mortgage densities of those tracts which were over 25 percent black in 1963 and therefore may be considered to have been racially consoli-dated at the time of the program; those which had become 25 percent black within the past five years and were in various stages of racial transition; and those which were not yet 25 percent black but where

Table 37. Mortgage Density in Tracts with Black Inhabitants,
Controlled for Stage of Racial Transition, 1967-68[a] (Percent)

Mortgage density	Stage of racial transition[b] Consolidated	Transitional	Early transitional
1	71.6	0.0	100.0
2	21.7	64.3	0.0
3	4.3	14.3	0.0
4	2.2	14.3	0.0
5	0.0	7.1	0.0
	(99.8)	(100.0)	(100.0)
N=	(46)	(14)	(2)

[a]Data on transition from Real Estate Research Corporation, Chicago, Illinois. The author is grateful to Anthony Downs, vice-president.
[b]Consolidated: Over 25 percent black in 1963
Transitional: Became 25 percent black, 1964-68.
Early transitional: Under 25 percent black in 1968, but some recent black residents.

black residents had moved within the past year. The results here are strikingly clear. In no case did a tract already in the process of racial transition fail to receive funds under the program. On the other hand, no money was loaned to provide blacks with homes in all-white neighborhoods. This last fact is consistent with the historic role of institutional lenders, as well as with the passivity toward integration expressed in the interviews. But the heavy concentration of funds in transition tracts calls into question the special contribution of the program in the area of home loans.

In chapter V it was shown that between 1955–64 life insurance money was in fact available in limited but increased amounts to middle-income tracts, particularly those on the border areas of racial transition. The tracts in transition with densities above two (table 37), are in the community areas of Morgan Park, Auburn Gresham, Washington Heights, Englewood, and West Englewood. The last two have already been discussed. The first three are communities with a median family income in 1966 near $10,000, $4,000 above the average for nonwhites. Moreover, the average price of the homes in these areas, from $20,000 to $22,000, place them in moderate- rather than low-income housing according to FHA ceilings and as applied by the program's staff, and our interviews suggest that the homes for which mortgages were written were priced considerably above these averages.

What then, did the Urban Investments Program actually accomplish in the area of home lending? It provided little for the black homeowner in the blighted core and was most effective in extending mortgages to moderate-income home purchasers at the point of racial transition—a section of the market already serviced by normal financing. Its most unique benefit, perhaps, was to shield black homeowners from the effects of the general pullout of the life industry from the home lending field.

Unfortunately, the data on apartments is based primarily on the Chicago interviews and is less systematic. Without exception, however, the multiunit loans reported by mortgage officers and correspondents in the interviews confirms the unworkability of low-income buildings in the core. Three categories of investment were mentioned. First, loans located outside the blighted area: one stock insurer, for example, took a mortgage on a 215-unit building in the community area of South Shore, renting for $110 for a three-room apartment, slightly higher than the prevailing rate in this middle-income transitional neighborhood. Second, this same insurance company loaned money on two buildings in Woodlawn, a low-income core area. Here the rents were approximately $10 per room higher than the community average. Finally, another large stock insurer had committed $4,000,000 for the

rehabilitation of 450 apartment units in the ghetto area of Grand Bou-
levard. The rehabilitated units would rent for $110–140 a month; the
average median rent for that community in 1966 was $83. All of these
mortgages were at market rates, which at the time were between 7¾
and 8 percent.

Most of these apartments, moreover, contained one and one-half to
three rooms. A mortgage correspondent was asked whether he considered such apartments suitable for a family: "Well," he replied, "what's
really needed is to change their whole family structure, and we can't do
that. But we know that in a three room apartment they *will* put a
family, and we're giving them a new bathroom, clean walls and some
other things to hold the family unit together. And we're giving the
owner an opportunity to upgrade his building." With the exception of
the rehabilitation project, which was owned by a nonprofit foundation,
all of the owners of the apartments cited in the interviews were white.
Some correspondents said that they were looking for black owners of
mortgage-worthy apartment buildings but were having a hard time finding them. In the meantime, given the high rents and the deleterious
effects of over-crowding, it may be argued that the white owner was the
main beneficiary of these loans.

By March 1, 1971, with all of the first billion and two-thirds of the
second billion committed or dispersed, the Clearinghouse reported the
provision of 6,221 housing units in Illinois. Assuming for the moment
that the program had the effect of actually expanding the used housing
supply above what it would have been already, this figure must be
compared with the 15,239 dilapidated (i.e., unsafe) and 56,557 deteriorating (i.e., needing major repairs and plumbing) units occupied by
nonwhites in the city of Chicago in the preceding census.[26]

The subtleties of residential lending seem almost simple, however,
when compared with investments to provide jobs and services in the
core. Here the vagueness of the criteria and the social structure of the
ghetto combined to create a veritable kaleidoscope of variations, of
which the following, together with some comments by the life insurance mortgage officers in charge of the loans, are merely a sampling:

1) To white owners of an industrial, commercial, or service establishment located in a black area employing white workers: e.g., a supermarket on the South Side which had been damaged in a riot and which
employed white clerks. "We helped the community in an important
way, by providing that facility."

2) To white owners of an industrial, commercial, or service establish-

[26] Evelyn M. Kitagawa and Karl E. Taeuber (eds.), *Local Community Fact Book, Chicago
Metropolitan Area, 1960* (Chicago: Chicago Community Inventory, University of Chicago,
1967), p. 282.

ment located in a black area employing black workers: e.g., a shopping center on the South Side, with national chain stores as major tenants but with black management and clerks.

3) To white owners of a factory or commercial establishment located in a white area but employing black workers: e.g., an industrial park located in the area of the stockyards, which will be the relocation site for a refrigeration plant, a manufacturer, a food processor, and some other companies. "These won't necessarily provide new jobs at first, but the space should allow eventual doubling of employment. It will draw labor from the East, the black areas. The nearby whites have employment, that's no problem."

4) To white owners of a building located in a black area housing a black-owned company employing black workers: e.g., to the owners of a building built to the specifications of a black-owned cosmetic firm employing twenty.

5) To black owners of an industrial, commercial, or service establishment located in a black area employing black workers: "Usually our commitments are to blacks doing second things;" e.g., a nursing home in Gary, which will expand into a new building; and a laundry, which is to move out of a frame shack into a new building and will employ up to 25 workers—"a small beacon at 56th and State."

6) To black owners of a building in a black area housing white-owned companies employing black workers: e.g., a building owned by a group of investors including a black mortgage banker, renting to a branch of a white insurance company, a white mutual fund, and some small black companies, including the mortgage banker. These combinations could be extended with many more examples—a black doctor's clinic, a white-owned vocational training school, and so on.

Several officers urged that the race of the owner and the employees was irrelevant to the purposes of the program, if the establishment, by not moving away, served to stabilize the community or provided shopping and service facilities. Others, however, were more sensitive to the social nuances, and their thoughts indicate the complexities of the program. One large mutual company, for example, reviewed a loan similar to (1) above, but involving a white-owned market housed in a white-owned building. The market had been picketed and its windows broken but, determined to stay in business, it's owner went to the landlord, proposed improvements, and offered to extend the lease. The landlord turned to the life insurance company for additional capital and received a loan. After second thoughts, however, the company decided that it didn't fit into the program—"you haven't helped anyone in a direct way"—and excluded the amount from the fulfillment of its pledge.

Even more complex problems were raised by loans to black owners, as in (5) or (6). For example, the same life company just mentioned was working on yet a different racial variation. A group of black investors was buying a parcel of land in a redevelopment area, and they were negotiating with a white-owned paper box company to relocate on the site, put in a new building, and expand its employment, which would be predominantly white. The loan officer explained:

Now, this would fit into the program—a new facility where a facility is required. The credit would be the box company. But here's where the program is crazy. The loan is for $200,000 and the tenant, the company, might have a net worth of $70,000. So we'd be like going into partnership.

And what should the interest rate be on this deal? 7½ to 8 per cent is the market rate. They argue for the lower rate, that with the cost of financing lower, the rents could be lower as an inducement to come in. But when you work out the math, at 8 per cent the group is making 11 per cent on their investment, and if we do it at 7½ it's up to 15 per cent. So where does our big-heartedness end and stop?

We're now lining the pockets of colored guys who have money. We're going way out anyway.

We can call it an inner-core deal, but . . .

And if we look at the box company with white employees, we're back to the supermarket problems.

He went on: "We're actively seeking loans. We said we're going to do it. That's why you have to decide who it is you're really helping."

As with housing, it is difficult to estimate the benefits to the core areas through these commercial investments. The Clearinghouse staff attempted to keep a total of jobs provided, but they added together new jobs and those "retained" through relocation on plant expansion, refinancing, and relocation. The interviews indicated, however, that a good majority of the jobs were in the "retained" category. The staff figure on employment for Illinois in February 1971, with the entire first billion and two-thirds of the second billion committed, was 7,919 jobs newly provided or retained. While it is unreasonable to dismiss these figures, it is not clear what to make of them. Even assuming that all of the "retained" jobs would have moved out to the suburbs without life insurance money, the 7,919 figure cannot escape comparison with the approximately 50,000 unemployed persons living in Chicago's ten poorest communities in 1966, to say nothing of elsewhere in the city, and the indeterminant thousands of jobs which, according to this logic, face the threat of plant removal.[27]

No data are available for Chicago or Illinois specifically on how the ownership dilemmas were resolved and, of course, no data at all according to the intricate categories we have discussed. But the Clearinghouse staff did estimate minority ownership for the program as a whole

[27]Computed from data in Pierre de Vise, *Chicago's Widening Color Gap* (Chicago: Inter-university Social Research Committee, 1967), pp. 60–61.

when approximately $1,400,000 had been committed. The factories receiving loans were almost entirely white-owned. Something over 75 percent of the medical clinics and 85 percent of the nursing homes were white-owned. One-third of the number of loans made to retail stores, supermarkets, and shopping centers are estimated "to have assisted minority owners." Judging by the experience in Chicago, this last group would include a large proportion of white-owned shopping centers with a few black tenants—though fewer than one-third; the prime leases are reserved for national retail chains. Moreover, since many company reports did not indicate the race of the owner, and since it may be guessed that loans to blacks would be more often specified than those to whites, the Clearinghouse figures are probably a general overestimation of black ownership.

Although racial attitudes may not be completely ruled out as a constraint in successfully furthering black capitalism, every single one of the company officers and correspondents interviewed had attempted to find black entrepreneurs who were sufficiently experienced and commercially positioned to benefit from market-rate funds. But with the paucity of such persons, and the reluctance to provide risky equity ("seed") capital for new ventures—traditionally the role of banks rather than insurance companies, as insurance men continually pointed out—the money inevitably served to reinforce the racial status quo in ghetto commerce and industry.

What is again striking is the apparent lack of long-range considerations of black capitalism's viability. Indeed, the second billion placed a much greater emphasis on job-creating and service projects and in particular on the needs of "urban businessmen and minority entrepreneurs" (see table 38). The pursuit of this course, despite early signs of frustration, may be explained in several ways, and no doubt each of

Table 38. Amount and Percent Dispersed for Housing and Job-creating Enterprises by Urban Investments Program, March 1969 and March 1971 (in Thousands)[a]

	(1) Amount 3/69	(2) % Total	(3) Amount 3/71	(4) % Total	(5) % of increase (3)-(1)	(6) % Change compared to 1st 2-yr. pd.
Housing	$681,506	75.7	1,120,367	68.6	50.3	− 35.6
Job-creating	219,203	24.3	513,352	31.4	49.7	+134.2
Total	900,709	100.0	1,633,719	100.0	100.0	—

[a]From *Urban Investment Report* (American Life Convention; Life Insurance Association of America).

them played a part. First, there was the ideological attachment to the concept of bootstrap free enterprise as necessary to the social and economic development of the urban core: repeated reference was made to "the need for a sound economic base in the community." Second, there was belief that the Nixon administration was interested in black capitalism and would adapt certain guaranteed small-business loan programs to the procedures of the insurance lenders. Third, there was the temptation of the rate: while the black entrepreneur was being hunted, loans in the meantime to national supermarket chains and white factories were bringing 7¾ percent to 8 percent—frequently with "kickers" on the borrower's profits.

The factor of impact perceptibility which influenced company participation also played a role in the industry's decision not to continue the program with a third billion dollars. In the interviews no one mentioned the discouraging statistics on jobs and housing cited here; but disappointments were more diffusely felt. A trade association officer summarized these reactions: first, the industry was disappointed that other members of the financial community had not come forward with their own programs, "which would have made everyone's effort more effective." Second, there had been little success in linking up with federal programs, particularly guarantees for the higher yielding, ideologically preferred commercial loans: in April 1970 Treasury Secretary Kennedy had told the industry that the President now wanted more funds for housing rather than black capitalism; some guarantees were obtained from the SBA, but "the red tape was unbelievable." Wedded to a "conservative stance"—the companies never forgot this was "other people's money," and the industry shied away from venture capital. "We went into this all starry eyed," said the official, "but, particularly in our realization of the need for a sound economic base for the community, we were largely frustrated." Instead the staff was searching for a new project, perhaps ambulatory care centers, in the field of health already familiar to the industry.

Moreover, political factors which had been an important inspiration for the program's beginning, now contributed to its end. A new Republican administration—indeed, one elected with wide industry support, including the highly publicized personal contributions of Chicago life insurance magnate Clement F. Stone—had cooled the political winds. The interest of the public press in the industry's beneficence had waned: whereas the first billion-dollar pledge was given front page coverage by metropolitan newspapers, the second had been buried in the financial pages. Finally, in the words of the trade association official, "the cash flow situation in the companies wasn't getting any better."

V

The Urban Investments Program may now be reconsidered in terms of the components of policy which we have analyzed in chapters II and V. While the two billions eventually committed amounted to a mere six-tenths of one percent of the industry's assets, it was nonetheless a purposeful redirection of credit from normal investments to investments defined by social criteria. That these social criteria were distorted by the procedural drift toward profits does not in itself distinguish the program from government policy—as shown, for example, by the long history of public housing which has consistently benefited the so-called rich poor. Nor is there a distinction in the fact that the social purposes were linked to certain political exigencies—compromise being the sine qua non of American legislation. To be sure, the program was grafted onto an industry organization geared to the goals of growth and profits, and was therefore vulnerable to submersion through the sheer weight of accustomed procedures. But, as the experience of the FHA demonstrates, such diversion is hardly foreign to government.

Where the Urban Investments Program does differ from the government model, however, is in the element of coercion. For what the program points up is not simply the definite distaste among businessmen for relinquishing investment autonomy, but rather the total absence of the authoritative dimension in the sphere of private industry. This is not to deny the very real elements of force which a company exercises over its employees or over its competitors; the process of allocating credit may itself be understood, ultimately, as partaking of force. But no company, or group of companies, or trade association is able to dictate positive policy to other companies and expect that it will be carried out against their will. Companies may be forced by market pressures to follow the leader, but this is an adjustment in the interest of the companies' business survival and has nothing to do with positive policymaking as such. Failing to submit and going out of business does not constitute compliance, any more than a company shutting its doors rather than obeying a government law constitutes compliance.

The radically voluntary nature of the program is evident at two junctures. First, the establishment of the program and the decision of companies to participate in the pledge was entirely uncoerced. True, the social, and particularly the political, climate were the conditions of action, but they did not in themselves prescribe any particular course. Also, public relations benefits to individual companies might have been an inducement to participate, but these were marginal, could have backfired, and, in any case, were minimized in the interests of a united industry front. Second, the choice and terms of investments was wholly at company discretion with virtually no central coordination. In the end this meant the choice of adhering to market rates or sacrificing yield to the original common objectives, a choice made universally in favor of the company and its private business goals at the expense of the program, and with the unplanned impact of the procedures as they have been described. This says nothing about a company which might have embarked on a carefully executed, low-yield program on its own— but such a plan would not have satisfied the political purposes of social responsibility and, of course, it still would have been entirely voluntary.

The question of autonomy, moreover, is related to the matter of the constituency. In a government program, the constituency is understood to include the segment of the population intended to receive the benefits of the policy; even in the case of benefits accruing to a group not acknowledged in the plan, this group may still be conceived of as a constituency of the program. In this sense there was a constituency to the Urban Investments Program: first the residents of the blighted core, later middle-class blacks and their white landlords and local businessmen. That the life insurance industry has other, perhaps more favored "constituencies"—company executives, stockholders, and employees, even policyholders—with competing interests, does not distinguish private industry from the potpourri of government policies, with their separate, sometimes favored, constituencies. But what is distinctive about the government case is the active or at least potentially active nature of constituencies. Government policy is predicated on constituency support, and in this narrow, semantic, but highly significant sense, is responsible. The Urban Investments Program, on the other hand, was premised on no such active constituency relationship, and in fact companies feared its development.

The role of the social content of the inner city to the life insurance program has so far been described primarily in its passive mood. The dilapidation, the inflated home prices, the lack of business experience of the black entrepreneur and the ever-present hegemony of the white one, twisted the program from social change to the financing of the status quo. But in the highly politicized atmosphere of the late 1960s, and in the midst of the ghetto which had precipitated the program in the first place, active community response was necessarily a factor, albeit one the industry scrupulously avoided.

This atmosphere permeated the Chicago interviews. At its least organized, the community had communicated a simple hostility to the white lender. One correspondent spoke of "a new attitude, a new breed":

Five or six years ago, a white liberal was welcome. Now some of these people have the attitude that there's going to be big money here and they don't want it to be the white man.

It's tough. You get kicked enough times and you don't want to go back. I sent my appraiser out to Lawndale a couple of weeks ago, and they ran him out of there.

With somewhat more group consciousness, there had been the demand for privileged, compensatory treatment rather than the use of straightforward market rates. Said another correspondent: "I've met with some of these community organizations. . . . These Negroes claim they want to be treated exactly the same, no discrimination. But when you try to deal with them financially, on a regular basis, they don't like it."

Worse, there was the specter of actual organized confrontation. This had been conjured up not in the program itself but, equally palpable, in the case of an earlier, highly profitable investment made by a brother life insurer in a large, middle-income housing project in the heart of black Chicago. The complex known as Lake Meadows, the pride of both the company and the Chicago Urban Renewal Agency's leader, Mayor Richard Daley, had been built by the New York Life Insurance Company in 1961. In August 1968 the Lake Meadows Residents Council had organized a rent strike to protest high rents and the poor condition of the building. The dispute had gone to the courts after the insurance company's management had agreed to meet with tenants individually but not as a group.

Although he didn't mention it by name, it was clearly Lake Meadows which the treasurer of an Illinois mutual company had in mind when he said,

A lot of companies have been scared off. There's a lot of adverse publicity coming out of the area. I was just yesterday talking to our mortgage manager. In a particular one in question the occupants banded together and among other things, demanded interest on the month's advance rent they had put up for deposit when they moved in.

This doesn't exactly do anything to make things easier. And this type of action gets a lot of publicity among investment people. You can argue whether it's right or wrong, but there are certain practices in the investment community that are what they are.

When someone is looking for a supply of capital, don't beat the supplier over the head with a sledge hammer. We work with people too. We're as sensitive as the next guy to being beat up or thrown down the stairs. You don't go back for more. And more violence today will just postpone the eventual solution. I'd say this is a fairly common attitude among investment people.

Several executives indicated that it was the fear of such activism which had inhibited any large-scale investment, particularly one which would concentrate great numbers of people, such as a high-rise apartment building: for example, "Well, high rise gets us back to the Robert

Taylor Homes. And I don't just mean policing and so forth. But, if we own it, our maintenance has to be twice as good as everyone else's. . . . Before long there's a move to get the big guy with the black mustache."

In the desire to find some means of coordination and a more effective response to social needs, a few large companies sought to utilize the short-circuit of government agencies. Indeed, the industry's contacts with the FHA and the SBA contained something of this. But the route had the disadvantage of connecting the company to the highly charged constituency relations of the government itself. For example, one company had made sizable allocations to two black mortgage bankers and had arranged to make a joint public announcement with Mayor Daley. But on the day planned, Mayor Daley made a "shoot to kill" statement regarding civil disorders, and one of the bankers refused to have his picture alongside the Mayor in the newspapers. Another company had attempted, unsuccessfully, to work with the Chicago Dwelling Authority in its scattered lot-building program: "A typical example of the government trying to do something. They were paying gang members to guard the lots after the foundations were torn up a couple of times. It was pretty crazy."

Government, for its part, had everything to gain and little to lose by acquiring the resources of the life companies for its own programs. Thus, when the Urban Investments Program was announced, city officials in the Office of Community Development promptly contacted life companies operating in the area and invited them to meet, along with the Lawndale Community Conference and the Midwest Community Council, to "make known the needs of the community and its desire to get a piece of the action." But the liaison was not fruitful. Community members' requests for seed money, a not-for-profit consulting corporation, and a full-time business counseling service were beyond the companies' purposes. "All they're really doing commercially is putting money in newer areas," said the city official in charge, "and there's no change in the interest rates."

One high Chicago housing official took a generally dim view of the program:

> They held out this program to the inner cities and it was trumpeted from the White House. They're not instituting programs. They're not really planning anything. Their explanation is that they're in the mortgage business, they don't want to get mixed up with architects, et cetera.
> Shopping centers? One, there is no evidence of a scarcity of commercial financing in Chicago. If there's no center in the area all the better for them. With mortgages, they're hemmed in by laws and the rest. With a shopping center, they're looking for speculation on their leases. How can they lose?
> Jobs? Are these factories that *already* are in Chicago?
> Sure, land values are high for housing in Chicago. But that's true of all major

cities. And if land in Lawndale is inflated, say, 10 per cent, how about inflation on the Lake Shore and the Loop? Look at John Hancock. Why didn't they build that big building in Lawndale if they're so damned worried about land values?

This man had tried to get a life insurance company to pick up the mortgage on some modular homes on the South Side: "Their answer: bring us the FHA insurance. But in that case, who needs them?" And here the impotence of government, as it was described in chapter II in terms of the mobility of capital and the rigidity of legal jurisdiction, was manifest. The author asked the official whether certain political associations of City Hall with life insurance men might not be used for persuasion. He replied: "Look, you can't put the bite on people like that. They help out in other ways—they pay personal taxes, property taxes and the rest; what're you gonna do—blast 'em? They could always pick up their marbles and go elsewhere."

Finally, there is the problem of the shape of the black community which, it was argued in chapter I, has been an obstacle to government techniques of cooptation. The life insurance industry faced the same bewildering picture. One large domestic company was hoping to provide a "major project," such as a residential park complex or a job training facility in Woodlawn:

> But there are so many groups, so many various representatives, we don't know who to align ourselves with. I don't want to mention anyone by name. [Probe: the Woodlawn (community) Organization?] They would be one, and the Blackstone Rangers [a local gang], and others. There are so many affiliations.
>
> We don't want the project to be a debacle, something that causes a bad public reaction. There's even the simple problem of protecting the property from damage.

And an excerpt from the *Urban Investment Report* illustrates the problem of shapelessness in the case of a project in Brooklyn's Bedford-Stuyvesant area:

> The frozen ground, a bitter wind and temperatures near zero kept the outdoor ceremonies brief for the ground-breaking of the Medgar Evers Houses on January 28, 1971. The speeches inside the neighboring Summer Avenue armory were hotter and longer.
>
> First to speak were two ladies not on the program, each carrying signs, one which said "Apartments are Apartheid" and the other proclaiming "Model Cities are a Trick on the People." They protested the planned construction of the 312-unit complex because many long-time residents of the neighborhood had been forced to relocate when their houses had been condemned and then razed. These residents, many of them elderly and poor, had not been relocated in adequate housing or paid enough money to provide decent housing for themselves. The replies of the speakers were sympathetic to the protestors and critical of the situation in New York City, where the housing shortage is so severe that hardship is certain to result from any destruction of existing residences.
>
> After singing the National Anthem and "We Shall Overcome," the 150 guests at the ceremony heard Henry G. Parks, Jr., the president of the black-owned Parks Sausage Inc., speak on the role of private business in urban problems. Reverend William Jones, the pastor of the church acting as one of the sponsors, could not

appear as the next speaker because he was leading a sit-in at the corporate headquarters of A & P in an effort to improve A & P's record of minority hiring and
promotion. The main speaker was Mrs. Myrlie Evers, widow of the Mississippi
NAACP leader who was shot and killed by a sniper outside his home in 1963.

Among those attending the ceremonies were representatives of the three life
insurance companies making the permanent loan and the New York bank making
the construction loan.

In fact, this project was undertaken after numerous disputes among
local community groups, and between the city and the groups, over
whether the neighborhoods should consist of low-income housing or
should be economically mixed had resulted in the cancellation of a
similar 221(d)(3) project in Harlem.

The question of shapelessness raises the additional issue of legitimacy, a vital concern for an analysis of corporate social responsibility.
This will be taken up in the next chapter. Here it may be simply
remarked that "responsibility" in the Urban Investments Program may
conceivably have referred to some extremely general and passive entity,
such as responsibility to "society." But in respect to the particular members of society for whom the investments were originally intended, the
program was strictly noblesse oblige, or at least to the extent that the
life insurance industry could make it so.

CHAPTER **VII**

CONCLUSIONS

Senator Proxmire: Mr. Beal, . . . We are delighted to have you represent the great insurance companies that have done such a marvelous job.

This is the best example of real business statesmanship that we have had in a long time, the fact that you have made this enormous commitment of funds.

Would you favor a suggestion made at these hearings for the establishment of a joint Federal-industry financial planning council to develop ghetto investment programs on a voluntary basis?

Mr. Beal: If it were completely voluntary, yes.

Senator Proxmire: One of the reasons I ask this is because this is a method which has been used in France with considerable success and we have noted the great amount of investment funds there are, the insurance industry has done a superb job of showing it is practical, and can be done. And it is our feeling that if you could have a program of this kind, with some kind of system involved of providing voluntary quotas which these groups could try to match or meet, we might get some action.

Mr. Beal: Well, it is when you get into the business of establishing the quotas and so on that we would get concerned.

Senator Proxmire: You are afraid it is not voluntary then?

Mr. Beal: I would be afraid it would become a regimented, tightly regulated system, and would destroy the great advantages and benefits we have had from the voluntary approach.[1]

The October 1968 hearings of the Senate Subcommittee on Financial Institutions, from which the above exchange is an excerpt, indicate the possible reemergence of credit as a major political issue in the 1970s. The urban crisis is an appropriate context for looking again at some of our findings. For if the argument of the Introduction to this book is valid, if in fact the relations between corporate business and the govern-

[1]U.S. Congress, Senate Subcommittee on Financial Institutions of the Committee on Banking and Currency, *Hearings, Financial Institutions and the Urban Crisis*, 90th Cong., 2nd Sess., 1968, p. 160.

ment are strained by the failure of traditional methods in coping with black America's demand for equality, then the status quo may be conditioned largely on business' ability to provide an effective private response, particularly in the inner city.

The hearings also illustrate the life insurance industry's penchant for "the voluntary approach" which maintains autonomous company control over its assets. This has been a constant objective of life insurance politics and its protection the main inducement to socially conscious investment. By considering autonomy in relation to the inner city, its role in the industry may be further examined.

I

Although even the briefest sketch of the needs of the inner city and its population is impossible here, the main dimensions of any conceivable solution may be indicated in order to avoid the generalities so often encumbering discussions of social responsibility. The first dimension is duration: projects to aid the inner city are likely to reach over a longer period of time than attempts to cope with other controversies currently besetting corporate business. The change to a noncombustion engine will be expensive, but after it is done the company may resume production, perhaps with a consumer representative on its board of directors and a plan of management efficiency to recover costs; but a program of minority training or a mixed-income housing development demands the nourishment of decades. Second is scale. One patch of wilderness preserved or somewhat purer water are steps in a desired direction; but a handful of apartment houses or auto dealerships are unlikely to survive the social contaminations of the ghetto. Third is the dimension of strategy. Companies may proceed sporadically and by their own devices to meet standards of product safety and truth in advertising; but urban renewal, relocation of businesses, and black capitalism must not work at cross-purposes if they are to work at all; job training and business aids must be properly timed; transportation and child-care must be provided where needed.

Having stated the problem, it is tempting to simply express pessimism that any corporate business effort can be sufficiently persistent, large-scale, and strategically coordinated, and leave matters there. But since any solution will be a question of more or less, the case of the Urban Investments Program may add perspective. To begin with, the political conditions under which this and similar life insurance projects have been undertaken serve to emphasize rather than mute company autonomy and thereby diminish the industry's potential for social effectiveness. The contingency of industry action on government pressures, the tendency to view programs as preempting drastic public initiatives, has meant that companies preserve their options by making only short-range commitments. It may also have heightened ideological concern for voluntary action and company independence.

Likewise, the industry's political aim in the program of presenting a united front through the broadest possible company participation worked against setting specific investment goals or requirements which might reduce company support. The fixed dollar amount of the pledge encouraged each company to invest individually its pro rata share, rather than providing for any comprehensive assessment of urban needs and resources. Finally, this lack of any broad strategy into which a company might fit its contribution accentuated the elusiveness of concrete social results and had the effect of depressing management enthusiasm and support.

The Urban Investments Program, moreover, points to another dimension of the inner city: the difficulty in establishing the support within the community necessary for project implementation. This difficulty was demonstrated in various ways, most bluntly when mortgage appraisers were physically ejected from neighborhoods. In some cases a measure of support was purchased with money, as when one company hired a local gang to guard housing foundations which had been repeatedly torn apart. But more often it could be sought only at a price few companies were willing to pay—the participation of community groups in determining the direction of a particular project.[2]

And even at this high price, support was hard to obtain. In chapter I it was argued that the shapelessness of the Black Revolution—its factional irregularity and the amorphousness of leadership and issues—has stymied long-studied government responses to interest group demands. The factor of shapelessness was no less a frustration to the life insurance industry. Larger projects, such as 221(d)(3) housing, where government participation required community representation, were delayed and in some cases cancelled because of intergroup rivalry and quarrels. And the inherent conflict-ridden social structure of the ghetto may have been made even more chaotic by the short-term, provisional and fragmented program which provided little incentive for compromise. The lack of coordination promoted wildcat actions, as it were, in the form of vandalism. A genuine urban strategy will require and perhaps receive community support, but an uncertain, apparently arbitrary series of investments can be expected only to increase frustration and hostility.

[2] On the reluctance of business leaders generally to deal with inner-city neighborhood organizations in planning and administering projects, see Jules Cohen, "Is Business Meeting the Challenge of Urban Affairs," *Harvard Business Review* (March–April 1970): 68 ff. Cohen also remarks on the fact that businessmen he interviewed were depressed about what they had been able to accomplish.

The role of company autonomy, then, is something of a paradox. It is to preserve their range of investment discretion that life insurance managers instituted the Urban Investments Program. But this discretion was shared no more readily with fellow companies or community groups than with government agencies, and this reluctance undermined support for the program and hence its success. It would be an exaggeration to say that the life insurance industry by its attachment to autonomy failed to alleviate the social conditions prompting government pressures, for no such grandiose achievement was contemplated; the idea was to demonstrate good will, make some contribution to the inner city, and perhaps induce other industries to do the same. But to the extent that a private solution to the ghetto will be made up of a multitude of similar programs, there is this additional factor of self-defeat in the voluntary approach.

II

It remains to reiterate the life insurance industry's preoccupation with autonomy. In chapter II it was demonstrated that the industry has historically exerted its best energies to thwart any attempts by the states or the federal government to channel asset investment by mandatory legislation. The elaborate network of lobbyists and insurance men in government, described in chapter III, the obfuscation and isolation of life insurance policy by bogus technicality, the threats to shift capital away from the offending jurisdiction—all work for the passage and administration of laws that expand and endorse company discretion. And, of course, the Urban Investments Program was another part of this strategy.

In chapter IV it was shown that the discretion allowed management by stockholder and policyholder passivity and the absence of effective price competition among companies has not significantly modified the goal of profits or its complement, asset growth. Indeed, increasing profits are the mechanism which provides an ever-widening scope to the life company's business function, which is to produce investment choices. This is not to say that these decisions are devoid of social content or impact; on the contrary. Chapter V illustrated how investment attitudes favorable to suburbanites and fellow corporations and unfavorable to black citizens are associated with rather striking social patterns and changes in the metropolitan area of Chicago. But neither these attitudes nor the patterns and changes themselves are in any sense goals akin to autonomy and profit. When in the Urban Investments Program an effort was made to cleanse investment procedures of racial bias without imposing any specific new goals, the habits of underwriting channeled funds straight to the most profitable or peripheral segments of the ghetto community, most of which were already served adequately in financial markets.

While this study has been limited to the life insurance industry, present business trends suggest that the facts plainly contradicting Galbraith's hypothesis of social responsibility may extend to other industries of like "maturity." To the extent that manufacturing corporations become increasingly diversified, their higher stations are occupied by technocrats of choice, persons less closely identified with a particular product line than with financial balance sheets. Conglomerate companies are nothing so much as creations of sheer financial wizardry, and they are managed largely on that basis.[3]

III

These observations have implications for government policy. Thus far most plans and proposals for harnessing the controls of credit to the requirements of the inner city have been entirely voluntary, or, as they were designated in chapter II, inducing measures, generally employing some kind of subsidy or tax incentive. However, once the instincts of the life insurance industry are understood as preserving one, autonomy and two, profits, it appears unlikely that such measures will be successful. For one thing, the more planned and coordinated the subsidized programs are, the less likely they will attract participation. Second, since subsidies endorse the goal of profit, regular company investment procedures can be expected to consistently pass over projects with low expected yields and to be totally unsuited for choosing among those with no presubsidy yields, indeterminant yields, or losses. These same limitations inhibit the use of tax incentives, which have an added disadvantage in that they work best where taxes are high, and life insurance taxes are relatively low.[4]

From the point of view of policy, leaving complicated political questions aside, it is likely that no move toward an aggressive credit strategy will be made until the incomes strategy—to raise the buying power of the ghetto population by job training, a guaranteed annual income, and so on—has been proven a failure.[5] Should the government attempt to

---

[3] For an introduction to conglomerates, see Morton S. Baratz, *The American Business System in Transition* (New York: Thomas Y. Crowell Company, 1970), especially chapter 3.

[4] Tax incentive schemes also encourage the rapid turnover of rental property to secure the tax advantages and thus are an inducement to reduce maintenance and other costs. For a concise treatment of public policy options in the area of housing, see Dick Netzer, *Economics and Urban Problems* (New York: Basic Books, 1970), chapter 4.

[5] An important exception is the proposal made by Governor Rockefeller of New York that savings banks be required to invest a specified amount in conventional housing mortgages in

assume situational control through mandatory investment policies, however, it is probable that the life insurance industry will be a primary target. Unlike savings and loan associations, life insurance companies obtain their funds through the sale of a contract which has a specialized use, and are thus less sensitive to the withdrawal of their "depositors." Unlike banks, life companies receive their funds for the long-term, and cash flows are highly predictable and suitable for long-range planning. Insurance companies in France, India, and elsewhere have been nationalized for these reasons; nationalization of life insurance has been part of the British Labour Party's platform on and off since 1950. Moreover, the constitutionality of federal regulation of insurance funds has been established by the South-Eastern Underwriters decision, and there are precedents for national involvement in insurance with Medicare and Social Security—two measures originally opposed by the life insurance industry with understandable zeal.

In the questions submitted to witnesses prior to the hearings cited earlier, Senator Proxmire inquired about "legislation requiring financial institutions to allocate a certain percentage of their resources to inner city areas," and "to what extent . . . new financial institutions (are) called for to specialize in investments in the ghetto?"[6] It is useful to speculate briefly on the form such a new relationship between the government and the life insurance industry might take, not in order to endorse a particular plan but rather to further elucidate the limitations of present investment practices. One of the most frequently offered proposals has been for some type of community development bank or corporation to supplement existing credit markets and to plan and oversee inner-city investment.[7] A major stumbling block to such an institution, however, is funding, since the means by which similar development banks have been funded—voluntary contributions to the World Bank, or users' deposits in various kinds of cooperatives—are either not likely to be forthcoming or else intrinsically difficult given the marginal economies of ghetto families.

Life insurance funds, on the other hand, are well suited to such a plan. In addition to the features already mentioned, life insurance policies carry a fixed rate of interest assumed for the entire period of the insured's "deposit," providing a convenient method for setting the in-

New York. The proposal was drafted by State Superintendent of Banks Frank Wille, who left shortly afterward to become chairman of the Federal Deposit Insurance Corporation. For details and some reactions, see *New York Times*, April 9, 1970.

[6] U.S. Congress, *Hearings, Financial Institutions and the Urban Crisis*, p. 2.

[7] See Richard S. Rosenbloom and Robin Marris, eds., *Social Innovation in the City* (Cambridge, Mass.: Harvard University Program on Technology and Society, 1968), especially Rosenbloom, "Corporations for Urban Development."

terest rate at which the development bank would pay the life company for the use of its money. It could be required by law that, say, one-third of the annual investible funds of the industry—in 1970 this amount would have been something over seventeen billion dollars—be invested in federally guaranteed securities of the development corporation, earning 3 to 3½ percent. This would leave a sizable portion of industry assets at the companies' discretion, maintaining the incentive for policy sales, but would provide a base from which the bank could begin to operate. Perhaps some system could be implemented by which companies could later redeem their securities for mortgages and notes, in order to avoid the consequences of turning the government into an immense creditor to the black and the poor.

The manner in which such a bank might operate suggests an answer to a question raised in chapter V: whether credit is by its very nature a conservative social tool. Certainly credit differs from grants-in-aid in the expectation of a monetary return. In its simple form, it requires collateral—a home for a mortgage loan, etc. Since only those persons with some collateral to provide are eligible for its benefits, credit is here at its most conservative. In its more dynamic form credit is extended for goods or services not yet in existence. But here too there is a bias in favor of borrowers with business skills and experience—the bias illustrated by the Urban Investments Program's abortive attempt to fund black inner-city businesses. Both of these conservative biases rest, however, on the practice of evaluating applications for loans individually, rather than evaluating the composite credit status of comprehensive categories of loans. Thus, in chapter V, risky mortgages are not accepted along with solid ones to create an *aggregate* margin of safety; instead, each possible investment is considered on its own merits for a *maximum* margin which would be entirely superfluous if the company's aim were solvency rather than profits.

A development bank could take the more comprehensive view and balance risks, an advantage relevant to the question of whether ghetto investments can make a profit for the lender. The answer is probably yes and no: the potential of technological innovations in housing construction is still unknown; middle-class housing can pay its way; some businesses are profitable in a shorter time than others. As inelegant as this is, it points to the crucial role for an agency able to consider each proposed project in terms of its contribution to overall development and to provide subsidies in some cases, or finance at higher rates. Furthermore, there would be the advantages of external economies, the actual economic supports provided individual enterprises by development as a whole, which do not accrue to the incremental decisions of life insurance or similar investments. The allocations to the Englewood community in the Urban Investments Program, which were synchronized with a healthy infusion of urban renewal funds, demonstrate the additional positive effects of planned expenditures to act as a developmental threshold to attract and utilize additional private investment.

IV

There is some reluctance to take up the knotty problem of legitimacy this late in the day, but it is a problem closely related to the issue of social responsibility, one given primary importance by students of the corporation, and which may perhaps benefit from a viewpoint prompted by the foregoing study. In chapter I the idea was rejected that the status of business in society is in any sense threatened by charges of "illegitimacy" arising from the fact of its diffuse and passive ownership. But this idea should be reconsidered as part of a larger argument, that managers indeed overstep their legitimacy when they engage in projects of social responsibility like the Urban Investments Program. The indictment is by now familiar: business managers have not been authorized by any law of either the market or the state, or by any constituency inside or outside the corporation, to impose their own conceptions of the good life or the just society on the general public. Nor are they accountable for their actions after they are done.[8]

Although the study of the life insurance industry provides support for the specifics of the indictment, it strongly suggests that the emphasis on social responsibility as the focus of concern is entirely misplaced. Life insurance managers did opt for particpation in the Urban Investments Program along with fellow companies, and without consultation with their policyholders and stockholders; they sought to encourage black capitalism and avoided disturbing neighborhood racial patterns; and they were never called before anybody to answer for the generally discouraging results. But the point of the discussion of mortgage decisions since 1935 in chapter V was precisely to illustrate the entirely unplanned social consequences—including consequences for the inner city—of investment-as-usual. Life company executives were no more constrained or accountable in these business decisions than they were in the comparatively trivial investment of the two billion dollar pledges.

In fairness it must be admitted that some critics of corporate social responsibility are well aware that regular business activities are likewise tottering on the brink of their definitions of legitimacy. Thus Friedrich Hayek, for example, would reinvigorate the rights and obligations of

---

[8] For a summary of these arguments, see Clarence C. Walton, *Corporate Social Responsibilities* (Belmont, Calif.: Wadsworth Publishing Company, 1967), chapter 3.

stockholders, and Milton Friedman has called for the strengthening of market competition.[9] As it happens, to repeat, the life insurance industry lacks both. But it is instructive to speculate on how matters might stand if the case were otherwise.

Suppose that the life company investments described were, as a matter of course, reported in detail to stockholders in a monthly letter, accompanied by the names of the department heads involved, who would then stand as a slate in the annual elections of company officers. Assume, moreover, that the majority of stockholders conscientiously scrutinized and evaluated these investments. Ought they therefore to constitute, by virtue of having purchased stock in the company, a legislature to vote on questions of wide societal impact? Company executives would then be accountable, but not to the public at large which must bear the brunt of their decisions. Surely, this would be carrying even the most conservative of republican precepts too far.

Alternatively, consider a life insurance industry in which companies compete to provide insurance at the lowest cost and thus are compelled to obtain maximum yields on their investments. Although enterprises and segments of the economy would vie with one another for financing, much of the public affected by these credit decisions would not be in the bidding, and particularly not those citizens who can make no demand whatever in monetary terms. But even more important is the fact that in the life insurance case managers do seek maximum profits, just as if they were forced to do so by the market; yet there is still a substantial margin of discretion as to what criteria are applied in specific choices—criteria, as we have seen, by no means strictly economic in nature.

Maximum profits, yes; but what of the criteria for choosing to finance a plant in one location rather than another, or for rating the members of one ethnic group a higher loan risk than another, or the myriad of other social determinations which wielding the controls of credit entails? These criteria or rules of behavior carve out a constituency for a company which is far more comprehensive than merely its stockholders or the consumers of its products.[10] And this is the case generally, not only in projects of purposive social engineering.

[9]Hayek is quoted in ibid., pp. 64–67; Milton Friedman, *Capitalism and Freedom* (Chicago: University of Chicago Press, 1962), pp. 120 ff. and passim. For a provocative case study of business as usual, see Grant McConnell, *Steel and the Presidency, 1962* (New York: W. W. Norton & Company, 1963) and McConnell's comments on legitimacy in chapter 6.

[10]Some critics of the corporation have advocated providing companies with systems of representation of the various groups affected by its decisions. See, for example, Abram Chayes, "The Modern Corporation and the Rule of Law," in Edward S. Mason (ed.), *The Corporation in Modern Society* (New York: Atheneum, 1966), pp. 40–41. This approach is implied in recent attempts by citizen reformers to put a black member on the board of directors in companies such as General Motors, as well as a consumer member, an employee member, and so on. The

These observations suggest, then, that it is the criteria or rules of choice which are in greatest need of legitimacy, rather than the rotating columns of executives who make the actual decisions. Viewed in this light, programs for shareholder democracy and restoring the forces of the market may be seen not as justifying corporate managers by finding a constituency to which they will be accountable, so much as enforcing one rule or criterion of choice—maximum profits—and grounding this rule in property rights or the philosophical faith in perfect competition. Moreover, once it is understood that it is the criteria that are at issue, the quest for legitimacy may proceed in a different direction. For now legitimacy attaches not to specific categories of business decisions, but to the many laws and conventions which society prescribes for the conduct of its affairs.

The setting of criteria has its ultimate expression through the organs of the state. The state has frequently changed the rules by which business is conducted—through antitrust, public regulation, zoning, minimum wage, laws against discrimination in hiring, and the rest. But more often the state has abdicated this function to the companies, providing that within designated limits business may make decisions according to its own criteria. This abdication has been based in part on certain assumptions concerning economic limitations to business power, but in the face of increasing doubts about the validity of these assumptions, government itself could pass a law requiring corporations to seek maximum profits and eschew philanthropy.[11] This would achieve the same remedy for the ambiguities of managerialism as would plans for increased competition and stockholder control, but now the edict would issue from the corporations' larger constituency through its most representative institutions. However, this would still not eliminate the social criteria involved in any ordinary business decision, whether it pertain to pricing, investment, employment, technology for production.

In the case of life insurance investment, the state has repeatedly considered the establishment of various criteria in the form of mandatory legislation and has generally turned away from such measures. Does this then grant legitimacy to the criteria employed by the industry? The answer is complex, and lies deep in the processes of legislation

---

life insurance case, however, suggests that factors in both business and the broader community will defeat schemes of genuine representation. And it is just as well, since a business sector claiming such representation would realize the worst fears of a long line of political thinkers beginning with Hobbes, of a network of competing governments boring from within the body politic. Under these circumstances the problem would not simply be legitimacy but counter-legitimacy.

[11] On profit maximization as a rule of law, see Eugene V. Rostow, "To Whom and for What Ends is Corporate Management Responsible?" in Edward S. Mason (ed.), *The Corporation in Modern Society*, pp. 69–71.

and the basic fairness of the representational system. This study has raised some troubling questions about the life insurance industry's lobbying activities and its manipulation of public dialogue on insurance affairs, as well as certain structures of government which frustrate and narrow the scope of public policy.

The legitimacy of privately established criteria, moreover, is inevitably threatened when the public perceives them as hindering the achievement of some pressing public task.[12] Seen in this perspective, the relevant question is not whether business may legitimately undertake programs of social responsibility, but how necessary and how successful programs of social responsibility will be in preserving the legitimacy of autonomous business decisions generally. The reconstruction of the inner city and the wider issue of black equality of which it is a part is such a task, and the study of the life insurance industry has diagnosed a stalemate. Government, in order to cope with black demands and relieve the public disquietude produced by the persistence of the ghetto, may require the situational controls of credit held by the industry. The industry uses a variety of political tactics to foreclose and preempt government initiative, while continuing to direct resources away from the areas of most urgent need. To the extent that this situation characterizes business-government relations as a whole, the failure to move off dead center threatens the legitimacy not simply of corporate business, but of the entire political order.

[12]The threat would seem to be especially strong in circumstances like life insurance, where there is little appeal to the sanctity of private property. It is interesting that toward the end of the Urban Investments Program several large life companies began to stress in their advertising the place of investments in the life insurance business and the contributions of company investments to the economy. One of the largest mutuals, for example, advertized that its policyholders "own a piece of the rock"—the rock being the trade mark of the company—and therefore own an interest in the companies in which the company has invested. However preposterous this claim is in legal terms, it may one day pay off handsomely in voters' opposition to government tampering with "their" assets.

BIBLIOGRAPHY

BOOKS

Appleman, John Allen. *Insurance Law and Practice.* Kansas City, Mo.: Vernon Law Book Company, 1941–70.

Arendt, Hannah. *The Human Condition.* Garden City, N.Y.: Anchor Books, 1959.

Baratz, Morton S. *The American Business System in Transition.* New York: Thomas Y. Crowell Company, 1970.

Barnard, Chester I. *The Functions of the Executive.* Cambridge, Mass.: Harvard University Press, 1938.

Bauer, Raymond A., de Sola Pool, Ithiel, and Dexter, Lewis Anthony. *American Business and Public Policy: The Politics of Foreign Trade.* New York: Atherton Press, 1963.

Baumhart, Raymond, S. J. *An Honest Profit.* New York: Holt, Rinehart & Winston, 1968.

Belth, Joseph M. *The Retail Price Structure in American Life Insurance.* Bloomington, Ind.: The Foundation for the School of Business, Indiana University, 1966.

Bennett, Walter H. *The History of the National Association of Insurance Agents.* Cincinnati, Ohio: The National Underwriter Co., 1954.

Berle, Adolf A. *The American Economic Republic.* New York: Harcourt, Brace & World, 1965.

――――. *The 20th Century Capitalist Revolution.* New York: Harcourt, Brace & World, 1954.

Beyer, Glenn H. *Housing and Society.* New York: The Macmillan Company, 1965.

Boulding, Kenneth E. *A Reconstruction of Economics.* New York: John Wiley and Sons, 1950.

Brady, Robert A. *Business As a System of Power.* New York: Columbia University Press, 1947.

Brandeis, Louis D. *Business—A Profession.* Boston, Mass.: Small, Maynard and Co., 1914.

――――. *Other People's Money.* New York: Harper & Row, 1967.

Brimmer, Andrew F. *Life Insurance Companies in the Capital Market.* East Lansing, Mich.: Michigan State University Press, 1962.

Buley, R. Carlyle. *The American Life Convention 1906–1952: A Study in the History of Life Insurance.* New York: Appleton-Century-Crofts, 1963.
———. *The Equitable Life Assurance Society of the United States, 1859–1964.* New York: Appleton-Century-Crofts, 1967.
Cameron, Rondo. *Banking in the Early Stages of Industrialization.* New York: Oxford University Press, 1967.
Carr, Edward Hallett. *History of Soviet Russia, II: The Bolshevik Revolution.* Harmondsworth, England: Penguin Books, 1966.
Cater, Douglas. *Power in Washington.* New York: Random House, 1966.
Center, Charles C., and Heins, Richard M. *Insurance and Government.* New York: McGraw-Hill Book Company, 1962.
Clayton, George, and Osborn, W. T. *Insurance Company Investment.* London: George Allen and Unwin, 1965.
Congressional Quarterly Almanac. Washington, D.C.: Congressional Quarterly, Inc., 1945.
Crenson, Matthew A. *The Un-politics of Air Pollution.* Baltimore: The John Hopkins University Press, 1971.
Dacey, Norman F. *What's Wrong With Your Life Insurance.* New York: The Crowell-Collier Press, 1962.
de Vise, Pierre. *Chicago's Widening Color Gap.* Chicago: Interuniversity Social Research Committee, 1967.
Downs, Anthony. *Urban Problems and Prospects.* Chicago: Markham Publishing Company, 1970.
Drucker, Peter F. *The Future of Industrial Man.* New York: The John Day Company, 1942.
Edwards, G. W. *The Evolution of Finance Capitalism.* London: Longmans, Green and Co., 1938.
Engler, Robert. *The Politics of Oil.* Chicago: Phoenix Books, The University of Chicago Press, 1967.
Epstein, Edwin M. *The Corporation in American Politics.* Englewood Cliffs, N.J.: Prentice-Hall, 1969.
Faulkner, Harold U. *The Decline of Laissez Faire, 1897–1917.* New York: Harper and Row, 1969.
Finn, David. *The Corporate Oligarch.* New York: Simon and Schuster, 1969.
Friedman, Milton. *Capitalism and Freedom.* Chicago: University of Chicago Press, 1962.
Galbraith, John Kenneth. *The New Industrial State.* New York: Houghton Mifflin Company, 1967.
Garnett, R. G. *A Century of Co-Operative Insurance.* London: George Allen and Unwin, 1968.
Gephart, W. F. *Insurance and the State.* New York: The Macmillan Company, 1913.
Gollin, James. *Pay Now, Die Later.* New York: Penguin Books, 1966.
Goodrich, Carter (ed.). *The Government and the Economy.* Indianapolis: The Bobbs-Merrill Company, 1967.
Gordon, Robert A. *Business Leadership in the Large Corporation.* 2nd edition. Berkeley, Calif: University of California Press, 1961.
Grebler, Leo, Blank, David M., and Winnick, Louis. *Capital Formation in Residential Real Estate: Trends and Prospects.* Princeton, N.J.: Princeton University Press, 1956.
Hacker, Louis M. *The Course of American Economic Growth and Development.* New York: John Wiley & Sons, 1970.
Hammond, Bray. *Banks and Politics in America.* Princeton, N.J.: Princeton University Press, 1967.

Hartz, Louis. *Economic Policy and Democratic Thought: Pennsylvania 1776–1860.* Cambridge, Mass.: Harvard University Press, 1948.

Hicks, John. *A Theory of Economic History.* London: Oxford University Press, 1969.

Hobsbaum, E. J. *Primitive Rebels.* New York: W. W. Norton & Company, 1965.

Housing a Nation. Washington, D.C.: Congressional Quarterly Service, Inc., 1966.

Jacob, Herbert, and Vines, Kenneth N. *Politics in the American States: A Comparative Analysis.* Boston, Mass.: Little, Brown and Co., 1967.

James, Marquis. *The Metropolitan Life, A Study in Business Growth.* New York: Viking Press, 1947.

Jewell, Malcolm. *The State Legislature: Politics and Practice.* 2nd edition. New York: Random House, 1969.

Josephson, Halsey D. *Discrimination.* New York: Wesley Press, 1960.

Keller, Morton. *The Life Insurance Enterprise, 1885–1910: A Study in the Limits of Corporate Power.* Cambridge, Mass.: Belknap Press, Harvard University Press, 1963.

Kimball, Spencer L. *Insurance and Public Policy: A Study in the Legal Implementation of Social and Economic Public Policy.* Madison, Wis.: University of Wisconsin Press, 1960.

Kitagawa, Evelyn M., and Tauber, Karl B. (eds.). *Local Community Fact Book, Chicago Metropolitan Area, 1960.* Chicago: Chicago Community Inventory, University of Chicago, 1967.

Knowles, Louis L., and Prewitt, Kenneth (eds.). *Institutional Racism in America.* Englewood Cliffs, N.J.: Prenctice-Hall, 1969.

Kraemer, P. E. *The Societal State.* Meppel, The Netherlands: J. A. Boom En Zoon, 1966.

Lekachman, Robert. *The Age of Keynes.* New York: Vintage Books, 1966.

Levitt, Kari. *Silent Surrender: The American Economic Empire in Canada.* New York: Liveright, 1971.

Life Insurance Fact Book 1967. New York: Institute of Life Insurance, 1967.

Life Insurance Fact Book 1968. New York: Institute of Life Insurance, 1968.

Life Insurance Fact Book 1969. New York: Institute of Life Insurance, 1969.

Life Insurance Fact Book 1970. New York: Institute of Life Insurance, 1970.

MacLean, Joseph M. *Modern Life Insurance.* 9th edition. New York: McGraw-Hill Book Company, 1962.

Martindale Hubbel Law Directory, Illinois section. Vol. II. Summit, N.J.: Martindale Hubbell, 1968.

Mason, Edward S. (ed.). *The Corporation in Modern Society.* New York: Atheneum, 1966.

May, Earl Chapin, and Ousler, Will. *The Prudential: A Story of Human Security.* Garden City, N.J.: Doubleday and Co., 1950.

McCahan, David. *Investment of Life Insurance Funds.* Homewood, Ill.. Richard D. Irwin, 1953.

McConnell, Grant. *Private Power and American Democracy.* New York: Alfred A. Knopf, 1966.

　　　Steel and the Presidency, 1962. New York: Norton and Company, 1963.

Milbraith, Lester M. *The Washington Lobbyists.* Chicago: Rand McNally and Company, 1963.

Mortimer, Charles G. *The Purposeful Pursuit of Profits and Growth of Business.* New York: McGraw-Hill Book Company, 1965.

Myrdal, Gunnar. *The Political Element in the Development of Economic Theory.* Cambridge, Mass.: Harvard University Press, 1954.

Netzer, Dick. *Economics and Urban Problems.* New York: Basic Books, 1970.

Nicholas, H. G. *The British General Election of 1950.* London: Macmillan & Co., 1951.

Nossiter, Bernard. *The Mythmakers.* Boston: Beacon Press, 1964.
Oates, James F., Jr. *Business and Social Change: Life Insurance Looks to the Future.* New York: McGraw-Hill Book Company, 1968.
Olson, Mancur. *Logic of Collective Action: Public Goods and the Theory of Groups.* New York: Schoken Books, 1968.
Osofsky, Gilbert. *Harlem: The Making of a Ghetto.* New York: Harper and Row, 1966.
Parsons, Talcott, and Smelzer, Neil J. *Economy and Society.* New York: The Free Press, 1965.
Patterson, Edwin Wilhite. *The Insurance Commissioner in the United States: A Study in Administrative Law and Practice.* Cambridge, Mass.: Harvard University Press, 1927.
Pease, Robert M. (ed.). *Mortgage Banking.* 2nd edition. New York: McGraw-Hill Book Company, 1965.
Reagan, Michael D. *The Managed Economy.* Fair Lawn, N.J.: Oxford University Press, 1963.
Rosenbloom, Richard S., and Marris, Robin (eds.). *Social Innovation in the City.* Cambridge, Mass.: Harvard University Program on Technology and Society, 1968.
Rothschild, K. W. *Power in Economics.* Baltimore: Penguin Books, 1971.
Saulnier, R. J. *Urban Mortgage Lending by Life Insurance Companies.* New York: National Bureau of Economic Research, 1950.
Saulnier, R. J., Halcrow, Harold G., and Jacoby, Neil H. *Federal Lending and Loan Insurance.* Princeton, N.J.: Princeton University Press, 1958.
Sawyer, Elmer Warren. *Insurance as Interstate Commerce.* New York: McGraw-Hill Book Company, 1945.
Schultz, Robert E. *Life Insurance Housing Projects.* Homewood, Ill.: Richard D. Irwin, 1957.
Schumpeter, Joseph A. *Theory of Economic Development.* Fair Lawn, N.J.: Oxford University Press, 1970.
Shonfield, Andrew. *Modern Capitalism: The Changing Balance of Public and Private Power.* Fair Lawn, N.J.: Oxford University Press, 1965.
Snider, H. Wayne. *Life Insurance Investment in Commercial Real Estate.* Homewood, Ill.: Richard D. Irwin, 1956.
Stalson, J. Owen. *Marketing Life Insurance: Its History in America.* Cambridge, Mass.: Harvard University Press, 1942.
Steiner, Gilbert Y., and Gove, Samuel K. *Legislative Politics in Illinois.* Urbana, Ill.: University of Illinois Press, 1960.
Sutton, Francis X., Harris, Seymour E., Kaysen, Carl, and Tobin, James. *The American Business Creed.* New York: Schocken Books, 1962.
Tebbel, Robert. *The Slum Makers.* New York: Dial Press, 1963.
Thompson, E. P. *The Making of the English Working Class.* New York: Pantheon Books, 1963.
Tullock, Gordon. *Private Wants, Public Means.* New York: Basic Books, 1970.
U.S. National Advisory Commission on Civil Disorders. *Report.* New York: Bantam Books, 1968.
Veblen, Thorstein. *Absentee Ownership and Business Enterprise in Recent Times.* Boston, Mass.: Beacon Press, 1967.
       . *The Instinct of Workmanship and the State of the Industrial Arts.* New York: Viking Press, 1946.
       . *The Theory of Business Enterprise.* New York: Mentor Books, 1958.
Walter, James E. *The Investment Process.* Boston, Mass.: Graduate School of Business Administration, Harvard University, 1962.
Walton, Clarence C. *Corporate Social Responsibilities.* Belmont, Calif.: Wadsworth Publishing Company, 1967.

Williamson, Harold F., and Smalley, Orange A. *Northwestern Mutual Life, A Century of Trusteeship.* Evanston, Ill.: Northwestern University Press, 1957.

Wirth, Louis, and Bernet, Eleanor, H. (eds.). *Local Community Fact Book of Chicago.* Chicago: University of Chicago Press, 1949.

Zartman, Lester. *The Investments of Life Insurance Companies.* New York: Henry Holt & Company, 1906.

PERIODICALS

A Red Umbrella in High Wind. *Fortune* (August 1965): 139 ff.

Abrams, Charles. Segregation, Housing and the Horne Case. *The Reporter* 13, no. 5, October 6, 1955, p. 30.

Cohen, Jules. Is Business Meeting the Challenge of Urban Affairs. *Harvard Business Review* (March-April 1970): 68 ff.

Congressional Digest 23 (October 1944): 255.

Decisions. *Columbia Law Review* 44, no. 4 (July 1944).

Donovan, James B. Regulation of Insurance under the McCarran Act. *Law and Contemporary Problems* 14, no. 4 (Autumn 1940): 472-92.

Friedman, Lawrence M. Government and Slum Housing. *Law and Contemporary Problems* 32, no. 2 (Spring 1967): 357-70.

Graham, Howard Jay. The Conspiracy Theory of the Fourteenth Amendment, Part 2. *Yale Law Journal* 48 (December 1938): 171-94.

Impact of Investment Regulation on the Life Insurance Industry. *Insurance Law Journal* (July 1965).

Insurance, 1966-69.

Life Insurance: $84 Billion Dilemma. *Fortune* (February 1955): 112 ff.

Lowi, Theodore J. American Business, Public Policy, Case Studies and Political Theory. *World Politics* 16, no. 4 (July 1964): 677-715.

March, James G. The Business Firm as a Political Coalition. *Journal of Politics* 24 (1962).

Monsen, R. J., and Downs, Anthony. A Theory of Large Managerial Firms. *Journal of Political Economy* (June 1965): 227 ff.

The National Underwriter (Life edition), 1967-69.

The New York Times, 1967-69.

Nolan, Martin. A Belated Effort to Save Our Cities. *The Reporter* 37, no. 11, December 28, 1967, pp. 16 ff.

Riley, John W. Social Research and Life Insurance. (Special issue of *The American Behavioral Scientist*), 1963.

Scariano, Anthony. Changes for Automobile Claims? *Law Forum* (Fall 1967): 596-99.

Sheehan, Robert. Life Insurance's Almighty Leap into Equities. *Fortune* (October 1968): 142 ff.

Sheppard, C. W. Owsley, and Class, Robert. Shady Insurance Firms Can Thrive Under State Laws. *Chicago American,* October 3, 1966.

Simon, Herbert A. Theories of Decision-Making in Economics and Behavioral Science. *American Economic Review* (June 1959): 253-85.

Travis, Dempsey. Boycott. *Focus Midwest* 3, nos. 8 and 9, pp. 16-17.

Wade, Martin O., Jr. The NAIC and State Insurance Department Functions. *Insurance Law Journal* 356 (September 1952): 538-87.

Wall Street Journal, 1967-69.

PUBLIC DOCUMENTS

Bolton, John F., Jr. *Annual Report by the Director of the Department of Insurance,* 1967.

_____. *Annual Report by the Director of the Department of Insurance,* 1968.

State of New York Insurance Department. *Report of the Special Committee on Insurance Holding Companies*, 1968.

U.S. Bureau of Census. *Seventeenth Census of the United States: 1950. Population. and Housing Census Tracts.* Final Report PHC (1)-26, Chicago, Illinois. Washington, D.C., 1962.

U.S. Bureau of Census. *Seventeenth Census of the United States: 1950. Population.* Vol. III. *Census Tract Statistics.* Washington, D.C.: Government Printing Office, 1953.

U.S. Bureau of Census. *Sixteenth Census of the United States: 1940. Population and Housing for Census Tracts and Community Areas, Chicago, Illinois.* Washington, D.C.: Government Printing Office, 1943.

U.S. Bureau of the Census. *Statistical Abstract of the United States: 1970.* Washington, D.C.: Government Printing Office, 1970.

U.S. Congress. *Hearings before the Temporary National Economic Committee, Congress of the United States.* 76th Cong., 1st and 2nd Sess., 1940.

U.S. Cong. House Antitrust Subcommittee of the Committee on the Judiciary. Staff Report. "Interlocks in Corporate Management." 89th Cong., 1st Sess., 1965.

U.S. Congress. Senate Subcommittee on Financial Institutions of the Committee in Banking and Currency. *Hearings, Financial Institutions and the Urban Crisis.* 90th Cong., 2nd Sess., 1968.

U.S. Congress. Senate and House Committees on the Judiciary. *Joint Hearings, Insurance.* 78th Cong., 2nd Sess., pp. 634–36.

U.S. Temporary National Economic Committee. Investigation of the Concentration of Economic Power. Monograph 28. Gerhard A. Gesell and Ernest J. Howe. *Study of Legal Reserve Life Insurance Companies.* 76th Cong., 3rd Sess., 1941.

PAMPHLETS AND
UNPUBLISHED MATERIALS

Andrews, James H. *Private Groups in Illinois Government: Final Report and Background Papers, Assembly on Private Groups in Illinois Government.* University of Illinois Bulletin, vol. LXII, no. 63. Urbana, Ill.: University of Illinois Press, 1965.

Beard, Winston C. *The Effects of State Investment Requirements for Life Insurance Companies.* Prepared for the Arkansas Insurance Commissioner by the University of Arkansas College of Business Administration, Industrial Relations, and Extension Center in cooperation with the Arkansas Industrial Development Commission, 1958. (Mimeographed.)

"The Financial and Economic Effects of Geographical Restrictions Upon the Investment Politics of Life Insurance Companies." Ph.D. dissertation, Department of Economics, University of Illinois, 1961.

Boies, W. H. "The Legal Status of Mutual Life Insurance Policy-holders." (Mimeographed.)

Bolton, John F., Jr. "The Illinois Program: A Two Year Plan to Modernize Regulation of the Insurance Industry: A Regulatory White Paper Prepared for the Use of Members of the 75th Illinois General Assembly," 1967. (Mimeographed.)

Certified Stenographic Report of Proceedings Had at the Public Hearing of the Joint House of Representatives and Senate of the State of Illinois Insurance Study Committee, April 14, A.D. 1967, Chicago, Illinois. (Mimeographed.)

"The Contract Buyers League Demands Justice." Prepared by the Contract Buyers League of Chicago and distributed December 1968. (Mimeographed.)

Jones, Lawrence D. "Portfolio Objectives, External Constraints, and the Postwar Investment Behavior of Life Insurance Companies." Ph.D. dissertation, Department of Economics, Harvard University, September 1959.

"Mortgage Availability in Racially Transitional Areas." Prepared by the Chicago Commission on Human Relations, presented at a public hearing of the Commission on August 9, 1967. (Mimeographed.)

"1967 Legislation Explanation." Distributed by the Department of Insurance. (Mimeographed.)

Proceedings of the Sixtieth Annual Meeting of the Legal Section of the American Life Convention, 1967.

Puth, Robert C. "Supreme Life: A History of a Negro Life Insurance Company." Ph.D. disseration, Department of Economics, Northwestern University, 1967.

"Report of the Urban Problems Committee to the Board of Directors of the Life Insurance Association of America (as revised and adopted by the Board at its meeting on August 18, 1967). (Mimeographed.)

Urban Investment Report. American Life Convention and Life Insurance Association of America. Nos. 1-14. April 1970 to March 1971. (Mimeographed.)

Wright, Kenneth M., and Parks, Robert H. *1967 Economic and Investment Report.* New York: Life Insurance Association of America, 1967.

INDEX

This book was composed in Baskerville text
by the Jones Composition Company from a
design by Alan Tyson. It was printed
on 60-lb. Sebago paper and bound
in Columbia Bayside Chambray cloth by
The Maple Press Company.

Library of Congress Cataloging in Publication Data

Orren, Karren
    Corporate power and social change:

    Bibliography: p.
    1. Insurance, Life—United States. I. Title.
HG8958.077   338.4'7'368973   73-8118
ISBN 0-8018-1507-X